Racial Worldmaking

Racial Worldmaking

The Power of Popular Fiction

Mark C. Jerng

FORDHAM UNIVERSITY PRESS
New York 2018

Fordham University Press also publishes its books in a variety of electronic formats. Some content that appears in print may not be available in electronic books.

Visit us online at www.fordhampress.com.

Library of Congress Cataloging-in-Publication Data available online at http://catalog.loc.gov.

Printed in the United States of America

20 19 18 5 4 3 2 1

First edition

for Liane, Seneca, and Chloe

CONTENTS

Racial Worldmaking

INTRODUCTION

Racial Worldmaking

Popular fiction and racial representation. Put together, these two phrases likely conjure in your mind the most explicitly racist images and regressive fantasies in the American and British cultural imaginary. The black rapist of plantation romance. The evil Asian villain in science fiction. Fantasies of ridding the world of invading Orcs. Yellow hordes threatening to engulf the globe. Twentieth-century popular fictions such as Thomas Dixon's *Birth of the Nation*, Robert Howard's Conan the Barbarian stories, M. P. Shiel's *The Yellow Wave*, among others, are famous for disseminating some of the basest tendencies of humankind: xenophobia, misogyny, and racism. What can an exploration of these popular genre fictions possibly offer twenty-first-century race critique? What can it show besides the dark forces of ignorance and prejudice that antiracism must repeatedly cure?

The gambit of this book is that such an exploration is indispensable at this time. Far from being regressive remainders of white supremacy, biological racism, and political race hatred that can be written off as the extremism of the few, these genre fictions are at the center of what I call *racial worldmaking*. Racial worldmaking is my phrase for narrative and interpretive strategies that shape how readers notice race so as to build, anticipate, and organize the world. These strategies prompt us to notice race in unlikely sites and in unexpected ways. They locate race at the level of context, atmosphere, sequence, and narrative explanation—levels, that is, other than the biological representation of bodies or the social categorization of persons. Thus, their effectiveness in producing the conditions of racism lies not so much in the conventional sense of discriminating against specific persons; rather, it consists in getting us to embed race into our expectations for how the world operates. Ignoring it or concentrating only on how these fictions reflect already existing racial ideologies destines us to our ongoing participation in the structures of our racial worlds.

My theory of racial worldmaking as narrative and interpretive strategies for constructing relationships between noticing race and building worlds stems from two main interventions that I explain below. The first is that race critique has overemphasized the visual epistemology of race and its bases in scientific racism and comparative anatomy. I emphasize instead the *salience of race*: we are taught when, where, and how race is something to notice. Noticing race in some contexts and not others shapes how we organize situations, forms of reasoning, and expectations about what is going to happen. The second is that fictional and nonfictional genres do not just express or represent race as if race is a given, prior content. Genre and race should instead be conceptualized as deeply interrelated ways of building-in knowledge of the world. Here I develop the senses in which race has an organizing and shaping force that is often associated with genre.

In the parts that follow, I describe and analyze practices of racial worldmaking across four configurations of race and genre: (1) yellow peril future war stories; (2) plantation romances of Reconstruction; (3) sword and sorcery and racial capitalism; (4) alternate history and racial jurisprudence. Within each part of the book, I examine the shaping of formal features and narrative strategies within subgenres of science fiction, romance, and fantasy in relation to discursive possibilities that emerge from prominent historical dramas of racial reorganization. But genre here is not the vehicle for race as sociohistorical content. The mechanisms of genre and race operate together in making available certain knowledges about and projections of the world. Throughout I am interested in the cognitive effects of truth and authority produced by these popular genres. I explore their overlap with writings in the disciplines of history, anthropology, economics, and law in order to argue that they achieve these effects *by activating certain ways of perceiving and cognizing race.* Moreover, I show how popular fictions are shaped and reshaped in relation to other ways of producing racial meanings.

In order to set the stage for these arguments, I clarify my two main critical interventions mentioned above. First, I develop an approach to race based around racial salience by doing an immanent critique of Michael Omi and Howard Winant's racial formation theory—still one of the most influential approaches to race today. Second, I theorize how genre and race are linked and not separate entities, and how they work to build, anticipate, and organize the world. I situate this approach in relation to other literary approaches to race, ones that are most sensitive to race's formal, linguistic, and rhetorical dimensions. I conclude my introduction by developing the implications of my approach for rethinking prominent historical explanations of the transformation of racial meaning in the twentieth century. These two methodological interventions work together: in order to analyze the dynamics of *racial salience*, our approach to thinking about race in literature and the social sciences needs to develop a vocabulary that is alive to the way in which race not only shapes what does happen, but what potentially can happen. This question of *when, where, and how* we notice race rethinks our usual critical habits for reading race. What emerges, as we will see, is a renewed emphasis on the activity of noticing race as opposed to seeing it. Clarifying the distinction between "noticing" and "seeing" takes us to Michael Omi and Howard Winant's important work.

Noticing Race

> By noticing race we can begin to challenge racism.
>
> Michael Omi and Howard Winant, *Racial Formation in the United States*

In one sense, Omi and Winant's phrase in the epigraph has lost any critical edge it might once have had when it was published in the 1994 edition of their landmark *Racial Formation in the United States.* The powerful demonstrations of systematic racial inequalities and police brutality across social media over roughly the past decade (witnessing, of course, a much longer history of antiblack racism) have made "noticing race" in order to "challenge racism" almost obsolete. Black Lives Matter and other related movements against police killings of black people as well as the prison-industrial complex have heightened recognition of these practices that organize the present. They have spearheaded conversations about police reform, racial justice, and racial stratification. Conversely, the repeated rejoinders that "race matters" and "black lives matter," as well as the eloquent and sophisticated arguments that pinpoint practices of racism, are still explained away through interpretive frameworks that weigh race as one factor against others or displace race onto a different context in order to demonstrate its nonapplicability. In the case of police brutality, the condemnation of specific individuals or groups apart from larger social practices still serves as a way to disavow racial realities. As Ta-Nehisi Coates writes in *Between the World and Me*, "the phrase 'police reform' has come into vogue, and the actions of our publicly appointed guardians have attracted attention presidential and pedestrian. You may have heard the talk of diversity, sensitivity training and body cameras. These are all fine and applicable, but they understate the task and allow the citizens of this country to pretend that there is real distance between their own attitudes and those of the ones appointed to protect them."[1] With an ethos of color-blindness, race neutrality, and universalism still serving as horizons for progress, noticing race in increasingly sophisticated ways can still challenge conceptions in a landscape in which this distancing is prevalent.

The critical possibilities of "noticing race . . . to challenge racism" have been limited by a discursive landscape in which the hypervisibility and disavowal of racialized realities coexist. For example, in the debates about the role of race in the subprime mortgage crisis, various working papers determined that race was essentially a nonfactor by showing that racial demographics did not produce a statistically determinable causal factor or that other factors such as geography, income, and so on, played more of a role than race.[2] Equally, another set of papers argued that race was the underlying factor in the subprime mortgage crisis.[3] Gary Dymski sums up the status of these arguments well: "race is both ever-present and absent . . . some will see the effects of disparate racial treatment and outcomes everywhere; others will deny the importance of race in social and economic processes."[4] In the realm of cultural representation, this logic reigns as well in evaluations of some of our most popular forms of entertainment. The controversy over the representation of the Na'vi in the blockbuster movie *Avatar* is a vivid example. One article neatly sums up arguments that *Avatar* is a racist and imperialist fantasy of white men saving Native Americans. Responses to the article ridicule its claims, one in particular stating that "It is the HUMAN RACE that is referred to, that means all of us regardless of colour, nationality . . . I would also like to point out that the Na'vi are BLUE!"[5] As these two examples show, seeing whether race is an operative factor in any economic process or cultural representation is not a simple matter of "seeing" conventional markers of race and linking them to practices of inequality. Rather, it is a product of a discursive and narrative process in which what counts as race is itself being shaped.

The arguments described above are overdetermined by an either/or logic, one in which race is either there or not. As Susan Koshy puts it, "our social schemas . . . offer us only two options: we are in the racial order or we are out of it."[6] However, this is not just an impasse between individuals who choose to see race versus those who refuse to see it. We must look at how our methods for noticing race in the first place have *contributed* to this limitation in "our social schemas." For example, as I describe more fully in Part III, Gary Becker in *The Economics of Discrimination* creates a model for measuring the impact of race on economic processes, a model whose influence can be seen across legal and social science frameworks. The model compares two economic states, one with race as a factor and one without it. Such a method relies on locating race in a certain way such that we can imagine a world with or without race. Becker's method is an example where these "there–not there" conflicts around analyzing race are already produced within the methodology for determining racism in the first place.

A similar either-or logic is produced by the methodology of legal thinking in the form of the necessity to demonstrate intent and causality, what Imani Perry calls "an extraordinarily difficult standard to meet" that "often requires a 'smoking gun.'"[7] Race is either seen at the level of a "smoking gun" or it is not seen at all. Despite the move to include the disproportionate effects on marginalized populations as evidence for discrimination within legal decision making, it remains extremely difficult to identify the effects of racism in institutional and structural terms in the courtroom. As I argue in Part IV, one reason is the ubiquity of counterfactual reasoning in the legal context, a favorite tool in tort law because of its presumed efficacy in isolating causes: if x had not happened, then y would not have happened, thus establishing x as a salient and important cause for y. This mode of thought is repeatedly used in equal protection jurisprudence as a way to produce a race-neutral stance that relegates the perception of race (in certain instances) to the background.

These frameworks, it is important to underscore, emerged as a way to *account* for race in response to the lack of attention to race. When Becker wrote *The Economics of Discrimination*, he was among the earliest group of economics scholars attempting to show the effects of race within economic practices and market processes. The inclusion of disparate impact or de facto racism in addition to de jure racism was an effort to account for race in more capacious ways than the earlier, more limited frameworks. But as I have outlined above and demonstrate further in later chapters, when economic and legal thinking are practicing their due diligence, they do not just incorporate race as a factor in their analyses; rather, they shape the sequences and narrative explanations by which race will be rendered salient or relegated to the background. We must now attend to the perceptual framework put into place by the most dominant approach in antiracist scholarship over the past thirty years: racial formation and the social construction thesis.

At the core of Omi and Winant's theory of racial formation over all three editions of *Racial Formation in the United States* is that race operates on two levels: the micro-level of attributing difference and classifying persons based on race and the macro-level of social organization and structure, for example, an unequal distribution of wealth or unequal practices of incarceration. This methodology relies on a set of correspondences in which one activity can be linked to another through some mutually determining relationship: "We conceive of racial formation processes as occurring through a linkage between structure and signification."[8] The trajectory of the argument suggests a linkage between significations on identities and bodies with a more diffuse sense of social structure: race is "a concept which signifies and symbolizes sociopolitical conflicts and interests in reference to different types of human bodies."[9] However, the phrase "in reference to" opens up two related points of ambiguity. One is the primacy of the already given visuality of race as bodily difference. Omi and Winant's argument is often based on the activity of noticing people at the level of physical characteristics. The foundational point of reference for this moment of perception is the "perceived corporeal and phenotypic markers of difference."[10] These already given markers are the raw material upon which racial meanings act. Within this mode of perception specified in the theory of racial formation, there is no room for thinking beyond the priority of the already visualized body.

As Osagie Obasogie argues, what is outside their framework (and the framework of the generation of social constructionist writing on race that followed Omi and Winant's thesis) is the way we are trained discursively to see the visual salience of race. In other words, contrary to most social constructionist theorizations, the visuality of race is not "anterior to" the social process.[11] Rather, the assumed visuality of racial difference on the body is itself something that is *rendered* visible and *made* salient through a set of social practices. Obasogie sums up this gap: "The social constructionist approach in general, and race theory in law and the social sciences in particular, have largely looked at how meanings attach to bodies without spending much time on how these racialized bodies become visually salient in the first place."[12] Obasogie's critique highlights the assumptions of a social constructionist approach that looks at how meanings attach to bodies all the while presuming the self-evidence of the body as well as the representational apparatus. These assumptions have been a defining ground of race critique across law, the social sciences, and literary analysis. Obasogie's intervention opens up a mode of critique that analyzes the "social practices" that "produce our very ability to see race."[13] To be sure, Omi and Winant specify that race cannot "even be *noticed* without reference . . . to social structure."[14] But this process of "reference" brings us back to how racial meanings are attached to bodies and the "perceived corporeal and phenotypic markers of difference."

The second point of ambiguity is related to this process of reference—the ambiguity of the terms used to characterize the relationship between structure and representation: "links," "connects," "shapes," and "based on." In Omi and Winant, "racial projects link signification and structure"; they also "shape the ways in which social structures are racially signified and the ways that racial meanings are embedded in social structures."[15] The words "links" and "based on" imply a more positivist or deterministic way in which meaning at the level of social structure "links" to signification at the level of the body, even as "shape" opens up a potentially more dynamic relationship. This more deterministic formulation can be found in their definition of a racial project as racist: "a racial project can be defined as racist if it *creates or reproduces structures of domination based on racial significations and identities.*"[16] But race, as Omi and Winant state, is "*more* than racism,"[17] and this methodological reliance on "linking" limits our capacity to think in more depth about this shaping force of race as a social fact that exceeds the parameters we currently have for demonstrating and proving racism. The success of Omi and Winant's racial formation thesis is that it has taught us to see race very clearly in terms of specific links between structure and racial categories. But the modes of perception they put in place must themselves be supplemented by attending to the often nonvisual ways in which race is "noticed."

I highlight these perceptual frameworks in order to articulate a methodology that gets past the "there–not there" impasse, one that does not hinge on linkages between what we have noticed but rather on a deeper understanding of our practices of noticing race and their impact on how we inhabit and participate in the world. A crucial term for this methodology is "salience." Linda Martín Alcoff uses "salience" in order to remark on race's "compelling social reality": "in the very midst of our contemporary skepticism toward race stands the compelling social reality that race, or racialised identities, have as much political, sociological and economic salience as they ever had."[18] "Salience" does not just denote visibility but also "protruding" and "standing out." This aspect of salience returns us to other senses of "noticing" that have less to do with observing what is already there and more to do with "pointing out," "mentioning," or "referring to." Noticing something (a fact, an idea) *as salient* changes a sense of one's surroundings: it is to "become aware of what is happening."[19] We can think of "noticing race" in terms of this shifting relation to context: how, when, and how much do we notice race; how, when, and why race "stands out" and becomes actualizable in any situation; how race becomes an organizing factor in generating context. The question of salience suggests that race is something around which a scene or situation can cohere.

My critique of the dominant social science approach to race replaces racial formation with the dynamics of racial salience. It shifts attention from analyzing the linkage between structure and signification to analyzing when and how we notice race. Instead of looking for an overdetermined point or link between two realms, we are analyzing acts of attention, pointing out, or mentioning that shape contexts.[20] As I argue below, narrative modes of storytelling are filled with such acts of organizing perception. Analyzing race along these lines is not an exercise in the recognition of racial ideologies. Recognizing racial ideologies is inevitably a project in discovering what we already know, an activity of deriving the present from the past. Instead, we can describe the methodology being practiced here as analyzing our *participation* in race: What worlds are generated through racial meanings? What contexts, situations, and explanations are made possible by racial speculation? Brian Massumi identifies the importance of participation: "We become conscious of a situation in its midst, already actively engaged in it. Our awareness is always of an already ongoing participation in an unfolding relation. . . . *Participation precedes recognition*."[21] Racial thinking pervades our participation in and even our prospective generation of the world as an ongoing temporal unfolding. Unlike recognition, the dynamic of participation cannot be extracted as a settled, discrete moment that is seemingly ready-made to be analyzed. Participation is structured yet contingent, mobile and emergent, the accumulation and ordering of meaning over time.

This model more accurately gets at the potency of race in producing the organizing assumptions through which we move around in the world. It draws on a tradition of theory that sees racism less in terms of beliefs and attitudes or even retrospective rationalizations, and more as a discourse or worldview that is a way of looking, perceiving, and interpreting.[22] But it differs in theorizing the speculative modes of thought specific to the apprehension of race and world. Once we shift our analysis to how the salience of race is produced, we can show the ways in which we are taught to notice race not just on bodies but as social facts embedded in our temporal organization of experience. To return to the examples of police brutality so prominent at the time of this writing, the acquittal or refusal to charge police officers involved in the killings of black people often rest on the relocation of racial salience. Judge McCulloch who presided over the acquittal of Darren Wilson, the officer who killed Michael Brown on August 9, 2014, responded after the acquittal: "No young man should ever be killed by a police officer, but no police officer should ever be put in that position."[23] What I want to remark on here is not the race-neutral language of these two sentences but rather the displacement from "young man" into "that position." The language of "that position" institutes a narrative of necessity and justification that speaks to the ways in which a racialized repertory of judgments has been embedded into the situation. It is the knowledge built into understanding the phrase "that position" through which racism functions as justification. The key to understanding these dynamics of narrative discourse is the intertwined consideration of race and genre: race at the level of its genre-like organizing force and genre formations in their dependence on the capacities of race. The concept of genre helps us consider more closely how sequences are interpreted, how contexts are generated, and how statements gain explanatory force. Thinking genre and race together extends understandings of Omi and Winant's terms "shape" and "embedded" in describing the interrelation between meaning and structure. This is because we *participate in genres* in order to form and organize our sense of the world.

Genre-Race Configurations: A Methodological Approach

Genre fiction, popular fiction, pulp, junk fiction: these terms often designate cheap, mass-market books catering to an audience that wants fast, entertaining, plot-driven formulas of adventure, romance, suspense, and melodrama. Scott McCracken historicizes and differentiates popular genre fiction in this contemporary sense as a "product of the industrial age, mechanically reproduced alongside other goods, services, and cultural artefacts" beginning in the late nineteenth century.[24] The mass market and circulation of popular fiction was made possible by changing technologies of printing and publishing, everything from dime westerns to serialized adventure stories and the pulp magazines of weird fiction, oriental tales, and amazing stories to the mass-market paperbacks of today.

In this broad field, genre is most often used to designate the formulaic and the conventional, a way of classifying stories and prescribing a sense of what to expect. In a historical romance, one does not expect aliens to come down from outer space. In a western, one does not expect to see a sorcerer performing magic. The definition of genre used here derives from a long history of genre as a taxonomic and classifying device: a way to put texts into different categories based on their expressive properties, their mode of presentation, formal devices, the kind of action presented, and so on.[25] The classic distinctions between epic, dramatic, and lyric, as well as the listing of different genres that are each specifically appropriate to their content and audience come to mind. Genre in this taxonomic sense becomes a way for publishers to market certain kinds of books to their audiences, a way for readers to identify a consistent kind of story that they like to read, a way for writers to spin off multiple iterations that guarantee an audience. In this sense, the way in which genre is defined through the dynamics of mass-market fiction follows some of the main assumptions of traditional genre theory: that a text is "in" a genre, that it belongs to a genre in the sense that it is a particular instance of a general type, that it contains certain features that correspond to essential rules of the genre. For example, these assumptions underlie debates about whether to classify Kazuo Ishiguro's *The Buried Giant* as fantasy, as well as critical projects built around identifying the origins and/or properties of any given genre.

The weaknesses of genre as taxonomy are apparent anytime one actually tries to define a genre. As the exceptions, hybrids, and limit cases to any taxonomic approach show, it is impossible *not* to mix genres. Here is Jacques Derrida's reframing of this question in his essay "The Law of Genre": "a text would not *belong* to any genre. Every text *participates* in one or several genres, there is no genreless text, there is always a genre and genres, yet such participation never amounts to belonging."[26] The distinction between participation and belonging is the difference between an open-ended relation of citation and a closed relation of being a part of something already defined. Wai Chee Dimock follows this line of reasoning when she describes genre as a field of knowledge or incipience "with countless examples but no solidity to speak of."[27]

My own use of genre borrows from John Frow's work, which opens a space in between the use of genre as taxonomy and the madness of genre described by Derrida.[28] Frow focuses on multiple dimensions of reading and experience in which genres are implicated:

1. *The relationship between text and genre:* genres are not a static set of features or stable classes that govern texts; conversely, texts do not belong to a genre: "texts work upon genres as much as they are shaped by them, genres are open classes, and participation in a genre takes many different forms."
2. *The relationship between genre and reader:* no text is ever unframed; our experience of a text is organized in advance by expectations of what kind of text it is—whether that be a headline in a newspaper, a poem selected in an anthology, a mass-market paperback sold at an airport bookstore. Genres are thus "frames" that establish the protocols for reading any given text.
3. *The relationship between genre and rhetorical situation:* genres respond to the structures of information in which they are embedded and out of which genres are themselves constituted. As Frow puts it, "Genres organise verbal and non-verbal discourse, together with the actions that accompany them, and how they contribute to the social structuring of meaning."
4. *The relationship between genre and composing the world*: genres make available a set of knowledges that are activated by readers; texts construct worlds that are "generically specific." They do so in several ways: the projection of coherent worlds through the selection and organization of a particular thematic structure, the implication of the reader in presupposing a set of background knowledges, and formal features such as syntactic structure and narrative patterning.[29]

Understood as such, genres are not a fixed set of tropes, rules, or conventions. They dynamically shape meanings and expectations at the same time that they are shaped by them. It is not that everything is a genre. More precisely, genres are everywhere as fields and frames with which to organize meaning. They produce effects of truth and authority through the projection of their "generically specific" worlds.

This "generically specific" world is the construction of imaginary or fictional worlds as an effect of the work of art as a whole. For example, some of the most popular worlds constructed through narrative, like J. R. R. Tolkien's Middle Earth in the *Lord of the Rings* trilogy or Margaret Mitchell's plantation Tara in *Gone with the Wind*, take on a life of their own and have such force that they construct many of the givens and assumptions by which people understand their own history and present reality.

They are generically specific worlds in multiple senses: how they are projected by the text, how they implicate the reader, how they interact with the actual world. They teach readers what to expect, how to understand a protagonist's situation, and how to put together the causal sequence—in short, how to participate in the narrative telling. Generically specific worlds involve, as Eric Hayot observes in *On Literary Worlds*, an "arrangement of significances and relations" that distributes importance on multiple levels of narrative meaning.[30] Moreover, they consist of the time and space relations that generate a sense of worldedness and that prompt readers to connect and extend meanings in certain ways.[31]

This understanding of genre recognizes overlaps between the narrative storyworlds in which we are immersed and the ongoing world-building activities of the "actual" world. It does not occur just at the level of the text acting on the reader. The reader also acts on the text and within a social situation. Narrative theorists have taken up possible-worlds theory in order to consider the ontological status of our possible, imaginary, and fictional worlds and their relationship to the actual world. As Mark Wolf puts it in *Building Imaginary Worlds*, "Possible worlds theory places the 'actual world' at the center of the hierarchy of worlds, and 'possible worlds' around it, that are said to be 'accessible' to the actual world. These worlds are then used to formulate statements regarding possibility and necessity."[32] David Herman notes the intersection between imaginary worlds and actual worlds in this way: "Narratives do not merely evoke worlds; precisely by inviting interpreters to construct and inhabit such worlds, they also intervene in a field of discourses, a range of representational strategies, a constellation of ways of seeing—and sometimes a set of competing narratives, as in a courtroom trial, a political campaign, or a family dispute."[33] Both Herman and Thomas Pavel see the "actual" world alongside many or all of its other possible worlds or world-versions, whereby the inhabitation of fictional worlds can "intervene in" our modes of experiencing the "actual" world. Wolf describes this potential use of fictional worlds this way: "Worlds extend beyond the stories that occur in them, inviting speculation and exploration through imaginative means. They are realms of possibility, a mix of familiar and unfamiliar, permutations of wish, dread, and dream, and other kinds of existence that can make us more aware of the circumstances and conditions of the actual world we inhabit."[34] One of the best illustrations of this is participatory fan culture where readers act out, actualize, and subvert textual worlds.[35] Genres as practices of worldmaking attends to meaning-generation from many sites: authors, readers, editors, and structures of information and everyday discourse.

This notion of worldmaking has long been theorized within science fiction (SF) criticism. Darko Suvin makes the new cognitive construction of the "cosmic and social totality of each tale" one of the necessary conditions of SF proper.[36] I focus in particular on the processes of this cognitive construction, whereby genres "build-in" knowledges across text, reader, and situation. As Robert Gerrig comprehensively describes in *Experiencing Narrative Worlds*, narrative genres involve readers in all kinds of temporal organizations of the world for creating coherence and making sense. Gerrig lists the prospective and retrospective cognitive activities involved in this temporal processing: the "search for causal relations and that those causal relations, once recovered, provide much of the global coherence of memory representations"; a framing set of schemas that allows readers to "organize the information in accordance with that structure"; the staging of certain hopes and preferences for the reader as they replot the events of the narrative; the demand on the reader to "construct a context—different from the here and now—that enables them to understand the fictional text"; the cues by which authors encode a certain set of expected attitudes and qualities that the reader is expected to hold.[37] These activities of constructing contexts, encoding preferences, and organizing information are all things that readers do quickly.

As this description makes clear, the kind of knowledge that is "built in" is knowledge not merely to compose the present but also to speculate on both past and future conditions. We might say that genre trains us equally well not just in the act of, say, imagining a flower,[38] but in what Adrian Piper calls the "modal imagination": acts of envisioning what is possible through extending experience and the application of concepts both forward and backward in time. "We need," Piper writes, "modal imagination in order to extend our conception of reality—and, in particular, of human beings—beyond the immediate experience in the indexical present; and we need to do this in order to preserve the significance of human interaction."[39] Without our modal imagination, we would have a profoundly bereft understanding of our experiences and social relations: "Without the capacity to envisage events or states of affairs other than those we ourselves were experiencing or had experienced, we would be unable to identify our experiences in terms of universally applicable concepts . . . because the application of each extends past the experiences we have actually had forward into a possible future and backward into a counterfactually possible past."[40]

These speculative operations through which we extend our conception of reality are crucial ways to navigate and make judgments about the world.

They go beyond the operations of picturing the solidity of an object in that they represent imaginative operations through which we organize experience and understand events not as discrete things but according to their consequences. The modal imagination *extends* reality beyond the here and now; a nonmodal understanding of reality, by contrast, is deeply impoverished precisely because of the inability to make sense of experiences across time and different circumstances. For Mark Currie, these imaginative acts are at the heart of all narrative because it involves not just retrospection but anticipation: narrative involves a mode of "continuous anticipation in which we attach significance to present moments."[41] Anticipation here is experiencing the present as an object of an imagined future history. We do this all the time: every time we capture a moment (your child's theatrical performance, your experiences as a tourist) for future posterity, we are engaging in this anticipation of retrospection, or what Veronica Hollinger neatly calls "looking forward in order to look backward."[42]

This understanding of narrative genres as crucial to the activity of "building-in" or making available certain knowledges has, ironically, not been applied to popular genre fictions because of their presumed boundedness to rulelike conventions. For me, far from being the most formulaic and conventional examples of genre, popular genre fictions provide some of the clearest examples of the process of generating worlds with their own rules, meanings, and expectations. The infamous participation and readerly involvement in popular genres are predicated on a great deal of attention to the landscapes, rules, and judgments embedded in the worlds created. The "page-turner" quality of genre fiction hinges on its ability to be keyed to readers' temporal experiences of their worlds in continually forming and revising anticipations, expectations, and coherence. Ordinarily these traits are denigrated for producing a cheap and naïve readerly pleasure. Pierre Bourdieu characterizes the moral and emotional involvement in popular genres: "The desire to enter into the game, identifying with the characters' joys and sufferings, worrying about their fate, espousing their hopes and ideals, living their life, is based on a form of *investment*, a sort of deliberate 'naivety,' ingenuousness, good-natured credulity . . . which tends to accept formal experiments and specifically artistic effects only to the extent that they can be forgotten and do not get in the way of the substance of the work."[43]

However, these aspects of genre fiction—participation, involvement, investment—can be seen in terms of, and not in opposition to, "specifically artistic effects." The "genre" in genre fiction is crucial for shaping the world of reference and thereby constructing anticipatory cognitions. Precisely because of their commodity form and the particular forms of readership engendered, popular fictions rely to an unusually high degree on the rules and conventions of their respective genres in building their worlds of reference. The storyworlds of popular fiction are organizations of meaning that are intensely self-reflexive and intertextual with regard to specific precursors and readerships within the genre. Moreover, the highly codified and purposeful ways of staging the readerly pleasures within these works highlight the minute differences between works as they organize slightly differing landscapes of meaning-making. In other words, it is precisely in what critics most demean about genre fiction that we find the complexity of its worldmaking practices.

Popular fictions excel in inviting readers to co-create and inhabit worlds. They play out relationships between the rules of the world and how readers and characters alike respond to these worlds. The genre fictions that I focus on all give weight to the relationship to the world over the psychological organization of the individual. "Science fiction," the author and critic Samuel Delany argues, "is far more concerned with the organization (and reorganization) of the object, i.e., the world, or the institutions through which we perceive it. It is concerned with the subject, certainly, but concerned with those aspects of it that are closer to the object: How is the subject excited, impinged on, contoured, and constituted by the object?"[44] Instead of funneling the story through the subject's development and psychology, science fiction orients readers to the material ways in which the world is organized, how situations and landscapes are composed, and how objects are arranged. Historical romances similarly hinge on the inhabiting of a distinct but similar world through which readers can pleasurably participate in its meaning-making structures. Thomas Roberts notes the decreased emphasis on complex individual psychologies and increased emphasis on reactions to varied circumstances: "What it presents is not a series of ethically neutral incidents but an exemplary type of reaction, a repertory of normative attitudes in the supreme crises of life."[45] Janice Radway demonstrates how believable the heroes and heroines of romance are because they are "distinguished clearly in the readers' minds by the peculiarity of their circumstances and by the specificity of their responses to events"; they are "realistic" in the sense that readers "are convinced by the narrative's display of their individual particularity."[46] Meanwhile, one of the signatures of secondary-world fantasy is its map of the fantasy world, along with detailed explanations of its peoples and different species ranging along scales from "primitive" to "civilized." In the characterizations above, Radway, Roberts, and Delany put their fingers on the activity of reacting and responding to, as well as being "contoured" by, a shifting world. With all three popular modes of storytelling, the emphasis is placed on reactions not consciousness, on objects not subjects, on circumstances and situations as they "excite" or "impinge" on subjects, in short on the anticipations and expectations of the world.

This understanding of genre in terms of organizing meaning, projecting coherent worlds, and building knowledge helps articulate a different relationship with race. Ordinarily, genre is a static set of rules or properties used by an author to express or subvert some racial content as theme, representation, or ideology. As such, race is the content to be acted on by genre. Genre has causal priority over race; it comes first and race second. However, once we think of genres as constructing worlds in the ways detailed above, we can see the dynamic interrelations between genre and race. Genres activate certain ways in which racial meaning will be used in the composition of a world—establishing situations and justifying actions while making others seem less possible or realizable. At the same time, race shapes genre. As a possible set of referents, as narrative anticipations, and as the social structuring of meanings, race composes expectations for what the world might look like and activates rules for knowing the world.

Genre and race thus are both *affordances* because they make available certain knowledges about the world and help us interact with it in certain ways. The perceptual psychologist J. J. Gibson defines "affordance" as a subjective object that makes certain ways of inhabiting and interacting with the world possible and actualizable.[47] A table is an affordance for placing my cup of coffee both because of its material properties (wood, plastic) and its cognizable properties (that the table is of a sufficient height—not too low, not too high; that the table is of a sufficient stability—it is even and not wobbly). As such, the table provides an affordance for somebody to use it in a certain way. Or to take a more perceptual example, the bathroom light strikes my retina at a certain angle that allows me to see my toothbrush but also puts the corner of the sink into shadow. My perception of the bathroom space is thus given a particular organization by this affordance. In saying that both genre and race are affordances, I am not saying that genre and race are the same thing. Rather, it is that they both have the capacity to frame situations and channel responses.

In articulating this relationship, even affinity, between genre and race, I build on recent scholarship across African American, Asian American, and U.S. Latino/Latina literary studies that has used genre and/or form as a critical tool with which to treat questions of race. These contributions are twofold. One, formal considerations are used to critique realism and the referential reading practices engendered by it. As De Witt Douglas Kilgore states, race studies has long privileged social realism as the "mode that best captures the texture and meaning of the black experience."[48] Stephen Sohn considers the construction of "fictional worlds" through the lens of narrative perspective and the distance or disjunction between authorial identity and fictional content.[49] Frederick Luis Aldama uses narrative and cognitive approaches to complicate how race is used to generate certain cognitions and affects.[50] Two, greater attention to intersections between genre fiction and race complicates our understandings of the histories of race and its ideological assumptions. For example, John Rieder argues for the formative role of colonial imaginaries on the emergence of science fiction.[51] Isiah Lavender tracks how the different representational techniques of SF might refer to histories of race relations and figure or refigure its dominant ideologies.[52] Betsy Huang radically expands our applications of genre by thinking of Asian American writing as itself generic, existing within a set of expectations and conventions that both prescribe the possibilities of Asian American stories and become a site for their radical rewriting.[53] Like this scholarship, I am interested in how an attention to genre rethinks the referential reading practices that conventionally identify when a book is about race and when it is not, when racial meanings are generated and when they are not. *Racial Worldmaking* participates, too, in the excavation of popular genres for the distinct ways in which they articulate racial modes of thought.

The most recent broader paradigm to utilize concepts of form in relation to the question of race is Colleen Lye's notion of "racial form." By "racial form," Lye is not referring to literary techniques or conventions per se—an analysis based on the catalog of formal innovations or strategies that would be tied to the author's deployment/sophistication. She is referring to form as both social and aesthetic. For her, Raymond Williams's notion of form as a social relationship is crucial. According to Williams, the telling of a story, the writing of a poem, the reading of a scene are already social relationships. These processes are made possible by certain modes of address and certain social organizations that set soft limits around its presentation. This understanding of form gets us into a deeper historical materialism by thinking about how its mode of presentation is contoured in and as a social relationship. It helps us, Lye argues, keep in mind the notion of race as an "active social relation rather than a transhistorical abstraction."[54]

My own sense of the interrelations between genre and race builds on this notion of race as an "active social relation," for I am most interested in the ways that both genre and race figure *participation*: when a text participates in genre and race, it is making available certain ways of reading, perception, and cognition and not others. In understanding this notion of participation, we can add to the critiques of referential reading practices above. If our typical procedures for reading race have involved unraveling *what* race signifies, the reformulation of genre and race above shifts the analysis to *when* race signifies and *when* in the midst of organizing experience "forward into a possible future and backward into a counterfactually possible past" we confer significance on race. Doing so reminds us of the limitations in thinking race as solely a classificatory operation of thought. It reminds us that reading race need not consist solely of an activity of linking its referents to a set of denotations and connotations that produce hierarchical judgments. It allows us to shift our focus to how racial referents and meanings are arranged and distributed across the space and time of the textual world. Yes, while reading one still pays attention to statements about race, race as a descriptor, race as a referent to some historical event, legal context, or social situation. But one also pays attention to how all of these elements are arranged and used to frame the inhabiting and making of the textual world. I borrow from narratological approaches in order to think about how race is a part of the narrative structure of causality, its composition of space-time relations, its manipulation of what a reader knows, and its shifting of foreground and background. That means a greater attention to how race operates as a "subjectless discourse," used to regulate and organize situations, not just refer to bodies and subjects.[55] That requires a greater attention to how genre and race interact in our modes of storytelling[56] and to how these elements compose units of meaning such as sequence and context. Sequence is a unit that is temporally longer than description; context is a unit that focuses on the spatial parameters of how and when race might be used to compose a set of expectations.

Racial Worldmaking thus demonstrates how certain popular fictions have played a significant and overlooked role in teaching readers how to form racial meanings. Popular genres are read mainly as derivative phenomena—reinforcing, popularizing, or proliferating already existing modes of racial discrimination. For example, the future war genre is routinely described in terms of its extreme representation of already existing orientalist sentiments. But far from just replicating or reproducing the reigning racial ideologies of the moment, these genre formations prompt cognitive acts that have to do with our prospective generation of the world. One might briefly describe my critical method as analyzing all of the nonvisual ways in which race works with genre in building, anticipating, and organizing the world. Each part looks back at key influential moments in the emergence of these genre formations as well as the historical variability within the genre in order to see particular racial ways of knowing taking shape. By focusing on the narrative mechanisms by which these genres embed race in the reader's capacity to recount the past and imagine the future, we can see the development of racial modes of thought that have escaped our attention because they are not dependent on the biological or cultural visibility of bodily difference. *They carry out their effects whether race is seen or not.*

Worlds of Black and Asiatic Racialization

I take the emergence, development, and proliferation of popular fiction from the late nineteenth century to the present as the historical period of my book. I do so to make connections between the widely circulated imaginings of popular fiction and the racial logics of the twentieth century.[57] The four parts of this book collectively focus on Asiatic racialization and antiblack racism primarily in the United States during this time period. The selection of these particular racial logics is not meant to preclude attention to other racial groups, histories, or political formations of racism either within the United States or globally. Indeed, the theorization of racial worldmaking potentially puts these sites in conversation with recent work on Chicanafuturism, Blackfoot physics, and/or indigenous work on temporality—work that calls attention to various world-building practices that contest the racialized terms of the world.[58] But the selection of these particular practices of racial worldmaking oriented around African Americans and Chinese and Japanese Americans is not arbitrary either. It points to the prominent role of the legacies of the Russo-Japanese War, U.S. Civil War, and World War II in the production and framing of social knowledge about race in the twentieth century. It also highlights the particular importance of legal and economic discourse from the 1950s through the present that concentrates on black-white relations in the framing of debates about race relations in the United States, even as these frames erase the presence and histories of other racial groups. Even the most recent and prominent affirmative action and reverse discrimination cases continue to adhere to paradigms built around African American political struggle and, most recently, Asian Americans' contested claims to racial formation.[59] The *Ricci v. Distefano* reverse discrimination case that I consider in Part IV lists a Hispanic firefighter in addition to the white firefighters as one whose rights have been violated due to affirmative action policies. But nowhere in the oral testimony is the Hispanic firefighter highlighted or made visible. Only the situations and positions of white firefighters are described. My selection is not intended here to perpetuate these reductive paradigms. It is, rather, to notice how the *salience* of particular groups and identities project certain organizations of meaning at the expense of others.

Asiatic racialization has long been positioned as a wedge or third term to complicate the use of binary black-white models to cover the whole question of race relations. Important scholarship has traced various moments of Afro-Asian solidarity and unity, primarily around the historical moment of Third World internationalism.[60] Equally important are analyses that focus on Asianness in a triangulated relationship or as a mediated position between black and white through which the politics of race are carried out.[61] Labor histories often point to the substitutive role that Asians have played in reproducing exploitable labor after the U.S. Civil War.[62] My interest in focusing on African American and Asian American racialization has less to do with these moments of solidarity, contestation, or substitution. As Lye detects, this important scholarly work still relies for the most part on positing Asiatic racialization as deriving from antiblack racism.[63] My aim here is not to compare the development of Asiatic racialization and antiblackness in the sense of either analogy or influence.[64] I am more interested in locating the multiple racial logics emerging from these specific histories and the particularly salient role they have played in knowledges of race at the level of historical truth, economic thinking, and legal procedure. There are moments of convergence and overlap, to be sure. But my interest is in how this overlap creates new narrative and rhetorical possibilities that then proliferate in the making of racial worlds. The presence of these two sites across these genre fictions no doubt speaks to the powerful way in which large-scale events such as the Russo-Japanese War, the global attention to black-white relations in the United States and the U.S. civil rights movement, and World War II and the bombing of Pearl Harbor captured and were used to capture the popular "modal imagination" of race.

Finally, this juxtaposition of black and Asiatic racialization provides a useful test case because of the widely divergent relationships that they have to the field of racial referentiality. As we will see, the terms of Asiatic racialization have often included the vaguest, most disembodied referents—fog, flood, peril—while the terms of black racialization have often included the most concrete, embodied actions. I complicate this picture in the chapters that follow, but this juxtaposition allows me to highlight the relationship between the distribution of racial referents and racial salience. In some genre-race configurations such as future war/yellow peril and sword and sorcery/economic discrimination, racial markers come to name an increasing number of things and the overall domain of racial reference is expanded. In other genre-race configurations, such as plantation romance/ Reconstruction and alternate history/civil rights jurisprudence, this domain is contracted or displaced. In both cases, the distribution of racial referents shapes when race is *noticed* and how salient it becomes in forming meaning.

Each of the genre-race configurations I focus on emerges at moments when the mechanisms of racial attribution based on biological understandings or on dominant political characterizations are no longer palatable or easily assumed. Each part shows the way in which these configurations create new frames for noticing *when* and *how* race is salient based in retrospection and prediction about the world. From the late nineteenth century to the mid-twentieth century, both scientific racism and political racist characterizations were already being critiqued. Scientific racism was critiqued even as it was just emerging in the mid-to-late nineteenth century, not necessarily by antiracists but by writers who were not content with limiting racial signification to aspects of biology, lineage, or somatic difference. Parts I and II show the ways in which future war and plantation romance genres responded to these critiques by developing new domains of racial reference and new ways of noticing race at the level of constructing histories and temporalities.

In Part I, "Yellow Peril Genres," these new narrative strategies became most clear in relation to the difficulty of characterizing Japanese power, technology, and modernity sparked by Japan's ascent onto the world stage in the Russo-Japanese War. I track the emergence of future history and future war in relation to the ascension of Japan as a modern technological power, an ascension that made it difficult to apply scientific and anthropological racism to the Japanese people. These works, which span across fiction, nonfictional treatises, and U.S. military documents develop new spatio-temporal logics for noticing race that do not rely on representations of race via biological difference. They draw on modes of thought from historiography, prediction, and futurology in order to narrate the future as if it has already happened. In doing so, they articulate ways of noticing race that are less individual and more global and give narrative logic to referents such as the "white world" and the "yellow flood." I argue that speculative works such as M. P. Shiel's *The Yellow Danger*, Homer Lea's *The Valor of Ignorance*, and H. G. Wells's *The War in the Air* create narrative logics whereby race denotes a world and acts as a world-organizing force. These modes of thought, and not the use of overt racist stereotypes, constitute the persistent legacy of this period for racial salience today.

Much like the future war genres analyzed in Part I, plantation romance/Reconstruction emerges at a moment when prior, taken-for-granted attributions of political racism have been unsettled. In Part II, "Plantation Romance," I situate the worldmaking practices of Margaret Mitchell's *Gone with the Wind* in relation to both its precursors (specifically Thomas Dixon's *The Leopard's Spots*) and its immediate followers (Frank Yerby's *The Foxes of Harrow*). By juxtaposing Dixon's *The Leopard's Spots* with *Gone with the Wind*, I demonstrate not a movement from overt racism to covert racism but rather a change in the way in which these works attribute race in the formation of narrative probability and necessity. I argue that *Gone with the Wind* transforms modes of racial perception inherited from earlier plantation romances so as to shape the contexts by which readers either notice race or not. By juxtaposing *Gone with the Wind* with *The Foxes of Harrow*, we see how they operate within the context of Civil War and Reconstruction historiography, a powerful generic formation at this time for "transforming document into narrative and narrative into explanation."[65] Frank Yerby counters Mitchell's plantation romance with his own, engaging readers in a different set of cognitive acts with regard to racial meaning in the postslavery, post-Reconstruction landscape of the U.S. South. In doing so, he gives us an early example of strategies of antiracist racial worldmaking.

Parts III and IV both address the shifting terms of how and when we notice race in relation to legal and economic debates surrounding civil rights legislation. I find characterizations of a shift from overt to covert racism—from de jure to de facto discrimination or from biological to cultural racism widely used to characterize this historical period—inadequate. Instead, we see a simultaneous narrowing of racial reference and a broadening of its signification at the level of processes of prediction and speculation. Racial meanings were being embedded in our narrative logics via legal reasoning and the imagination of economic subjects and the market. Part III traces the trajectory of "sword and sorcery" (S&S) from Robert Howard in the 1930s to the reissuing of Howard's stories in the 1950s, 1960s, and 1970s by L. Sprague de Camp, and finally to Samuel Delany's sword and sorcery series in the 1980s. This trajectory of sword and sorcery participates in two major transformations of racial meanings in the twentieth century: (1) the critique of scientific racism marked by the United Nations Educational, Scientific and Cultural Organization (UNESCO) statements on race in the 1950s and 1960s and (2) the development of an "economics of discrimination." Part III, Chapter 5 discusses S&S's relationship to the former. I argue that both sword and sorcery and the critique of scientific racism marshaled forth primarily through cultural anthropology relocated race to levels other than phenotypical differences. Even as certain uses of race to produce racism were critiqued, race was used as an ordering principle.

Part III, Chapter 6 highlights the representation of the market as one of S&S's principal world-building devices. I argue that racial salience is organized in relation to the market both within the genre of sword and sorcery and by economists themselves. The relationship between racial discrimination and the free market was widely debated in the 1960s and 1970s by economists and social scientists, and though the paradigms and arguments created by economists such as Gary Becker and Milton Friedman did not prevent antidiscrimination laws from being passed, they did create a new representational strategy for locating race so as to frame and shape decision-making practices. Sword and sorcery and popular economic thought both negotiate the problem of how and when to notice race in order to produce certain outcomes in the sphere of market exchanges. Here, Samuel Delany's S&S series revises the expectations and uses of race in order to envision alternative pathways to the embedding of racism in the market.

Part IV, "Alternate History," analyzes the genre of alternate history in relation to what Sora Han calls "racial jurisprudence," specifically cases concerning and codifying equal protection and the development of "strict scrutiny." It argues that a particularly crucial mode of thought for transforming the meaning and interpretation of race and racism at this time is the counterfactual, and it tracks the deployment of the counterfactual across both recent legal jurisprudence and alternate history, a genre whose popularity hinges on its most privileged counterfactual scenarios—what if the South had won the Civil War, and what if Germany and Japan won World War II? In Part IV, Chapter 7, I look at alternate histories of the Civil War, paying particular attention to the logics within the genre staged by Peter Tsouras and Harry Turtledove. I juxtapose my analysis of the poetics of their narrative explanations with recent anti–affirmative action and reverse discrimination jurisprudence. In *Ricci v. Distefano* (2009), I point to the role of counterfactual thinking in determining what counts as "fact" in the first place and in distributing racial meanings across the shifting divide between fact and fiction. A reading of Steven Barnes's *Lion's Blood* shows some of the ways in which the racial counterfactual can be inhabited in antiracist ways. In Part IV, Chapter 8, I survey alternate histories of World War II and track the divergent representations of a United States conquered by Japan versus a United States conquered by Germany.

I juxtapose these scenarios with the peculiar perceptual logics of "strict scrutiny" developed in *Korematsu v. United States* (1944). I read the similarities between Cyril Kornbluth's "Two Dooms" and Philip K. Dick's *The Man in the High Castle*, both of which imagine a United States divided between Germany and Japan, in order to show how these counterfactual scenarios rely on racism to provide the coherence of the world.

In my conclusion, "On the Possibilities of an Antiracist Racial Worldmaking," I turn to the work of W. E. B. Du Bois and track the multiple ways in which he works on the edges of genre, race, and world. Brief readings of *Black Reconstruction*, "The Comet," *Worlds of Color*, and *From Dusk to Dawn: Autobiography of a Race Concept*, track Du Bois's engagements with genre and world in order to rethink the mechanisms of historiography, alternate histories, science fiction, and romance. His work links up with other writers in this study such as Barnes, Delany, and Yerby who point to alternative visions of racial worldmaking.

I focus specifically on these genre-race configurations because they are clearly involved in shaping the cognitive activities of prediction, anticipation, and retrospection on the large scale of national and/or world history. The particular emergences and/or re-emergences of these configurations tell us something new about our histories of racial thought. In this way, my analysis of various modes of racial worldmaking leads finally toward rethinking prominent histories of race and racism in the twentieth and twenty-first centuries.

Extensions of Racial Thought in the Twentieth Century

In historicizing the concept of race as a formation of knowledge, we have relied on broad trajectories that track the different intellectual foundations of racial thought. Omi and Winant characterize the "*longue durée* of racial formation from religion to science to politics."[66] The development of scientific racism—first in the taxonomies and debates of natural history and then in the biological sciences—has been traced in various ways from the eighteenth century to the beginning of the twentieth century.[67] Many accounts of race in the twentieth century develop a trajectory from the hegemony of scientific racism to its demise and the emergence of "culturalist" frameworks of race and, most recently, the resurgence of scientific racism in the form of genomics.[68] These histories are broadly based on an account of the hegemony of scientific racism that developed in the mid-nineteenth century and lasted until the mid-twentieth century and the importance accorded to the body, skin, and other morphological and somatic characteristics. Within these histories, racial modes of thought are usually thought in terms of classification, mapping, and a means of linking the visible and the invisible. Grounded in these formations, social constructionist work shows how the race concept has served a variety of social and historical projects and emerged coterminous with "specific labor regimes; with slavery; with expanding capitalism, or with the bureaucratic normalizing technologies of modern states."[69]

The domain of political formations of race in the nineteenth and twentieth centuries is historicized along lines of a broad movement from overt to covert racism. George Frederickson narrates the twentieth century in terms of the rise and fall of overtly racist regimes:

> As we have seen, something that can be legitimately described as racism existed well before the twentieth or even the late nineteenth century. Prejudice and discrimination, fortified by ideologies claiming that the differences between human groups of apparently divergent ancestry are immutable and have implications for social inclusion or ranking, have a history that goes back to the late Middle Ages. But racist principles were not fully codified into laws effectively enforced by the state or made a central concern of public policy until the emergence of what I will call "overtly racist regimes" during the past century.[70]

Other accounts similarly reflect this framework of a shift from overt to covert racial regimes. John L. Jackson describes an arc from "blatant white racism" to a racism that is "hidden, secret, papered over with public niceties and politically correct jargon."[71] Similarly, Eduardo Bonilla-Silva recapitulates this distinction in his argument about "color-blind racism": "contemporary racial inequality is reproduced through 'new racism' practices that are subtle, institutional, and apparently nonracial. In contrast to the Jim Crow era, where racial inequality was enforced through overt means (e.g., signs saying 'No Niggers Welcomed Here' or shotgun diplomacy at the voting booth), today racial practices operate in a 'now you see it, now you don't' fashion."[72] Together, these two broad-based assumptions about histories of race and racism—one characterizing the role of science in shaping racial thought and the other characterizing a shift from overt to covert racism—form the backdrop to measuring any manifestation of race and racism.

These histories rely on assumptions about the visibility of race and on the capacity of race to produce classifications and categories of subjects.[73] This is because the emergence of modern biological notions of race resulted in the privileging of seeing and the body, the production of a mode of seeing that links "somatic differences to innate physical and mental characteristics or traits."[74] In questioning these historical assumptions, Ann Stoler argues that both so-called "overt" and "covert" racism participate in an "ocular obsession" as well as recapitulate a historically and conceptually problematic "contrast between a biologized somatic racism in the past and a more nuanced, complex, and culturally coded racism of the present."[75] Ibram X. Kendi critiques these assumptions from the angle of public policy, stating, "Old and new racist policies remained as overt as ever."[76] My critique of these histories and categories is similar to Paul Gilroy's understanding of all forms of race as being "raciologies," the "elaborate work in order to make the idea of 'race' epistemologically correct." Gilroy takes up the "view of 'race' as an active, dynamic idea or principle that assists in the constitution of social reality." Like Gilroy, I do not "concede the possibility that 'race' could be seen spontaneously, unmediated by technical and social processes." However, for me, this elaborate work is not limited to race as a series of "body ideas," nor are raciologies in any kind of crisis.[77] I highlight how race has become embedded in our "modal imagination" in many ways irrespective of bodies and subjects. Race is actualized via our speculative modes of thought, precisely our "capacity to envision what is possible in addition to what is actual" and our anticipatory conjoining of a present moment with a future one. As Kodwo Eshun observes, "power now operates predictively as much as retrospectively."[78] The economist Glenn Loury puts his finger on precisely this modal imagination of race when he defines race as a social-cognitive process: "Everything depends . . . on racially biased social cognitions that cause some *situations* to appear anomalous, disquieting, contrary to expectations, worthy of further investigation, inconsistent with the natural order of things—while other situations appear normal, about right, in keeping with what one might expect, consistent with the social world as we know it."[79]

The use of "expectations" above shows how racial ways of knowing are used to construct *situations* as knowable and predictable. Loury is careful to distinguish this process of social meaning-making from simply racial attitudes, as well as from race as a biological-taxonomic notion.[80] After giving an example of the cab driver who refuses to stop for young black men, Loury says that "we can see from this example that no *objective* racial taxonomy need be valid (the proportion of robbers in each group might have been the same) for the *subjective* use of racial classification to become warranted (cab drivers have a rational justification for their use of racial information). It is enough that influential social actors hold schemes of racial classification in their minds and act on those schemes."[81] Although Loury's emphasis is on the distinction between "objective racial taxonomy" and the "*subjective* use of racial classification," he is alert to the temporality of this process and the ways in which a proleptically imagined future (robbery) is used to structure the present.

Instead of characterizing race in the twentieth century in terms of broad shifts from overt to covert racism, this study tracks the coexistence and emergence of multiple regimes of racial perception and attribution that are not reducible to the visual body, individual, or group. As Kendi observes, if there has been racial progress in the challenging of racial inequality, there has simultaneously been racist progress. Racism is not a "backward" idea that is just trying to take us back to past forms of inequality. It is forward-looking, laying claim on our capacity to imagine the future. I track ways in which new racial modes of thought based in narrative processes of anticipation emerged, creating new forms of racial attribution in order to organize meaning. Race has become a crucial part of our modal imagination for determining what is possible. The methodology I offer in the following chapters has less to do with an analysis of how racialized bodies are linked to social structures, and more to do with how race shapes the conditions for what potentially can happen. As such, race is a peculiar object, dispersed and distributed in ways that organize the limits and parameters of the social field that is nothing less than the inhabitation of the world as a structure of expectations. It is to these processes of worldmaking that I now turn.

PART I

Yellow Peril Genres

CHAPTER 1

Worlds of Color

Racial worldmaking consists of narrative and interpretive strategies that embed race into our knowledge and expectations of the world. I begin with the most explicit example: the way in which "world" becomes operative as a category of racial meaning. We see this establishment of a new referential relationship in the application of racial predicates to the world itself, as in the phrases "white world," "colored world," or "yellow world." Such phrases sound odd in the early twenty-first century—what would it mean to attribute the characteristics of race to something as abstract as world? But they were ubiquitous in the late nineteenth and early twentieth century. In fact, we can trace their uses quite precisely. Using color designations to describe something so encompassing as a world in a racial sense was new during the years leading up to and after the Russo-Japanese War of 1904–5. Prior to this moment, the phrase "white world" is most often used either in stories about going to the Arctic in order to denote a field of snow, a world in which you are surrounded by the whiteness of the physical elements.[1] Or it was used in Christian religious tracts to denote heaven as a dazzlingly bright, white world.[2] But beginning in the late 1890s and 1900s, the terms "white world," "yellow world," and "brown world" started being deployed in the sense of a geopolitical reordering of the world.[3] This new referential relationship is most dramatically and influentially established in essays and arguments declaring a "conflict of color." It is extended in the renewal of "yellow peril" fears in the years leading up to and after the Russo-Japanese War.

This phraseology is not just an unusual blip in the history of racial discourse. That it emerges as a direct effect of writers describing and evaluating the meaning of the Russo-Japanese War is not a coincidence. The event of the war was represented as a signal reversal of racial expectations—against all odds, a "colored" nation defeated a "white" nation. This way of narrating the event forced a shift in the racial imaginary. The racial ideologies of superiority and inferiority did not suffice as explanations. The explanations that did emerge manifested new ways of apprehending race and producing racism. These new ways implicated both subjects of Asiatic and black racialization. In the nineteenth century, these two groups were, of course, already co-constructed at times via the categories of "coolie" and "slave" and through debates concerning immigration and citizenship in the United States.[4] Here, they are read through a new perceptual emphasis on the organization of the world.

What is remarkable about this mode of racial worldmaking is that it is not reducible to nineteenth-century scientific discourses on race and early nineteenth-century Romantic nationalist ways of speaking about racial essences, although it draws some of its logics from the latter, as well as from "climate-and-custom" racism, which I describe below. The referents that it deploys—"world," "flood," "danger," "wave," "disaster"—concentrate attention on a different kind of object. The typical objects of attention for nineteenth-century scientific racism and physical anthropology are the body and physical characteristics. For *volkische* nationalism, they are character, people, spirit, and/or nation. Here, the thing being described in terms of race is the world itself, an object that on the one hand constitutes everything around you, the totality of what can be grasped, and on the other hand is the most immediate sense of exterior reality. I argue that locating racial difference in both senses of "world" embeds race as a historical tendency and in our temporal structures for organizing the significant features and events of the world.

The application of predicate to thing shapes perception. The effective attachment of "yellow," "white," or "colored" to "world" prompts us toward an apprehension of "world" that is predicated on race as an ordering form. The philosopher Nelson Goodman describes this process in the context of making strong claims for the formative force of language on objects: "Whether a predicate applies to a given thing often depends . . . on the realm of discourse"; "establishment of the referential relationship is a matter of singling out certain properties for attention, of selecting associations with certain other objects. Verbal discourse is not least among the many factors that aid in founding and nurturing such associations."[5] This chapter tracks and analyzes this emergent understanding of race as denoting a world and race as a world-organizing force. First, I detail the ways of worldmaking shared by B. L. Putnam Weale, author of "The Conflict of Color" (1909) and Lothrop Stoddard in *The Rising Tide of Color* (1920). I tease out the implications of their linguistic and narrative techniques on our specific ways of knowing and inhabiting the world. Rather than place these works in a genealogy as prime examples of white supremacist discourse, I contextualize their work as responding to the Russo-Japanese War, the emergence of Japan as a power on the world stage, and the failure of dominant racial modes of thought to account for the Japanese. It is only with such an understanding that we can see the distinctiveness and influence of Weale's and Stoddard's deployments of race within and against the dominant racial ideologies of the time. We discover that their work is not so much the extreme extension of scientific racism and social Darwinism as it is a response to their limitations.

This response of building race into the world finds its most formally codified development in the "yellow peril." The majority of this chapter thus focuses on the renewal of yellow peril fears in the late nineteenth and early twentieth centuries in both nonfictional and fictional speculative work, including Charles Pearson's *National Life and Character: A Forecast* (1893), Homer Lea's *Valor of Ignorance* (1909), M. P. Shiel's *The Yellow Danger* (1898), and H. G. Wells's *The War in the Air* (1908). The yellow peril is conventionally defined as a set of overtly racist representations of Asiatics and the irrational formation of fears concerning disease, lowered standards of living, and the decay of Western (white) civilization when beset by large numbers of Asiatics.[6] But this chapter recasts the yellow peril not merely as a set of stock representations but as a genre that keys readers' temporal experiences of their worlds and projects coherent structures of meaning for the reader to inhabit.[7] Mobilizing future war stories, the yellow peril genre embeds the salience of racial difference in the cognitive activities of retrospection and prediction.

Reducing this mode of worldmaking to the given racist ideologies of the time is to overlook the production of race at levels other than biological or anthropological differences between persons. Analyzing the yellow peril as genre delineates the narrative strategies that instruct readers to notice race in curiously intangible, abstract ways. Those abstract ways, I argue, construct new ways of seeing, new objects of attention, and new ways of connecting diverse experiences such that one cannot frame the world without instituting racial difference in its composition. In other words, the coherence of the world as such, the coherence of a global perspective, is made to depend on certain built-in knowledges of race. "Color" takes on a certainty of representation through which the world becomes present "before oneself" as such.[8] Despite being known as the body of literature most responsible for sensationalizing particular racist representations of Asiatic persons, the yellow peril persists, I suggest, because of these more abstract ways of seeing the world and race together.

The Russo-Japanese War was immediately narrated as a conflict between the yellow race and the white race. Jack London's newspaper dispatches in May 1904 already staged the conflict in these terms: "The doubtful old world had shaken its head and said: 'The Japanese are Asiatic. Hitherto they have fought only Asiatics. But what showing will they make when they go up against our own kind, the white kind of the earth?' The Japanese have been very sensitive to this, and they have been fiery to prove themselves fit from the white man's point of view by facing white men. To prove themselves fit at the very start was enormously to add to their prestige and enormously to make Russia 'lose face' in the eyes of other Asiatic peoples."[9] It would seem a short step from the designation of yellow and white races to yellow and white worlds, where "worlds" is merely a spatial extension of peoples. However, the Japanese themselves occupied a deeply ambivalent relationship to racial categories. The Japanese were "civilized," "modern," and wielded technocratic power in ways that did not jive well with certain anthropological and scientific discourses that linked racialized peoples to primitivism via either physical characteristics or culture.[10] London expresses this inability to simply incorporate the Japanese and specifically the phenomenon of Japanese modernization within dominant modes of racial thought.[11]

London emphasizes the baffling nature of the Japanese and chides Americans for their presumptuous superiority and belief in knowledge:

> An American lady of my acquaintance, after residing for months in Japan, in response to a query as to how she liked the Japanese said: "They have no souls." In this she was wrong. The Japanese are just as much possessed of soul as she and the rest of her race. And far be it from me to infer that the Japanese soul is in the smallest way inferior to the Western soul. It may be even superior. You see, we do not know

> the Japanese soul, and what its value may be in the scheme of things. And yet that American lady's remark but emphasizes the point. So different was the Japanese soul from hers, so unutterably alien, so absolutely without any sort of kinship or means of communication, that to her there was no slightest sign of its existence.[12]

Unable to locate superiority along physical or anthropological lines, London emphasizes unknowability. To be sure, this is an early example of the now-familiar discourse of Asian deceit and inscrutability.[13] But while this makes the Japanese unrepresentable, it does not preclude them from being the object of speculation. In his essay "If Japan Wakens China," London turns the inability of Westerners and Americans to "know" the Japanese into a problem of forecasting: "When one man does not understand another man's mental processes, how can the one forecast the other's future actions? This is precisely the situation to-day between the white race and the Japanese."[14] This inability to know defines the particular speculative threat that they pose—"the other's future actions." Indeed, as Kenneth Hough argues, Japan's military efficiency during the Russo-Japanese war was highly exaggerated through these projective fantasies, setting off a futurological imagination of invasion.[15] London continues this essay with a scenario in which Japan provides the managerial spirit and ethos by which to mobilize the Chinese and engage in a "race-adventure."[16] In doing so, he provides a clue into the new modes of thought based on forecasting that emerge from the attachment of race to world.

Weale writes his article "The Conflict of Color: The World Today and How Color Divides It" in this spirit of forecasting, except he adds a crucial element: the use of race to denote world. In this 1909 article, first published in the serial *The World's Work* and subsequently republished as part of a widely reviewed book of the same title, Weale depicts both color as itself a motive force and the world as organized spatially in terms of color. Writing in 1909, Weale is clearly spurred by the recent Russo-Japanese War, highlighting in particular its racial implications. Noting the treaty between England and Japan at that time, Weale writes, "it [the treaty] was not, as has so often been erroneously stated, a fundamental departure in her foreign policy as a whole . . . it was a fundamental departure in her Asiatic policy—that is, in her policy in dealing with coloured races. *For the first time in her history, she [England] placed herself by formal treaty on an absolute equality with an Asiatic race.*"[17] Starting with sections on "The Yellow World," followed by the "Brown World" and the "Black Problem," Weale reimagines the world as a totality mapped and configured in terms of racial color designations. This redescription singling out color in order to visualize the world leads to the inevitability of conflict between these worlds: "the next two or three decades must see a most surprising struggle, which will decide what the relations between the yellow world and the white world shall be for a very long time."[18]

The terms "white world" and "yellow world" here are not simply an extension of the logics underlying terms such as "white kind," "white nation," and "colored nation." Eliminating the referent of the person or a political unit such as "nation" and using the color designation to directly refer to the world requires a new form of perception, one that elevates race from describing a people or a nation to being an organizing principle. Weale foregrounds this shift in perception by beginning his article with the figure of the map, replacing political and national descriptors with the use of racial designations to describe not merely territories but also blocs of geography, peoples, and ineffable, shared spirit. Weale writes:

> There are few more interesting studies in the world than the study of the map. For, if the truth be known, a big map of the world on Mercator's projection should be to-day to every intelligent person something very like a horoscope of the human race—a horoscope, it is true, not cast as astrologers ordain, yet nevertheless enabling students to know within certain limits what should and should not happen to the various racial divisions and groups composing the human species, since the manner in which these divisions and groups are now distributed over the face of the earth is virtually an index to a great deal of the world's future history.[19]

First centering the reader's attention on the map as a technology of perception, Weale shifts our mode of perception yet again by merging the "map" with a "horoscope." He thereby mixes the spatial register of the map with the temporal register of the horoscope. But this horoscope does not go from astrological sign to the future but rather from racial distribution to "future history." This passage encapsulates Weale's interpretive strategies. He engages in extrapolation in the sense that he is extending a present trend and continuing it into the future. He is not, however, just taking present "facts" but rather using the future posited "conflict of color" in order to identify a present tendency. He gives race a projective component whose explanatory power into the future simultaneously rewrites the present and the past. The phrase "future history" should be distinguished from its use as a term within the field of science fiction.[20] Here, it captures Weale's particular shaping of temporality in relation to race.

In order to gain that projective component, Weale replaces the physical boundaries that enclose and separate variously organized peoples with boundaries organized by race, articulating land, culture, tradition, and civilization into cohesive unities: "For real frontiers—real barriers to the swaying to and fro of peoples—are not rivers or mountains or seas or any of those physical features referred to in geography books—for those are only the frontiers of savages—but masses of men distributed in proper density, highly civilized, irrevocably locked to the soil by their culture and their clear, century-old title deeds, and sufficiently war-like to make their physical boundaries respected, should wanton aggression menace them. It is flesh and blood that really forms modern frontiers."[21] Making "real frontiers" into racial projections and retrospections ("clear, century-old title deeds"), Weale overwrites histories of national, religious, and imperial conflicts in order to create a new starting point for building in knowledge of the world. It is thus that Weale can lock the "yellow world" and the "white world" into a deadly struggle irrespective of the internal differences of geography, politics, demographics, and the like that are classified within the designations of "white" and "yellow."

When Weale asserts that flesh and blood create the real modern frontiers, he is inviting us to inhabit a different version of the world in two ways. First, he is not so much changing the entities themselves as he is weighting some kinds ("flesh and blood") more than others (geographical entities like mountains). Second, deriving frontiers from racial distribution rather than the other way around makes race (as opposed to a mountain or a river) into the given from which to produce further world-versions.[22] Translating the spatial order of the racially weighted map into the temporal sequence of future history builds race into our temporal frameworks of what will or might happen. Indeed, this redescription of the world generates new facts about the world, as Weale creates analyses of populations based on color (as opposed to nationality, geography, political territories, governments in power, etc.) in order to demonstrate the precarious position of the "white world" and the need for unity across "white" populations: "If, for the sake of clearness, one last table be given here, it will be seen at a glance how, when every living being in the world is counted, the odds against the white man may be said to remain roughly two to one. . . . Now, to maintain the present balance of power for very many years to come might not be such difficult work, were it not for the fact that Europe—using the word here not so much in its strict sense as in a racial sense—is a house divided against itself."[23] The phrase "house divided against itself" transposes the history of the U.S. Civil War forward to the

TOTAL POPULATION OF THE WORLD ACCORDING TO COLOUR.

Whites.	
1. Europe	453,500,000
2. North America	85,000,000
3. Australasia	6,000,000
4. South America (Argentine, Brazil, &c.)	20,000,000
5. Africa	1,500,000
	566,000,000
Mixed Whites.	
(Including Indians) Mexico, Cuba, and West Indies, Central and South America	40,000,000
Absolute Yellow, Brown and Black.	
1. Asia	947,000,000
2. Africa	140,000,000
3. Pacific	2,000,000
4. United States	10,000,000
	1,099,000,000 [1]
Grand total of the world's population	1,705,000,000

Figure 1.1. Total population of the world according to color. Reproduced from *The Conflict of Colour*, 111.

context of the Russo-Japanese War, constructing a different kind of temporal continuity. When race is used to designate increasingly abstract entities, it entails new modes of organizing the world and creating what counts as meaningful correspondences. This is not simply a mode of perception that relates physical to metaphysical difference as it pertains to the racialization of groups of persons. It is to use race as a horizon against which to order the significances of a multitude of other variables. Weale's reweighting and reordering uses color to grasp the space and time of the world.

When Lothrop Stoddard uses the term "white world" in his 1920 tract, *The Rising Tide of Colour against White World Supremacy*, he utilizes precisely the same worldmaking techniques as Weale. Stoddard's book is known for being foundational for white supremacist ideologies. It sounded a warning that the colored peoples of the world were going to overtake the hitherto dominant white race. Less remarked upon is the powerful way in which race is attached to the world, again, not as an extension of the logics by which it is used to describe peoples and cultures, but as a reordering of spatio-temporal coordinates through which to grasp the world. At the beginning of the first chapter, "The World of Color," Stoddard begins with the exact same figure of the map as Weale:

> The man who, on a quiet spring evening of the year—1914, opened his atlas to a political map of the world and pored over its many-tinted patterns probably got one fundamental impression: the overwhelming preponderance of the white race in the ordering of the world's affairs. . . . Study of the political map might thus apparently lead one to conclude that white world-predominance is immutable since the war's ordeal has still further broadened the territorial basis of its authority. At this point the reader is perhaps asking himself why this book was ever undertaken. The answer is: the dangerous delusion created by viewing world affairs solely from the angle of politics. The late war has taught many lessons as to the unstable and transitory character of even the most imposing political phenomena, while a better reading of history must bring home the truth that the basic factor in human affairs is not politics, but race."[24]

This reordering of derivation (deriving politics from race rather than the other way around) again is mobilized in order to enlarge the temporal scope of race. Stoddard proceeds by carefully enumerating the new patterns and newly relevant objects that emerge from such a perceptual shift:

> The force of this query is exemplified when we turn from the political to the racial map of the globe. What a transformation! Instead of a world politically nine-tenths white, we see a world of which only four-tenths at the most can be considered predominantly white in blood, the rest of the world being inhabited mainly by the other primary races of mankind—yellows, browns, blacks, and reds. Speaking by continents, Europe, North America to the Rio Grade, the southern portion of South America, the Siberian part of Asia, and Australasia constitute the real white world; while the bulk of Asia, virtually the whole of Africa, and most of Central and South America form the world of color. The respective areas of these two racially contrasted worlds are 22,000,000 square miles for the whites and 31,000,000 square miles for the colored races. Furthermore it must be remembered that fully one-third of the white area (notably Australasia and Siberia) is very thinly inhabited and is thus held by a very slender racial tenure—the only tenure which counts in the long run. The statistical disproportion between the white and colored worlds becomes still more marked when we turn from surveys of area to tables of population.[25]

Race as an organizing principle for dividing up the world yields something different than the "political map." It abstracts out quantities of miles and populations so as to create the unquantifiable sense of unified racial forces. It reorders the relevant properties and patterns that count in thinking both historically and in terms of the future world: the "only tenure which counts *in the long run*" is racial. Indeed, to underscore the precarious position of the white man, the chapter titled "The White Flood" changes metaphors so as not to emphasize "land" and thereby "property" but rather the problem of flow and diffusion.

Like Weale, for Stoddard this reordering of the world via race is sparked by the Russo-Japanese War. As Stoddard writes, "During the closing decades of the nineteenth century, to be sure, premonitory signs of a change in attitude began to appear. The yellow and brown races, at least . . . measured the white man with a more critical eye. . . . The upshot was the Russo-Japanese War of 1904, an event the momentous character of which is even now not fully appreciated."[26] Stoddard identifies in these years "premonitory signs of a change," but as we have seen, both Weale and Stoddard use interpretive techniques around race as a particular kind of extrapolative thought process. It is one that depends on a new referential practice of using "world" as an operative category of racial meaning. It is one in which race is used to project a future via a re-envisioning of present and past "givens": "when we turn from the political to the racial map of the globe. What a transformation!" These interpretive techniques are shared across works that have been more traditionally identified with yellow peril discourse, including Charles Pearson's *National Life and Character* and Brooks Adams's *Laws of Civilization and Decay*. But they are also supplemented by narrative strategies through the scenarios of future war fictions, including works by M. P. Shiel and H. G. Wells, among others.

In the next two sections, I take up all of these works collectively under what we might term the yellow peril genre. I do so in order to trace these new ways of apprehending race and world exemplified through Weale and Stoddard across works that have been otherwise divided into different subgenres: nonfictional history, international relations commentary, military history, and science fictional future war fiction. Grouped as such, whether or not it is a nonfictional work of history or a more science fictional extrapolation, we see multiple overlaps. Weale, for example, seems to be familiar with Capitaine Danrit's future war series *L'invasion noire* when he writes, "It is inconceivable, for instance, that Europe should ever succumb to a 'black' invasion."[27] Each of these works participates in the "forecast": they are not set in some future time but rather follow a development into the future. Moreover, these works all participate in using race to build in knowledge of the world's present and future.[28] I thus frame the yellow peril as genre instead of more typically as representation or discourse in order to foreground the process of projecting a generically specific world. It is a generically specific world populated by persons, to be sure, but also populated by the "yellow flood," "fog," the "black and yellow belt," and the "yellow wave." It is in understanding yellow peril as genre that we can see a longer history of instructing readers to notice race in ways that supplement the limitations of scientific racism's attention to the body or social Darwinism's attention to civilization. This growing abstraction of the objects of racialization facilitates new mechanisms for connecting actions and persons within an understanding of race as a world-organizing force.

Race as Forecast

Both Stoddard and Weale cite Charles Pearson's *National Life and Character: A Forecast* (1893). Amazingly, Weale calls out Pearson for the latter's racism. Weale asserts as a fundamental principle "that every civilised nation should be accorded the same equitable treatment, entirely irrespective of the questions of colour or creed."[29] In a footnote to this sentence, Weale writes, "There is to be found a very startling instance of race-prejudice at the beginning of Professor Pearson's book *National Life and Character*."[30] This is telling because it shows how Weale is operating under a principle in which "same equitable treatment . . . irrespective of the questions of colour" is already a governing norm of his discourse. The logics and language of race prejudice identified by Weale do not seem to include his own use of race as an organizing principle for denoting the world. This is not simply a disavowal of racism. Seen alongside Stoddard's citations of Pearson, we can locate the particularity of apprehending race that I detailed above in relation to other uses of racial meaning.

Stoddard cites Pearson's characterization of the Chinese: "The Australian thinker, Charles H. Pearson, wrote of the Chinese a generation ago in his epoch-making book, 'National Life and Character': 'Flexible as Jews, they can thrive on the mountain plateaux of Thibet and under the sun of Singapore; more versatile even than Jews, they are excellent laborers, and not without merit as soldiers and sailors; while they have a capacity for trade which no other nation of the East possesses. They do not need even the accident of a man of genius to develop their magnificent future.'"[31] He cites Pearson again later, noting his particular forecasting capacities: "Long ago, wise old Professor Pearson saw how the wind was blowing."[32]

When Stoddard cites Pearson's forecasting ability, he utilizes the language of nature and pulls out a particular moment in which race is seen in deeply environmental terms: "Flexible as Jews, they can thrive on the mountain plateaux of Thibet and under the sun of Singapore." To be sure, this sentence resonates with the language of social Darwinism. But it also utilizes the assumptions of climate-and-custom racism that, when read in the context of Pearson's work as a whole, points to the irreducibility of yellow peril discourse to scientific racism, which focuses on the anatomy and the body on the one hand and social Darwinism on the other.

Pearson's 1893 *National Life and Character: A Forecast* is widely considered one of the foundational works of yellow perilism. It was reputed to have been read by Kaiser Wilhelm II as inspiration for the painting he commissioned depicting Lord Buddha riding a Chinese dragon in the process of laying waste to a whole set of European cities.[33] The modern yellow peril literature, which constructed the threat of Chinese and Japanese peoples on Western civilization, did not date from Pearson. It emerged as early as the 1860s and some have argued even earlier: all the way back to Marco Polo's description of a "'swarming' bestial Mongol army."[34] The phrase "yellow peril" was ubiquitous in public discourse between 1870 and 1920, and especially during congressional debates over the 1882 Chinese exclusion act and the Russo-Japanese War. These two moments are typically narrated as stages in yellow peril discourse, as fears of Asiatics move from centering on Chinese immigration in and around 1882 to fixating on Japanese modern and military power in and around 1904.[35] Continuous across these distinct objects, the yellow peril has been defined as a set of stereotypes derived from the application of social Darwinist constructions of race and racism to Asiatics and the use of scientific racism to denigrate Asiatic bodies as unassimilable, degraded, or as an economic threat precisely because their bodies could, according to this discourse, survive on less.[36]

However, this historical understanding of the Japanese being substituted for the Chinese within the same racist logics and fears of yellow perilism does not get at the reconfiguration of race within a larger construction of worlds of color that emerges from this transfer of anxiety to the Japanese. Roger Daniels notes that in 1905, "the anti-Japanese movement escalated significantly."[37] This transfer of anxiety, however, emerges even earlier with the First Sino-Japanese War (1894–95). Yellow perilism in this period from the early 1890s through the 1920s, I argue, is characterized through a more "global" framing: a way of cognizing the modern geopolitical world system using particular interpretive strategies around history and figuration that go beyond formulations of the impossibility of assimilation built around scientific racism or even social Darwinist racism.[38] Indeed, within the yellow perilism of this period, what is striking is both the peculiar temporality and referentiality of the yellow peril. The peculiar temporality is encapsulated in phrases such as "the yellow peril was a peril after all!," "the yellow peril will be a reality," or a "new yellow peril."[39] In these phrases, the yellow peril is simultaneously posited as that which is about to happen; that which is happening now; and that which has already happened. It is somehow always on the horizon.

This horizonlike quality to the yellow peril leads me to the peculiar referentiality of yellow perilism. Its referents have not always, or exclusively, been human. They have included phrases such as "yellow flood," "yellow wave," "yellow world," or "the yellow peril in action."[40] William Wu notes the prevalence of water imagery in these fictions, but missing from his analysis is that these images are used not as metaphors for people but in creating new referents of racialized natural or geological processes.[41] This range of representation operates at a level beyond the human body and expands the range of possible things in the world open to being "Asiatic." The yellow peril's peculiar temporality and referentiality stand out because they defamiliarize a yellow peril genre typically characterized in terms of its overt racist representations of persons. Instead, these representational practices suggest the residual persistence of "climate and custom" racism, a mode of racial thought prevalent in the seventeenth and early eighteenth century, in which the proper object of inquiry is not the body per se but rather the environment or the weather itself. Its racial logics surprisingly did not seem to depend on characterizations at the level of the body or person. As I shall argue, this range of textual strategies articulates racial thinking to understandings of historicity and temporality.

Far from just inspiring the ideas behind the yellow peril, Pearson's work shows the narrative strategies built around extrapolation and prediction—the imagining of what is to come—that play such a large role in the construction of the yellow peril as genre. Crucially, Pearson's *National Life and Character* is subtitled "*A Forecast.*" Pearson begins his treatise by remarking on the sheer impossibility of predicting the future. Nevertheless, even as he notes the limitations of long-range forecasts, he asserts the perennial need to forecast trends in order to govern present decisions and policies. The example that he uses to demonstrate this necessity is the U.S. Civil War and the problem of forecasting what is going to happen with the large "coloured" population in the U.S. South. We thus immediately see how the question of race relations is both a privileged example but also an important figure for the extrapolative logics of predicting the future.

Pearson takes up earlier characterizations of Asiatic labor but expands them to codify yellow peril fears as a way to map out global dynamics of population growth, expansion, and resource use. The givens that are so crucial for Pearson's near-history are the referents of population, climate, and race. He deploys these referents within a framework of climate-and-custom racism. Climate-and-custom racism is the notion drawn from the discipline of eighteenth-century natural history that race was caused by climate, custom, and other changing conditions. For example, Pearson notes the question of "whether the capacity of European races to form new homes for themselves is not narrowly limited by climate, and by the circumstances of prior population."[42] The language cited by Stoddard above—that the Chinese can "thrive on the mountain plateaux of Thibet and under the sun of Singapore" is similarly an instance of linking climate, environment, and race in a causal and interlinked relationship. This language is remarkable because, as many historians of racial ideology have it, modern, more scientific notions of race centered on biology, the body, and anatomy have won out by this time. These notions have won out against the weaker climate arguments because climate-and-custom racism always allowed race to be a mutable concept. It allowed for plasticity, while biological racism could be more essentialist and fixed.[43] But Pearson and others at this time retain climate-and-custom assumptions as a residual form in their thought precisely because of this malleability and plasticity.

In other words, these writers turn this disadvantage from the point of view of biological racism into a particular advantage. That advantage is to give race a temporal, historical component that is utilized by the mode of prediction. One, unlike the domain of the body, its predictive component operates on the scale of populations and the spatial division of the globe. As Richard Thompson summarizes, "Pearson declared that the white man had just about exhausted all of the temperate areas of the world into which he could expand. Remaining temperate regions were in the hands of people of color who could underlive and out-multiply the white man."[44] Two, it allows race to be elevated into a historical tendency that operates at the level of a gradual, accumulative idea of time. As Pearson writes, "On the whole, it seems difficult to doubt that the black and yellow belt, which always encircles the globe between the Tropics, will extend its area, and deepen its color with time."[45] "Always encircles," "will extend" and "deepen its color with time": race, here seen as a geological and climatic agent, has a temporality that exists outside of events and particular sequences. The dominant verb tenses for this temporality are the present progressive and the already completed present: the Chinese "*already form* half the population predominating in Singapore and Perak"; they "*are beginning* to settle" and "*are supplanting*" the natives.[46] The temporality of race as a geological figure here is slow and gradual because it is always happening. The temporality that the Chinese are "already" doing what they are presently doing borrows its construction of time from geological and climactic processes that blur sequence. But as a geological agency it is vast and can also surprise us as something that has already happened or as something that seemingly emerges quickly. The effect is to think of race as a natural and historical force that works "in" and "on" the world in the same way as other natural tendencies.

Pearson declares that the black and yellow belts will "deepen its color with time." Reinhardt Koselleck's essays on history and time provide a clue into how this racial temporality is mobilized for historical prognosis. According to Koselleck, "prognoses are only possible because there are formal structures in history that are themselves repeated. . . . Without constants in the different levels of permanence within the multitude of factors contributing to the formation of events to come, it would be impossible to predict anything at all."[47] Koselleck helps us identify the "structural pre-givens" that "pre-exist such events in a different way from that implied by the chronological sense of 'before.'"[48] He gives us examples such as "constitutional forms, and modes of rule—which do not change from one day to the next and are the preconditions of political action," as well as "constellations of friend and foe," "considerations of space and geography," and "unconscious patterns of behavior."[49] These structures differ from the temporality of the event in that they are not caused by specific subjects and thereby cannot be reduced to individual persons—they are processual. They enter into everyday experience as a pre-given, intersubjective "factor."

The examples from Pearson above point to how he figures race as a temporal structure in Koselleck's sense of some precondition that does not change from one day to the next. The "color" that Pearson talks about is one that operates outside the domain of linear time: it has, to use Koselleck's terms, a "repeated applicability" that allows it to figure new developments; it has an exponential quality that exceeds the time of historical development; and because it is always there somewhere—in the ancient annals or in contemporary developments—it has a causal force irrespective of individual actions or events.[50] In this way, Pearson goes against the grain of modern scientific racism with its more essentializing language of character, biology, and heritability. Instead, the yellow peril genre with its structural pre-givens of population, climate, and race elevate the significance of race into a historical tendency and temporality embedded in nature. The yellow peril is both like soil erosion and like an earthquake: the conditions are always present, it is always happening, and we are waiting for it to happen.

Like Pearson, Brooks Adams's *Law of Civilization and Decay: An Essay on History* is often cited as a source of yellow perilism.[51] Adams similarly infuses race with a particular temporal structure, only here it is used more explicitly to retrospectively write historical outcomes:

> When the Romans first emerged from the mist of fable, they were already a race of landowners who held their property in severalty. . . . The Latins had little economic versatility; they lacked the instinct of the Greeks for commerce, or of the Syrians and Hindoos for manufactures. They were essentially landowners, and, when endowed with the acquisitive faculty, usurers. The latter early developed into distinct species, at once more subtle of intellect and more tenacious of life than the farmers, and on the disparity between these two types of men, the fate of all subsequent civilization has hinged.[52]

The mixture of notions of race as natural kinds with the dynamism of social processes as they are ordered and determined in part by these natural kinds is a peculiar brew. It allows Adams to articulate race as a powerful explanatory component of history and allows him to racialize social processes such as division of labor as an effect of race itself. It considerably expands the explanatory force of race and contributes as well to its dynamism in that its effects are now felt at multiple levels of social, political, and national formation.

As prediction, race becomes a concept with "structural potential" that organizes our grasping of the world. As Koselleck writes, "Concepts . . . contain structural potential. . . . Only concepts with a claim to durability, repeated applicability, and empirical realizability . . . open the way today for a formerly 'real' history to appear possible and to be represented as such."[53] To cite the examples of climate-and-custom racism in Pearson and Adam's works as instances of retrograde thought would be to ignore their cognitive function. The attribution and imagination of race through geographic processes give race that "structural potential" for making a history "appear possible." It gives the concept of race a "durability" and "repeated applicability" that allows it to produce the perfect future history: one that people see as inevitable. As Pearson writes,

> If we cannot change manifest destiny, we may at least adapt ourselves to it, and make it endurable. We may circumscribe the growth of

> China, though we cannot altogether arrest it; and if we cannot hope that Europeans will ever people Africa, we may at least so work that European ideas shall one day be paramount from the Red Sea to the Atlantic. . . . Two centuries hence it may be matter of serious concern to the world if Russia has been displaced by China on the Amoor, if France has not been able to colonise North Africa, or if England is not holding India.[54]

Pearson's yellow perilism makes the future present almost as if it were already happening.

Is the Yellow Peril "Real"?

If the yellow peril genre goes against the grain of modern scientific racism with its particular technologies of visualizing the racialized body, if it constructs the yellow peril as something more akin to a climate, then it would seem to run the danger of rendering the yellow peril unreal. After all, that was why biological racism supposedly succeeded climate-and-custom racism—in order to make race *less* variable. In fact, by the 1900s, outcries about the yellow peril were already getting old and journalists called attention to this "weakness" in the perilist scenario. Newspaper accounts continually reiterate the problem of just how "real" or "mythic" the yellow peril actually is. In a sarcastic column, one writer writes, "Oh, perils pink and perils green are dished up by each magazine; and yellow journals pant and roar about the perils at our door. . . . With perils here and perils there, and perils raging everywhere, one's bosom should be full of fears . . . and yet I must confess, my friend, that all the world looks good to me."[55] Others question the quasi-reality of the yellow peril, stating, "there is no such thing as the 'yellow peril' unless we [the United States] insist upon it."[56] In another report, Ambassador Edwin H. Conger states that the yellow peril is a "bugaboo" and that there is no such thing.[57] Other articles self-consciously talk about the use of color and how a "color" can apply to many different things—there are various jokes made about the relationship between the yellow peril and the yellow press and being "yellow," and so on.

How, then, does something unseen and to a large extent not able to be seen become cognized as a determined reality? If the "realness" of the yellow peril was often in question, then it is the textual and interpretive strategies in the yellow peril genre that work toward making it "real." They do so by utilizing the uncertain temporality and referentiality of the yellow peril to craft narrative effects of truth and authority. Even as the yellow peril is demystified in these newspaper articles, the imprecise temporal status of the yellow peril is continually on display in ways that both (a) relate present conditions to future possibilities or probabilities; and (b) highlight future possibilities in order to reformulate understandings of present conditions. The *Los Angeles Herald* quotes a Canadian legislator as saying, "If she can stir up and force an alliance with half-awakened China, the yellow peril will be a reality."[58] Here, the future possibility of Japanese and Chinese collaboration is used to highlight a present condition as already accomplished—that China is "half-awakened." Similarly, the imprecise referential status takes on cognitive effects of its own. In "Orientalism Is Spreading Danger," the yellow peril is linked to the mobilization of Chinese militia in the United States. In an article titled "'Yellow Peril' War Declared," the declaration of war here refers to an economic boycott on all Japanese and all things grown by Japanese persons, conflating military language with an economic event. On February 1, 1908, the headline "Presents New Yellow Peril" calls attention to the danger of Japanese missionaries converting Americans to Christianity.[59] Another article states, "The 'yellow peril' is accepted in Germany as a substantial fact, and it is believed that Japanese imitation has already resulted in injuring Germany's trade in the Far East."[60] In all of these instances, yellow peril is linked to widely divergent phenomena. The ubiquity and range of references are used to create various connections: they can link up a German idea with a particular American anxiety, or a local development (the Chinese militia in California) with a global one (the Russo-Japanese War). Such free-floating and uncertain uses of yellow peril generate authority by relating large-scale historical forces to local events and circumstances, thus making the latter understandable within a larger frame.

Phrases such as "the yellow peril will be a reality," the "*real* yellow peril," or the "yellow peril *in reality*," point to the status of the yellow peril as an act of projection that prepares the viewer and reader for its always-possible actualizability. The yellow peril is always on the verge of becoming real because the narrative organization of causality creates a "world picture" that makes sense via racial formations: "If she [Japan] can stir up and force an alliance with half-awakened China, the yellow peril will be a reality." If one part of the yellow peril genre involves establishing a new referential relationship between race and world that enables race to gain predictive force, then a complementary part of the genre uses narrative in order to render the yellow peril solid and real. I turn in Chapter 2 to modes of storytelling drawn from future war fictions. These works cut across and blur the lines between military history and science fiction. Texts including

Marsden Manson's *Yellow Peril in Action*, Homer Lea's *Valor of Ignorance*, M. P. Shiel's *Yellow Wave*, and H. G. Wells's *The War in the Air* extend the uncertain referentiality and temporality described above to channel the reader's energies of anticipation. What we are made to anticipate is nothing less than a world that is *only* able to be cognized *as* world through the figuration of racial conflict.

CHAPTER 2

Futures Past of Asiatic Racialization

Future War

Studies of future war stories have long acknowledged the prominent role that plots built around yellow peril fears from the 1880s through the 1930s have played in the genre.[1] But they have typically not pursued the connections between these modes of storytelling and the *new* global logics of race being developed. This is because the authors of these works are understood as simply capitalizing on existing racist sentiments, characterizations, and fears of Asiatic peoples. The genre in this sense becomes a vehicle for an already recognizable racist content—the deceptive, cruel Asiatic; the barbaric "coolie" who lowers standards of living and who can survive just on rice instead of meat. Similarly, Asian American studies have long recognized these stories as some of the prime examples of yellow peril discourse. But scholars have typically explained its overt racist representations by referring to scientific racism and social Darwinism. This chapter takes the body of literature typically thought to be most responsible for sensationalizing racist representations of Asiatic persons, and suggests instead we take a closer look at how race and genre interact to achieve certain cognitive effects. Such an analysis allows us to better understand the racial logics at play here because they act on us not solely through the representation of Asiatic persons but through convincing us that we live in a world in which the yellow peril is a present and future reality. Without doing so, we will continually trace the persistence of yellow peril fears in the present back to past images and ideologies instead of understanding the narrative strategies that have made our grasping of the world dependent on the spatio-temporal coherence of race.

The future war story's main defining characteristic is the construction of an inevitable conflict. As I. F. Clarke notes, the war-to-come narrative is an "anticipatory fiction" that was meant to make nations better prepared for war.[2] As such, they immerse readers in a temporality where one always has to be prepared because they are already belated, because forces of which they were unaware are already on the move. George Chesney's *The Battle of Dorking*, published in 1855, is generally understood as one of the first invasion novels, and it was widely read by the writers of yellow peril fiction. Narrated by a survivor of the "battle of Dorking" and set in England, the novel recounts the attack on England, the decimation of its navy, and the complete destruction of civilization and morals that it entails. It usually does not get cited as part of a yellow peril genealogy because it is not about Asian invasion. But it expresses three specific formal strategies that get taken up by later yellow peril invasion novels.

The first is the uncertain representation of the enemy. In *The Battle of Dorking*, Chesney plays with our narrative expectations by insisting on the vagueness of the enemy. The reader is never told where the enemy comes from or given any characteristics of the enemy. The story even plays with this desire, taking the reader close to seeing the enemy if it were not for the haziness of the fog over the English Channel:

> Now then, we thought, the battle will begin. But still there were no signs of the enemy; and the air, though hot and sultry, began to be very hazy, so that you could scarcely see the town below, and the hills opposite were merely a confused blur, in which no features could be distinctly made out. . . . While I was down at the brook, a column emerged from the town, making for our position. We thought for a moment it was the enemy, and you could not make out the colour of the uniforms for the dust; but it turned out to be our rearguard.[3]

The haziness renders unclear what features of the enemy identify them as such. Importantly, it is the "colour" of the uniforms that are singled out, but even this marker proves unreliable as it turns out to be not the enemy but their own "rearguard." As we will see, this moment of discerning the enemy gets replayed in yellow peril fictions in order to single out race as a way to perceptually organize a blurred scene.

The second is the uncertain "time" of the attack. The vagueness of the enemy is matched by the uncertain temporality of the invasion itself: there is no discrete moment in which the attack "happens." Though the narrator recounts, "It was, however, nearly three o'clock before the battle began," the battle's beginning is itself a confused point: "For twelve hours had we been waiting for the coming struggle, till at last it seemed almost as if the invasion were but a bad dream, and the enemy, as yet unseen by us, had no real existence."[4] A gunshot is fired and "this gun was apparently the signal to begin," but the troops fire for several hours without any return fire.[5] The battle comes precipitously, suddenly, and "now," but the narrator has no capacity to situate that "now." Instead, the beginning of the battle is dispersed across an uncertain time and an indiscernible enemy. The military action is both highly anticipated and belated in that its beginning is uncertain, and by the time they fire for the second time, a great deal of damage has already been done. The uncertain temporality of the battle facilitates a narrative explanation that imposes a different temporality for the events. The narrative thrust is that this world-changing event could have been avoided if England had only been a bit more aware, a little less lackadaisical in its preparations, a little less obsessed with industry, trade, and money. Early in the narrative, the excruciating moments of anticipation followed by the uncertain time of the battle were already rewritten in terms of something calculable and predictable: "The danger did not come on us unawares. It burst on us suddenly, 'tis true; but its coming was foreshadowed plainly enough to open our eyes, if we had not been wilfully blind. We English have only ourselves to blame for the humiliation which has been brought on the land."[6] This imposition of a different sense of time offers itself as the corrective to avoid the uncertain perils of the future.

The phrase "We English" signals the third crucial feature of the future war story. As Clarke explains, future war stories fostered an "exclusive sense of nationhood."[7] According to Clarke, Chesney borrowed from the brand of new historical fiction that "sought to reveal the intimate links between character and action, between the person and the nation."[8] In future war stories, then, the nation becomes a physical organism much like these nationalist histories. As Noah Guynn explains of Michelet's notion of history, history is "*national, total, organicist* history. He conceives of the past as a body in which each of the organs—geography, climate, institutions, laws, health, morals, ideas—is necessary for creating and sustaining the life of the people."[9] It is precisely in marshaling forth this organicist history that the future war story can "show that the projected events in his history of the coming invasion would follow from the faults and failings of the nation in 1871. These errors of the past—so evident, so avoidable, so serious—gained a powerful psychological spin from a future history that could handle disaster or victory with equal facility. . . . Victory happily and gloriously confirmed the national destiny; and defeat allowed for telling contrasts between the final disaster and the better days gone beyond recall."[10]

Future war stories thus have three related components—the figuration of the enemy as vague, a narrativization of temporality as anticipatory and belated, and a construction of history as organicist—that get deployed by yellow peril writers in order to project worlds. In his 1907 pamphlet, *The Yellow Peril in Action: A Possible Chapter in History*, Marsden Manson narrates the events of the near future as if they had already happened: "In 1908 the friction between the United States and China became severe."[11] Similar to Weale and Stoddard, the certainty of this future is used to get us to see present conditions in a different way: "The indifference with which our people and Congress regard the development of the commerce of the Pacific Ocean prompts the writer to point out some of the possibilities of a war and its effects upon that commerce and our industries."[12] Also like Weale and Stoddard, Manson uses a map to further adjust our sight. The pamphlet comes with a map that subordinates the land to a representation of the oceans in order to spatially show the potential military weaknesses of the United States. However, this map additionally draws on the strategies of future war stories in order to anticipate a "global" conflict. The "Map of the world Showing The Three Great Oceans as Units and our Unfortified Military Stations" envisions a world in which the threat of China is both unseen and looming everywhere over the entire Pacific Ocean. Indeed, while China is identified as the enemy from the beginning of this pamphlet, it is an enemy whose precise location is unclear: after a "dark and rainy night," "every drydock in the Bay of San Francisco had been mysteriously blown up."[13]

Moreover, the narration renders ambiguous whether or not the enemy is inside or outside the United States. Patriotic "roughs" attack innocent Chinese and Japanese living in the United States, thus sowing disorder. The national guard is employed to quell racial antagonisms within the territorial United States, but it is never proven that Japanese or Chinese immigrants are responsible. Crucially, the pamphlet never indulges in racist characterizations of these Chinese or Japanese laborers—indeed, Manson blames the "yellow press" for inciting violence, thus "bringing on . . .

a war practically taking the shape of a civil and foreign war combined."[14] However, the future war is shaped by the perception of racial conflict.

Manson's pamphlet is part future war fiction, part political pamphlet, and part military history. He was a civil engineer who otherwise wrote about climate change. But already we can see how race as an affordance for certain knowledges interacts with modes of storytelling in order to project the possibility of a "civil and foreign war combined." The linking of potential racial conflict involving "patriots" with the mapping of an unseen but omnipresent enemy composes a world in which the conditions for the "yellow peril in action" are already present. In contrast, Homer Lea's *Valor of Ignorance* was a work of military history and strategy. First published in 1909, former U.S. Army Chief-of-Staff Adna R. Chaffee and Major General J. P. Story wrote introductions testifying to the book's potential importance for military strategists. It was reprinted in 1942, at which point Lea was hailed as a "prophet of Pearl Harbor."[15] The 1942 preface by Clare Boothe emphasizes Lea's forecasting ability: "Turning the pages of this book, while the very war the author predicted is raging about us, one finds few words of comfort. The cloth is being cut much too close to the author's pattern."[16] She begins with an anecdote about a conversation between U.S. military officers in the Philippines discussing Lea's book: one major is quoted as saying, "I read him at West Point. Damned convincing militarily"; a colonel is quoted as saying, "Homer Lea was neither a mystic nor a prophet. He was a scientist. He studied the science of war—the fundamental laws of which are as immutable as those of any other science."[17] Boothe further notes how Lea's book was widely read in Japan, where it "went into twenty-four editions in one month" and was made "required reading for officers in all the services."[18] As we will see, its reputation as a crucial document in military organization relies in part on its specific shaping of race in relation to future war fiction.

In *Valor of Ignorance*, Lea mobilizes the organicist conception of history and nations characteristic of future war modes of storytelling: "As the body of man is made up of volitionless molecules allowing the natural course of age, disease and decay to destroy it, the body politic of a nation is an aggregation of rational beings, atoms supposedly possessed of the ability to reason, and who should, if they are obedient to laws governing national growth and deterioration, prolong the existence of a nation far beyond the years and greatness ordinarily allotted to it."[19] These "laws governing national growth and deterioration," moreover, are deployed in order to render racial conflict as the perspective through which to enframe the global. For Lea places race and natural kinds on a *greater scale* than that of nation: "From the time, six thousand years past, when the wild highlander rolled down from the mountains of Elam, and moulded with sword and brawn the Turanian shepherds into the Chaldean Empire, until within the last decade, when the Samurai of Nippon rose out of their islands in the Eastern Sea and carved for themselves a new empire on the Continent of Asia, there has been no cessation nor deviation from this inexorable law governing the formation and extinction of national entities."[20] "This inexorable law" refers to the previous sentences: "Wars—Victory—a nation. Wars—Destruction—dissolution."[21] But these abstract phrases are given substance through the collective actions of the "wild highlander," "Turanian shepherds," and the "Samurai of Nippon." In this way, race moves from the unit of the individual to the level of a national entity and finally becomes the "inexorable law governing the formation and extinction of national entities." This movement does not so much eradicate the importance of individual racial traits as it transforms them into organizing principles of history.

Lea pronounces: "Not only does the history of the political development of China resemble the history of the remainder of mankind, but has, perhaps, within itself the solemn prophecy of the world's political future."[22] This prophecy contained within China itself links an organicist conception of history to the scale of world movements and forces. A reviewer for the *Saturday Review* echoes and reinforces this way of projecting the world: "He was never an emotional 'Yellow Perilist'; he merely applied a theory of the history of man as a predatory animal to Japan in relation to the United States, and while details of the situation changed, his basic analysis remained unchanged up to Dec. 7, 1941."[23] This understanding of Lea in contradistinction to the "emotional 'Yellow Perilist'" is crucial because it divorces the work from conventionally understood irrational racism. It explains his narrative logics on different terms. Those terms are not ones that mimic Lea's clearly racist sentiments around the alienness of any person of non–Anglo Saxon ancestry on American soil.[24] Rather, they are terms that take up Lea's prophetic method, exemplified in his relocation of race to the level of foundational historical principles. In describing the perspective that is required for forecasting, Lea writes, "In considering the future of this Republic one must do so, not from the closets of its politicians, not from its alleyways with their frenzied crowds. . . . It must be regarded from the heights of universal history and empirical knowledge which appertains to national existence."[25] Empirical knowledge and universal history are united through the deployment of race as an enduring force and element. In explaining the "primordial" conditions for conflict between the

United States and Japan, Lea writes, "A great race is like a rock in the wash of the sea."[26]

Lea's obvious racism is easily dismissed. But the strength of his world-making strategies lies in the way that it embeds race into our temporal structures for organizing the world. This embedding must be distinguished from another common form of racialization found in future-war stories, that of a Darwinian logic of development. William Delisle Hay's 1881 future-war SF, *Three Hundred Years Hence; or, A Voice from Posterity* exemplifies this social Darwinist conception of race: "men's minds had become opened to the truth, had become sensible of the diversity of species, had become conscious of Nature's law of development. . . . The stern logic of facts proclaimed the Negro and the Chinaman below the level of the Caucasian, and incapacitated from advance towards his intellectual standard."[27] This social Darwinist framework is the one most often employed in order to make sense of yellow peril racism. However, as we have seen from the examples above, the yellow peril genre develops racial logics in an additional direction. They start from the referential vagueness of the Japanese and the Chinese and they render the yellow peril "real" by embedding this vagueness into the structures of historiography and anticipatory time at the level of the "world." The difference with Hay's statement above is that this embedding occurs whether or not we believe in racial hierarchy. Lea, Pearson, Adams, and Manson utilize the forecast in order to mobilize these "weaknesses" of racial theory and make them into a framework by which world events and processes only emerge through racial figuration.

Lea's prophecy making achieves its reality effect by shaping race in relation to anticipation. It self-consciously crafts a perspective that "regards" the future from the "heights" of universal history. When we turn to yellow peril future war fiction, we see these same emphases on crafting a particular global-racial perspective, one that makes racial conflict both abstract and immediate, both transcendent and inevitable. I take up in this next section M. P. Shiel's *The Yellow Danger* (1898) and H. G. Wells's *The War in the Air* (1908), novels that imagine a scenario in which Japan and China join forces to eradicate the West. They are part of a larger cadre of novels that accompanied yellow peril anxieties that include Pierton Dooner's *Last Days of the Republic* (1880), Jules Lermina's *La bataille de Strasbourg* (1895), Ferdinand Heinrich Grautoff's *Bansai!* (1908), J. H. Palmer's *The Invasion of New York; or, How Hawaii Was Annexed* (1897), and Jack London's "The Unparalleled Invasion" (1910), among others.[28] The particular scenario of Japan uniting with China is one that picks up steam with the First Sino-Japanese War (1894–95) and Russo-Japanese War (1904–5), as seen in essays such as Jack London's "If Japan Wakens China" and magazine and newspaper commentary on "Panmongolism," and "If Japan Wins," among many others.[29] Drawing on this scenario, Shiel and Wells both take the idea of the yellow peril to its logical extreme: all-encompassing global-racial conflict. What stands out in their works is their self-conscious negotiation with the problem of imagining the immediacy and reality of global-racial conflict. As we will see, both authors comment on the role of newspapers in producing the "'immediacy" of an event in order to negotiate this problem. The convergence of their strategies of representation with those of Lea and others surveyed in this chapter, *despite seeming ideological differences*, should give us pause. For it shows a set of textual strategies that have formed ways of seeing and reality effects that need not be linked to views of racial superiority.

Why We Are All Yellow Perilists

M. P. Shiel wrote some of the most well-known yellow peril future war fictions, capitalizing on the worldwide interest in China after the Sino-Japanese War (1894–95).[30] His first yellow peril story, *The Yellow Danger*, was serialized in the popular press in 1898 as *The Empress of the Earth: The Tale of the Yellow War*, and later republished in 1899 as *The Yellow Danger; or, What Might Happen If the Division of the Chinese Empire Should Estrange All European Countries*. He also wrote *The Yellow Wave* (1905), a book that specifically takes up the Russo-Japanese War, and *The Dragon*, serialized as "To Arms!" in 1913 and then republished as *The Yellow Peril* in 1929. *The Yellow Danger* was the most popular, reissued in the United States following its success in Britain. The plot is a familiar one: China and Japan manipulate international affairs to cause a war among all the European powers, only to pounce on the weakened powers in an attempt to obliterate them all. A plucky Englishman named John Hardy ends up outwitting the evil Asian mastermind, Dr. Yen How, and turns the tables, utilizing biological warfare in order to wipe out "nearly a hundred million yellow men."[31] *The Yellow Danger*'s plot, language, and timing place it squarely within the center of a "market for paranoid invasion science fiction" that "was robust in the 1890s."[32] Its formula of pitting John Hardy against Dr. Yen How seems to fit the mold of successful works in this genre that "reinscribed the logic of individual craft labor in the body of their heroic protagonists, clarifying once again the value of . . . manhood over coolieism."[33] The evil villain Dr. Yen How can be seen as a prototype for later cerebral, cruel, manipulative Asian figures such as Fu Manchu and Ming the Merciless.[34] The novel has the requisite scenes of torture, Asiatic cruelty, and romance that make it sensationalistic and lurid.[35]

And yet, although *The Yellow Danger* encapsulates the tenets of yellow perilism in its most sensationalist version, its fictional world corresponds with the nonfictional worlds projected by Pearson, Lea, and others. This correspondence of projected worlds has less to do with racism at the level of anthropology and biology and more to do with the implementation of narrative strategies and construction of a global perspective built on the uncertain temporality and referentiality of the yellow peril. Far from being an opposition between "manhood" and "coolieism," the struggle between Dr. Yen How and John Hardy is framed by their similar extraordinary capacities of foresight and their abilities to control time through their visions: "They two—the little Chinese doctor, and this consumptive English lad—held in their hands the destinies of the world. Each had his own idea of the shape which the future of the human race should take; each was determined that it should take the shape which he chose, and no other; and each was immensely strong."[36] John Hardy is not a rough portrait of English masculinity but rather "consumptive"; he has an asthma attack that nearly fells him in the middle of the novel. Ironically, he is distinguished not by being "hardy" but by having a good head for figures and foresight. Dr. Yen How is similarly not your prototypical representation: "He was not really a Chinaman—or rather, he was that, and more. He was the son of a Japanese father by a Chinese woman. He combined these antagonistic races in one man. In Dr. Yen How was the East"; "here was a man who simply breathed Western modernity, and who yet was an Eastern of the Easterns. His skin was more yellow than the yellow man's, and his brain was more white than the white man's."[37] He is a Sino-Japanese antagonist who combines virtually everything being said in the newspapers about the Japanese and their dual position as Asiatics and masters of modernity. What makes him a "new element in Chinese politics" is that he is the "far-seeing Oriental-European," a person whose power lies in his capacities for foretelling.[38]

Dr. Yen How's plots that drive the yellow peril scenario specifically rely on the manipulation of time in order to veil the reality of the global forces at play. In the plot, he manipulates when information is received by different nations, creating gaps in time such that the European nations fight one another while Japan and China mobilize their forces. This plot relies on the accelerated relationship between the time of newspapers and the formation of reality: "On the morning of the duel between *La Gloire* and the *Majestic* it was rumoured at an early hour in the neighbourhood of Fleet

Street that China had dismissed Sir Robert Hart from the Controllership of the Imperial Maritime Customs, and that a Russian was about to be appointed in his stead. The announcement appeared in the morning papers, and its almost immediate consequence was a rise of threepence per quarter in the price of bread." Later in the same chapter, "The *Evening News* it was which [*sic*], in a premature eleven o'clock fourth edition, applied the match to the latent mine of excitement which smouldered in the minds of the people."[39] The news does not report reality in these cases; it produces reality at an accelerated rate. Dr. Yen How capitalizes on the rapidity of these reports, rumors, and speculation in order to sow conflict among the European nations and thereby unleash the "real" yellow peril.

This situation represented *in* the narrative mirrors the material production *of* the narrative. Shiel was writing in the midst of these global conflicts and rumors. He drew on newspaper reports of these political affairs, often incorporating specific contemporaneous events and persons in the fictional work. In "The Dragon's Tale: M. P. Shiel on the Emergence of Modern China," Shiel critic John D. Squires maps out the many correspondences between contemporary articles and Shiel's writing: a newspaper summary of government policy statements in relation to the possible partition of China is paralleled by Shiel's scene of the British legislature issuing a policy statement in chapter 5; articles about England's naval position in Eastern waters are reflected in chapter 13, a chapter that appeared in the same month as those articles. Shiel, Squires demonstrates, was writing right alongside the newspaper headlines and reports. As such, the novel reflects the language with which these political conflicts were being narrated, creating a real-time correspondence between the development of the story and progression of these events. The "yellow peril" represented in the story thereby gains its coherence by being placed on the horizon of existing events being recounted in the daily papers.

However, even as the narrative gains its reality effect by using the accelerated time of mass publicity to construct the "immediacy" of events, it links this immediacy to the large-scale, slow-time referent of race in order to lend coherence to this world. In making his argument to put his plan into action, Yen How utilizes a much longer scale of time in order to establish the durability of race as an organizing force: 'Look forward five hundred, a thousand years, Marquis, and what do you see?' Answered Yen How. 'Is it not this?—the white man and the yellow man in their death-grip, contending for the earth. The white and the yellow—there are no others.'" In delineating the danger of trying to "follow" the white man, Yen How argues that "the longer you follow them, the farther they get away from you. Their rate of progress is continually increasing. Every day that passes over the world gives them an additional advantage over you. . . . Can't you see?—you are losing time!" In honing in on the necessity of striking now, Yen How uses the large-scale referent of population to slice up the world according to particular "constellations of friend and foe": "In the world to-day there are 408,000,000 Christians and—mark the figures—1,004,000,000 non-Christians."[40] Though Yen How's own division is built on religion, the novel uses East and West and "yellow" and "white" as operative frameworks for creating a global perspective on this conflict. These referents are like those that we have traced in Pearson and Lea: race as a durable force; population as a way to re-envision the world along racial, not political, lines; and long temporal durations. Each of these elements frames the "immediate" event of war within a long history of conflict between the white man and the yellow man, as if they have been battling each other for all time.[41]

This perspective, built on a longer sense of time and a global bird's-eye view, informs even the narration of individual battles. For example, in the middle of narrating a moment when a British naval battalion is waiting for their enemy to appear, the narrative is interrupted: "By eight o'clock thirty thousand troops with one hundred and ten guns, under Sir Evelyn Wood, were concentrated, and waiting for the enemy, and all through the night the number was being rapidly increased. But they waited in vain. England had been several times invaded by foreigners. The last occasion was in the year 1066, and that occasion Providence designed to be the last for ever. This land had since then nursed a race as superb and firm as the foot with which she spurned the breakers raving round her inviolate shores."[42] In tracing a history that goes all the way back to 1066 and following a continuity between that moment and a "race . . . superb and firm," the novel changes scales drastically. It moves from the individual (Sir Evelyn Wood) and a given set of troops at a specific point in time—time that is so crucial for a sense of immediacy—to the long structures of nation, race, and foreigner. These structures provide the causal explanations for framing this moment in the long run. The novel introduces another kind of time built around race in order to make a referent like the "yellow wave" both durable and immediate.

This reality effect relies, moreover, on the impossible perspective of the person who can see and foretell global events at a glance. That is the perspective of both Yen How and John Hardy. After the first battle between French and English warships that marks the first part of an intra-European conflict on which the "yellow races" capitalize, the narration conjures up the image of Yen How: "But if Dr. Yen How had been there to see that battle of the giants, and its result, the corners of his eyes would have wrinkled up into a very web of tickled merriment."[43] Yen How, of course, is the mastermind behind the events that lead up to this battle, so he is the virtual cause of the scene. Emerging even if phantasmatically right at the end of this battle, Yen How takes on the impossible narrative perspective of globality. John Hardy similarly assumes this narrative position of sight and foresight. In the culminating naval battle of the novel, Hardy coordinates every movement like a master military strategist, as if he has a bird's-eye view even though he is in the midst of the conflict: "And thus it has suddenly happened that the whole yellow fleet is packed into a mere bundle of ships whose crews can speak to each other, whose steersmen need be cautious to avoid collision. And when Hardy sees them so—herded together by his harsh and baleful forethought—like sheep driven into the penfold—he knows that the yellow wave is damned, and the greatest of his works is accomplished."[44] Race at the level of referents such as "yellow fleet" and "yellow wave" enframes this battle and renders it legible at the level of world conflict. These referents stand out because they build in the longer perspective and knowledge of race as history into the single battle.

Interestingly, this scene is quoted by a contemporaneous reviewer as evidence of Shiel's "full and convincing methods" that "make the encounters perfectly conceivable."[45] While Shiel's knowledge of naval battles and his capacity to represent them was lauded more generally, the selection of this passage—low as it is on detail and action, high in the emphasis on Hardy's sight—seems curious except through the lens of the reality effect just cited—that is, a reality effect that highlights race not at the level of individual bodies but at the level of global forces of time and organization, thus rendering the yellow wave into something that can be seen in the immediate future.

The well-worn plot and racism of *The Yellow Danger* was obvious to at least one contemporary reader. William T. Stead, a writer who otherwise expresses various race prejudices in his writings on Japan, reviews the novel: "It is this element which vitiates the value of the book. Race hatreds are the devil, and any one who develops them consciously or unconsciously, as Mr. Sheil [*sic*] seems to have done, is holding a candle to the devil with a vengeance."[46] But if these elements of race hatred were quite clear, they coexisted with other levels by which racial logics were used to create the reality effect of framing the world. In interweaving "contemporary personalities and events from each previous week's current events into a fantasy of world war,"[47] Shiel was certainly writing *The Yellow Danger* in haste. But this concurrence of the language and time of weekly serials and the language and time of the narrative is not merely one of influence. It is a shared projection of a world that relies on developing interconnections among race, time, and history. That this shared world does not require even the representation of an evil Asian mastermind is demonstrated in H. G. Wells's depiction of the same scenario in *The War in the Air* (1908).

H. G. Wells is known for his scientific romances and his depictions of war on a grand scale—most famously, *The War of the Worlds* and *The World Set Free*. Including *The War in the Air*, Wells calls these works "fantasias of possibility" where "each one takes some great creative tendency or group of tendencies, and develops its possible consequences in the future."[48] He was well aware of M. P. Shiel's work, having reviewed Shiel's earlier works not very kindly for the *Saturday Review*.[49] *The War in the Air* was published in 1908 shortly after the Russo-Japanese War and in the midst of the particular yellow peril anxieties that I have been tracing. But critically it is more known for its early representation of the airplane as a flying war machine and Wells's "forecast" of World War I and World War II. Patrick Parrinder captures this emphasis on Wells's dystopian forecast: "Wells's principal aim . . . was to link his intimations of the collapse of modern civilisation to the imminent development of aerial warfare."[50] Wells himself wrote that his book concerns how the flying machine "not only alters the methods of war but the consequences of war," those consequences being "social destruction." Emphasizing its success as forecast in 1921, Wells goes on to say, "After all that has happened since this fantasia of possibility was written, I do not think that there is much wrong with that thesis."[51] Even more clearly in his preface to the 1941 edition of *The War in the Air*, Wells famously writes that his epitaph should read: "I told you so. You *damned* fools.'"[52]

Jay Wynter is one of the few scholars to consider yellow peril anxieties in his introduction to the latest reprint of *The War in the Air*. But he understands them to be a vehicle for Wells's real aim of rendering the collapse of British and European civilization: "By bringing them [Chinese and Japanese] together in this novel in the form of an Asiatic confederation, Wells offered his readers a vision of British and European decline, which was his real destination. Wells . . . was too intelligent to buy into the vulgar prejudices of his day about race. Wells used them to shock his readers into taking a hard look at the European world in which they lived."[53] I am not interested in determining authors' prejudices but rather in more closely considering the function of the yellow peril scenario in *The War in the Air*.[54]

For as I have demonstrated above, the yellow peril genre was not just a set of "vulgar prejudices" but also a form of forecast and a set of strategies for building knowledge of race into visions of world conflict. Wells was not the only one forecasting world war at this time: this scenario was firmly in the province of the yellow peril genre.

Placing *The War in the Air* back in this context helps us see that it is a crucial demonstration of how the yellow peril genre frames the world. This is because it seems to strip yellow peril future war fiction of everything except its mechanisms of constructing a global, racial perspective. Unlike Shiel's novels, Wells does not begin his future war scenario with the clear strategy and deviousness of the oriental and the forecasting capacity of Yen How. Squires writes that *The War in the Air* is a "rewrite of *Empress* [*The Yellow Danger*] without Yen How."[55] That the novel even incorporates a yellow peril scenario like Shiel's is not made clear until relatively very late in the novel. It is almost as if the novel stumbles into representing a global conflict organized along racial lines. Finally, the work itself presents many moments in which it parodies the very language and ideologies that seem most responsible for the paranoiac visions of race war. And yet, it adheres to narrative strategies that make the legibility of the world depend on imagining racial referents tied to history, time, and the globe. For these reasons, it provides the clearest link between this capacity to cognize the vast scale of the world with the rendering of the yellow peril as real. The absence of the evil Asiatic mastermind in Wells's novel is crucial because it signals how Asiatic racialization can be represented through the assumptions built into making sense of the world irrespective of explicit representations of Asiatic agents.

The novel begins without a trace of Orientalism and instead with a vision of how industrial "Progress" is taking over the local ways and cultures of small town England. The novel centers on Bert Smallways, a character whose name already signals a "small," on-the-ground perspective, someone who is in over his head, caught up in a set of forces that are beyond him. As the novel progresses, Smallways's perspective literally ascends: first, he accidentally flies off in a balloon; then he finds himself on a German aircraft and in the midst of a battle, and then finally in the middle of a global conflict. In making his narrator literally ascend from a localized perspective on the ground to a more "global" perspective in the air, Wells positions us to "see" in a different way. Specifically, he positions us to "see" race and nation as forces within the terms of historiography and forecasting noted above:

> Bert Smallways was only one of countless millions in Europe and America and Asia who, instead of being rooted in the soil, were born struggling in a torrent they never clearly understood. . . . Particularly did the fine old tradition of patriotism get perverted and distorted in the rush of the new times. Instead of the sturdy establishment in prejudice of Bert's grandfather, to whom the word "Frenchified" was the ultimate term of contempt, there flowed through Bert's brain a squittering succession of thinly violent ideas about German competition, about the Yellow Danger, about the Black Peril, about the White Man's Burthen—that is to say Bert's preposterous right to muddle further the naturally very muddled politics of the entirely similar little cads to himself (except for a smear of brown) who smoked cigarettes and rode bicycles in Buluwayo, Kingston (Jamaica), or Bombay. These were Bert's "Subject Races," and he was ready to die—by proxy in the person of any one who cared to enlist—to maintain his hold upon that right. It kept him awake at nights to think that he might lose it.[56]

These referents—"German competition," "Yellow Danger," "Black Peril," "White Man's Burthen"—organize the sense of the environment in which Bert Smallways lives, inspiring him with tremendous fear of losing his rights as a white man even though what separated him from "similar little cads to himself" was merely a "smear of brown." The "squittering succession of thinly violent ideas" that keeps Bert "awake at nights" is clearly the subject of parody. However, the trajectory of the novel does not lead Bert or the reader toward a further distancing and critique of their organizing force. Rather, it leads us toward a greater immersion into a sense of the world organized by these thin, foggy referents.

The novel as a whole moves us narratively through the change in scale that marks the particular historiographical conventions of the future war genre and the referents on which people act and feel. Wells writes, "The development of Science had altered the scale of human affairs. By means of rapid mechanical traction it had brought men nearer together, so much nearer socially, economically, physically, that the old separations into nations and kingdoms were no longer possible, a newer, wider synthesis was not only needed but imperatively demanded."[57] The yellow peril stands in for this "newer, wider synthesis" that is "imperatively demanded." When the yellow peril scenario enters into the narrative, it both comes out of nowhere and all at once. It emerges late—already 230 pages in to the novel. Further, it has a temporality that is outside of a sequence of events: "The Japanese and Chinese have joined in. That's the great fact. That's the supreme fact. They've pounced into our little quarrels. . . . The Yellow Peril was a peril after all! They've got thousands of airships. They're all over the world."[58] The figuration of the immensity and largeness of the yellow peril is exactly what allows it to figure and enframe the world as a whole, positioning the reader and Bert Smallways to grasp the ungraspable.

With the lines "The Yellow Peril was a peril after all! . . . They're all over the world," Wells shows his recognition of the exaggerated language of the "yellow peril." But it also marks the entry of this novel into the global perspective that is only possible when the yellow peril is taken as real. The change in scale from "little quarrels" to being "all over the world" makes the idea of the yellow peril a precondition for grasping and cognizing a sense of the world. Smallways's movement toward this perspective and the knowledge it affords is emphasized: "Of all these world-forces and gigantic designs Bert Smallways knew nothing until he found himself in the very focus of it all and gaped down amazed on the spectacle of that giant herd of airships."[59] That the "giant herd of airships" is the graspable referent of "world-forces" has one more crucial narrative effect. Operating at the scale of the world, the Asiatic invasion becomes the only real thing going on at the level of history, completely erasing the German-American conflict as event: "The Asiatic invasion of America completely effaced the German-American conflict. It vanishes from history."[60] Wells represents the reality of the yellow peril in relation to its ability to give the reader a "touch" of the global.[61]

In the representation of this Asiatic threat, Wells thus produces a perspective divided between the "aerial" view through which the "realness" of the yellow peril as a world-force is rendered and a ground view of individual Asiatics. In the very few representations of individual Asiatics in this novel, they are seen at ground-level: when Bert is marooned on Goat Island after the battle that sets off the world war, he sees a "dead Chinaman" hanging from a tree.[62] There he is also chased by a group of Japanese soldiers with swords. The "dead Chinaman" is an uncanny, shadowy figure who Bert tries to avoid, but comically somehow always manages to stumble over again. The sword-wielding Japanese soldiers are completely incongruous in relation to the modern militarized power of the Japanese, again narrated more in a comic, uncanny vein that does not operate on the same scale as the Asiatic when embedded into the temporality of future war.

This division between the view from the ground and from the air captures a particular racial configuration in which familiar racial representations—the "Chinaman," the cruel Japanese—are rendered less visible in the face of a perceptual apparatus that articulates race at a world-historical level. These representations do not seem to fit in the diegetic world of the narrative. The yellow peril is not a peril after all in these comic, farcical moments of the narrative. However, the perspective from the air gives us the incoherence and fogginess of abstractions that are the real "movers" of history. Counterintuitively, the thin and foggy referents are *more* real than the representations on the ground. This is because the "global" perspective creates referents that are extrapolatable, that can be seen in motion with other referents on a worldwide scale. The unreality that is usually associated with the level of abstraction is the only "real" thing that is happening in the world: it is the "supreme fact."

As in *The Yellow Danger*, the role of newspapers and its relationship to the making of the "real" reflects this refiguring of a racialized world. Bert Smallways references this in his response to the coming war: "They've been saying things like this in the papers for a long time," he remarked. "Fancy it coming real!"[63] Within the narrative, newspapers mediate the representation of the two attacks on New York, first by the Germans and then by the "Asiatic invasion." The newspapers first produce a distanced view of war: "They saw war as they saw history, through an iridescent mist, deodorized, scented indeed, with all its essential cruelties tactfully hidden away."[64] The headlines continue to construct this distanced relationship to reality in "wonderfully illustrated accounts" of the war preparations, and Wells gives us the headlines: "The Secret of the Thunderbolt," "Washington Orders Five Hundred."[65] These headlines are suggestive in their lack of detail and in their ability to conjure forth whole scenarios and narratives. They shape a sense of reality and of the enemy not through detail but precisely through the fog of "fancy." Here, things come into view and come to be real at a distance. Details are lost and general emotions and spirits convey the realism of events. The chapter, which is unusual in its continual movement back and forth between newspaper headlines and novelistic narration, details the way in which large-scale global realities are mediated and understood to be real through the fog of distance, a distance that allows abstractions of nationhood and race to carry social force. When the attack does happen, what is emphasized is not its concrete details and effects but the fact that it was visible and present before the newspapers were able to represent it: "It beat," they declared, "the newspapers."[66] The reality of the event is still referenced in relation to the temporality of the newspapers. When it arrives, it arrives *as* the foggy abstractions it was represented to be: "Fancy it coming real!"

In his assessment of yellow peril invasion novels, William Wu notes the use of natural imagery—specifically water—that is prevalent in the broader genre of yellow peril fiction.[67] Wu concentrates his energy, however, on stereotypes of individuals or groups. But we can reread these images in terms of the way in which race is embedded into the temporal and historiographic structures of meaning-making. At the end of the initial battle that introduces the "Asiatic" element in *The War in the Air*, the narration turns toward the temporality of nature in order to articulate the "real" effects of race: "It seemed to him indeed that this must be the sunset of his race"; "And it went down the rapids like an empty sack and left the visible world to Asia, to yellow people beyond Christendom, to all that was terrible and strange! Remote over Canada receded the rest of that conflict and vanished beyond the range of his vision."[68] The language of "sunset," "receded," and "vanished" point to the horizons of racial feeling and being that are activated in relation to Asiatic racialization. It is a form of historiography that draws its energy from the nature imagery of race. The horizon of nature's vision plays the role of a structural force that drags the rest of history along behind it. In this way, conceptualizations of race and the arrangement of its referents work hand in hand with textual strategies that use abstraction, extrapolation, and the figuration of principles as history's facts for its reality effects. *The War in the Air*, despite stripping the yellow peril genre of much of its representational content, leaves us with a vision that can only grasp the world through that genre's machinery.

As Edlie Wong demonstrates, yellow perilism is alive and well in media, literature, and culture, primarily through the specter of Chinese economic dominance in the present.[69] At the representational level, these works most certainly "echo" Fu Manchu and other classic stereotypes of Asians from the early twentieth century,[70] but the relationship between the "new" yellow perilism and the "old" yellow perilism of the early twentieth century does not end there. Returning to one early moment in the old yellow perilism of the early twentieth century—the Japanese after the Russo-Japanese War—this chapter situates Asiatic racialization not within scientific racism or social Darwinism but within the worldmaking strategies of future war and extrapolation. I have shown how this yellow peril conceived as genre developed powerful new logics of race and temporality: the expansion of racial referentiality itself toward encompassing the world and the capacity to make our grasping of the world dependent on the figuration of the yellow peril. Here, race and genre work together as affordances for constructing a particular way of noticing race and building in knowledge of the world. In this sense, the renewed forms of yellow perilism are not simply the reiteration of stereotypes that are either holdovers from the past or newly articulated in relation to contemporary forms. They persist because the world-version put into place by Weale, Stoddard, Shiel, and others is still embedded in our grasping of the world. Without a critique of these strategies of worldmaking, we risk reproducing the epistemologies that render the yellow peril real and visible even as we critique its representational content.

This process of making future worlds involved acts of speculation both forward and backward. In Part II, I treat the plantation romance for its similar investments in shaping relations among the future, past, and present. Though well known for rhapsodizing about the past and constructing nostalgic visions that transported readers back to the halcyon days of slavery and white rule, in the early twentieth century the plantation romance played a forward-looking role, crafting future worlds on the basis of its speculative historiography. If the yellow peril genre responded to the challenge posed by the Russo-Japanese War on the larger architecture of racial thought and its capacity to project a world, the plantation romance responded to the challenge of Reconstruction.

PART II

Plantation Romance

CHAPTER 3

Romance and Racism after the Civil War

The plantation romance re-emerges with a vengeance in the early twentieth century, armed with new political projects. Far from dying out, it seems to have proliferated toward the late nineteenth and early twentieth century.[1] Its antebellum predecessors were famous, of course, for their proslavery ideologies often written in response to the enormous success of Harriet Beecher Stowe's *Uncle Tom's Cabin*. Drawing from the literary pastoral, these novels painted an idyllic landscape against which the benevolent planter, often beset by problems outside of his control, struggles to maintain existence. They commonly portray affectionate, loving relationships between masters and slaves.[2] As Chad Luck puts it, these novels "celebrate not just aristocratic ideals and Southern honor, but white supremacy and retrograde paternalism."[3] The postbellum plantation romance certainly retains many of these ideological positions, but in a world where slavery has been formally abolished in name, it takes on different objects of attention.[4] Unlike the antebellum plantation romance that was fighting in the midst of a discursive battle over slavery to maintain existing institutions and ways, the postbellum plantation romance is oriented both toward a more displaced past and a longer view of the future. This orientation is encapsulated in the new image of the plantation, itself mobilized by many of these fictions: now rundown or even destroyed by the war, the plantation itself has become not so much the center but a place in transition, moving toward an uncertain future.

This image is often used to wax elegiac, as it is in Thomas Nelson Page's "Marse Chan," a canonical example of postbellum plantation fiction.[5] My own interest is in one prominent cross-section of this re-emergence that does not just reiterate the conventions of its precursors. Rather, it performs a different narrative action, one that takes Reconstruction as its pivotal event. Each of the major novels that I discuss hinges on the transitions from the antebellum South to Reconstruction and a post-Reconstruction South. Occupying the space and time of transition, they represent the possibilities of both the past and the future in terms of distinct worlds. I focus first on two of the most influential and impactful examples of this project: Thomas Dixon's *The Leopard's Spots: A Romance of the White Man's Burden* (1902) and Margaret Mitchell's *Gone with the Wind* (1936). *The Leopard's Spots* was the first of a trilogy of Reconstruction romances that included *The Clansmen* (1905) and *The Traitor* (1907). It sold a hundred thousand copies within its first few months of publication and about a million copies overall. All three were sensations and *The Clansmen* became the basis for D. W. Griffith's *The Birth of a Nation. Gone with the Wind* was published thirty-four years after *The Leopard's Spots* and was even more of a sensation than its predecessors; it sold more than 750,000 copies in the first five months of its publication and has never been out of print. The title of the novel and its alternate possible title—*Tomorrow Is Another Day*—capture the tensions of looking backward and forward. In narrating the moment of transition, it constructs new logics for thinking about the intertwined relationship between the future of the U.S. South and the role of race in the making of the modern world. Finally, I analyze Frank Yerby's *Foxes of Harrow* (1946), a novel that followed *Gone with the Wind*'s success: it sold more than a million copies and was adapted as a feature film in 1947. Yerby, an African American writer who built his reputation on plantation romances and the genre of historical romance more broadly, evinces in his novel a keen awareness of the questions of historiography and figuration being played out within the twentieth-century reiteration of the genre.

No longer oriented around the project of defending slavery as such, plantation romances from the early to mid-twentieth century operate in the midst of transition where political and economic tools of white supremacy (such as voter suppression, the Ku Klux Klan, debt peonage) were being fashioned and refashioned in relation to new forms of rendering blackness and whiteness legible. The terrain of this transition is the battle over deciding and transmitting the meaning of Reconstruction. As Grace Hale argues, "Professional histories and memoirs and autobiography . . . brought the present into the past by basing interpretations of antebellum days on postbellum experience. 'History' was the first battlefield in the creation of modern southern whiteness. . . . History, a sense of the distance between the past and the present, became not only a time but a cultural space in which to craft a new southern order."[6] This battle over the telling of history resulted in the widespread narrative understanding of Reconstruction as a hopeless failure, and the reassertion of white aristocratic power as the benevolent fountain of virtue and civilization. Hale continues, "While Dixie may have long ago lost the war . . . the white South, its regional autobiography fixed in a plantation romance peopled with 'happy darkies,' noble masters, and doting mistresses, had won the peace."[7] If the plantation romance of the mid-nineteenth century was driven by the need to justify slavery and reimagine a world built around and through the institution of slavery in the face of ever-sharpening critiques,[8] this re-emergence worked to shape logics for new racial organizations.

Some critics might argue that works like Mitchell's and Yerby's are examples of the end of plantation fiction, a genre that had run its course and whose appeal at the time can be attributed to its old-fashioned, outmoded character.[9] To be sure, these works are belated examples. But in their very belatedness, these works incorporate and fully display the projected worlds of plantation romances. If Mitchell worked to institute modes of perception for new configurations of racial inequality, Yerby challenged those modes.[10] I thus focus on the processes whereby these works teach readers to locate race in particular ways. Like the narrative and interpretive strategies of the works I analyzed in the previous chapter, these novels often place racial markers in unusual places in order to build in knowledge of the projected world. Here, I place particular emphasis on the use of racial meanings in the construction of context. These narrative strategies create the conditions for divergent explanations of behavior, motive, and consequence. It is this cognitive work for which the plantation romance returns.

In this sense, these plantation romances are more similar than it might seem to the science fiction and fantasy genres. Like all the genres in this study, the plantation romance delves deep into historiography for its imaginative hold on readers. It does so in order to look forward by looking backward. In order, that is, to shape the givens from which to project and anticipate particular kinds of futures. Much like science fiction and fantasy, its narrative effects depend on constructing a coherent world with rules, conventions, and modes of evaluation. Finally, as in the other genres, racial meanings are not just a part of the representational content of these fictions but rather a built-in knowledge that is embedded into the shape, direction, and logics of the narrative. They are perceptual givens actively being shaped and reshaped within and through genre. In Part I, this process consists in reshaping race in between a biological racism and a social Darwinist worldview as an organizing principle for imagining both the globe and the future. In Part II, this process consists in re-engineering relations between blackness and whiteness from a political discrimination based on status to a discrimination that acts at the level of context in order to circumscribe historical possibility.

Epistemologies of Racial Worlds from Dixon to Mitchell

Exactly how representations of race function in *Gone with the Wind* have proven over the years to be a source of ambivalence and debate for critics and readers alike. Part of the ambivalence has to do with its place within the plantation romance tradition and whether or not it simply reiterates or instead updates its racist conventions. Malcolm Cowley famously called *Gone with the Wind* an "encyclopedia of the plantation legend," suggesting both its return to the racial politics of that genre and its belatedness: "it is all here, every last bale of cotton and bushel of moonlight, every last full measure of Southern female devotion working its lilywhite fingers uncomplainingly to the lily-white bone."[11] Other readers, though, have noted and contextualized the novel's departures from the plantation romance. Thomas Cripps writes how Mitchell set out to avoid the outrageousness of the plantation romance tradition represented by "Uncle Remus" even as she retained certain traditional conventions. Cripps situates the novel within a "growing national ambiguity in racial attitudes" as part of a middle ground between the nonacceptance of certain images and conventions passed on from D. W. Griffiths and as-yet-unformed images.[12] Diane Roberts nicely synthesizes some of these ambiguities when she writes that Mitchell "avoids the ugly, obvious racism of Thomas Dixon's Ku Klux Klan romances (which she, none the less, quite enjoyed in her youth) yet her novel represents blacks as faithful mammies, stupid servants or masterless, violent aggressors—when she deals with blacks at all."[13]

As Cripps' contextualization and Roberts' description suggest, the period of time between Dixon's trilogy and Mitchell's *Gone with the Wind* is conceived as a moment where racial discrimination was increasingly challenged at a national level. Writing after Dixon's "overt" racism that linked representations of depraved black character to the moral corruption of the body politic, Mitchell gives us a set of representations that are more difficult to measure because they have been detached from Dixon's representational practices.[14] It is no surprise, then, to see wide gaps among critics when it comes to reading race in *Gone with the Wind*, from those who see "race, and politics too" as "essentially negligible elements" or "largely background material" to those who read race at the level of Mitchell's imagery in order to show its subtle reinforcing of racial hierarchies.[15] Even as one critic can discuss the novel without mentioning race, another can write incredulously that "until recently most critics denied that the novel was about race at all."[16] This critical reception reminds us that deciding whether *Gone with the Wind* is "about race" is not straightforward but rather requires a more precise analysis of our own descriptive modes for determining when and how race is salient.

The interpretive strategy implicit in contrasting Mitchell and Dixon is the descriptive opposition between overt and covert racism. According to this schema, unlike Dixon's Ku Klux Klan romances and its "ugly, obvious racism," Mitchell constructs more coded, subtle ways of accomplishing the same ends of reinforcing racial difference, hierarchy, and inferiority. This framework should be familiar to us. Its heuristic power can be seen not just in the description of literary representation and authorial worldview but also in the characterization of historical periods, as in the movement from formal discrimination and Jim Crow to more subtle or coded mechanisms. However, as powerful as it is for describing continually emerging rhetorics of racial discrimination, this mode of description has its blind spots. It simplifies and narrows the uses of race, as if racial markers either explicitly degrade nonwhite peoples, do the same thing just simply in a more coded fashion, or do nothing at all and are thereby "neutral." As such, it fails to notice the multiple ways in which race can be used to build in knowledge for the comprehension of social structures. Within this broader field of possible uses, race does not just lead to racism when it is used to target, categorize, and label people. It also leads to racism when it is used to shape context and embed certain expectations of the world. Whether overt or covert, attributing racial significance as salient in some places or contexts (and not others) shapes the routes through which we organize our knowledge of the world.[17] The incoherence seen above in evaluating whether *Gone with the Wind* is "about race at all" is a symptom of our limited powers of description when wedded to conventional categories of overt racism, covert racism, and race neutrality.

In focusing on racial salience across each part of this book, I reframe longstanding questions at the intersection of racial and literary formation. Instead of being limited to the descriptive framework above, I notice race at multiple levels of narrative organization and fictional diegesis. All of the following are narrative strategies that prompt readers to use race in organizing the storyworld: the manipulation of the relationship between foreground and background, particular placements of figurative language, and ways in which narrator's knowledge is played against character's and reader's knowledge. Such an analysis, as I demonstrate below, gives us new insight into what these "late" plantation romances as a whole are doing in this early to mid-twentieth-century moment. *Gone with the Wind* does not simply "avoid the obvious racism" of Dixon by giving us more subtle representations; nor does it simply treat race relations as background. Each of the novels I treat struggle with their predecessors to "reconstruct" racial perceptions within a political landscape in which earlier racial attributions are no longer palatable. They constitute another aspect of racial worldmaking because they intervene in the popular imagination at the level of different narrative strategies for building race into our everyday interaction with social structures.

Both Dixon's *The Leopard's Spots* and *Gone with the Wind* dramatize Reconstruction as a blow to white Southerners and portray blacks as unfit for freedom or the cause of political corruption and misrule. Both novels narrate the transition from one world (antebellum South) to another (Reconstruction South), thus staging the problem of inhabiting this new world. But in order to get a clear sense of Mitchell's narrative strategies, we cannot take for granted even something so "obvious" or "given" as Thomas Dixon's racist representations. What are the narrative logics that make Dixon's racism "obvious"? Focusing just on the iconic image of the black rapist or the delineation of a noble, Anglo-Saxon heritage for which Dixon's novels are famous would be to miss out on exactly how these images interact with the reader's comprehension of not just the storyworld but also the transition from one projected world to another within the narrative. Descriptions of black people as brutish are just one part of the force of racism in Dixon's text. Its larger perceptual work is to connect characters and actions to reader's expectations such that race becomes not just a form of racist characterization but a way to inhabit the (new) world.

The immersiveness in *The Leopard's Spots* depends on rooting for two narratives of success: a poor white man gains political success on a platform of white supremacy as well as romantic success in winning the heart of the aptly named Sallie Worth. These dual narrative arcs are driven by what the story frames as a choice between two worlds. The novel begins with the end of the U.S. Civil War, the desolation of which "marked the end of an era."[18] Following a troupe of soldiers returning to North Carolina after the surrender of the Confederate armies, "they felt that the end of the world had come" and "now their feet seemed to falter as though they were not sure of the road."[19] The apocalyptic tone of Dixon's beginning places the reader precisely at the moment of transition in which an uncertain future awaits. Jeremy Wells observes that even within the short span that the narrative hones in on an individual and a particular "village," it alludes to "the world" five times and "the earth" twice.[20] Moreover, the status of this world is one that is pervaded by the changed status of the "Negro": "In every one of these soldier's hearts, and over all the earth hung the shadow of the freed Negro, transformed by the exigency of war from a Chattel to be bought and sold into a possible Beast to be feared and guarded. Around this dusky figure every white man's soul was keeping its grim vigil."[21] The change from "Chattel" to "Beast" makes blackness into a sign not of denigrated social and political status but into a sign of character. Moreover, as a sign of character it changes the landscape of the novel and recodes the possible actions within that world. It is a world in which the "freed Negro" is everywhere and one in which he must be vigilantly watched. This all-consuming presence of the Negro is materialized in the merging of the figurative registers of blackness with the denoting of black persons: "But the black cloud was already seen on the horizon. . . . The streets were black with Negroes."[22] With these lines, Dixon stages a setting in which the very presence of blackness changes the world.

The new salience of race here denotes a choice between two worlds—one that is morally lax and dissolute, overrun with degenerate black *and* white persons and one that is ordered, principled, and virtuous, made so because it is led by principled white persons. Most often, this racial framework is the main code through which we can follow, predict, and link characters' fates and actions to one another. When the reader encounters a black character depicted as slavish and dependent, one knows that their loyalty and honesty will be either rewarded or, conversely, they will be victimized by unprincipled persons within the terms of the narrative. When the reader encounters an unprincipled white person, they will most likely act within a vision of racial equality or at least integration. In other words, race becomes the central way with which to connect characters and actions to the novel's larger sense of justice or injustice. But this framework is refined in the reader's navigation of the romance narrative since it plays with our expectation that one's actions can be related to one's character in these ways.

In the romance, Charles Gaston and Allen McLeod struggle for the hand and heart of Sallie Worth. Part of the reader's involvement in this romance is that we know more than a couple of the key characters in the novel. While Gaston's character is being unjustly maligned by McLeod's rumors, insinuations, and charges, the reader knows better. Dixon makes the moral choice between McLeod and Gaston abundantly clear to the reader, while leaving pivotal characters such as Sallie Worth's father and the preacher's wife in the dark. Whiteness itself does not guarantee the quality of one's actions, as the principle antagonists in this novel are those white persons who gain power and money at the expense of the South by using the Negro vote and championing racial equality. As readers, we must decipher and see through the actions of certain characters in order to see their moral corruption. Readers experience the gap between their knowledge and the character's knowledge: the success of the romance requires that the characters be made to eventually see what we have always seen. Gaston's honesty and probity is finally recognized, making his vision of white supremacy into a moral ideal, while McLeod's political program has always relied on racial duplicity.

Within Dixon's "ugly, obvious racism" is a particular epistemology of using race to denote the moral status of the world. The narrative desire to see honesty and moral probity win is causally linked to the valuing of one political worldview (Gaston's white supremacy) over another (McLeod's use of Reconstruction for personal gain). The "obviousness" of the novel's racism, then, has two dimensions. One, the new status of blackness shapes possible actions and evaluations of those actions. Two, readers are required to employ antiblackness in the act of choosing a world built on moral probity rather than lassitude.

"Tomorrow is another day": Gone with the Wind*'s Future Individuality*

Against this description of the racial ways of knowing embedded in Dixon's novel, we can rethink what it means for Mitchell to "avoid" Dixon's "ugly, obvious racism." As noted above, for some critics she does so by placing race relations largely in the background, ancillary to the main romance plot of Scarlett O'Hara as opposed to being integral to the fulfillment of romance, as it is in Dixon. For others, Mitchell's novel differs from Dixon's because of the lack of an iconic "black rapist."[23] What these critics register is the way in which black characters are not as omnipresent in the storyworld of Mitchell's text. The presence of blackness does not contour every judgment and feeling in *Gone with the Wind* as it does in Dixon's *The Leopard's Spots.* However, contrasting Dixon's overt racism with the idea that race is in the background of *Gone with the Wind* simplifies both Dixon's and Mitchell's works. As seen in the "black cloud" example above, Dixon deploys race at multiple levels of figuration in order to construct race as a moral choice between different kinds of social and political worlds. Mitchell, too, shifts between literal and figurative registers of racial description, placing racial salience in the foreground and background at specific moments in order to shape the narrative functions of blackness and whiteness in the novel's world. Like *Leopard's Spots, Gone with the Wind* reformulates the relationship between character and action by reshaping the signifying potentials of blackness and whiteness. I analyze how, where, and when racial significance is deployed in constructing the background assumptions of the storyworld within which characters' moral and economic choices are made.

As opposed to making the hero's romantic and political aspirations coincide as in Dixon's *The Leopard's Spots,* Mitchell articulates race with particular pleasures of romance reading. As Riché Richardson argues in "Mammy's 'Mules,'" *Gone with the Wind* highlights how Scarlett navigates the marriage and courtship rules of the U.S. southern world that she inhabits and her calculated choices as to when these rules might be broken.[24] These rules that make up Scarlett's world are most evident when she bristles against them, for example, by going to Atlanta or dancing with Rhett as a widow. A great deal of the narrative drama and pleasure in *Gone with the Wind* revolves around this relationship between Scarlett's individual desires and the shifting rules of the world, whether they pertain to the rules of marriage or to the shifting racial rules during the transition from antebellum to postbellum South as figured in the novel. Scarlett is continually trying to make the world of the novel align with her private world of desires: marrying Ashley, surviving and saving Tara by building up her mill business, getting rid of Melanie.[25] The deployment of racial significance and descriptions are an important component of the background assumptions for evaluating these actions. Most importantly, this deployment itself shifts from the antebellum to the postbellum parts of the novel.

In the beginning of the novel before the U.S. Civil War, black characters are comfortably ensconced within the division between images of field hands and house "negroes." The former constitutes a backdrop that establishes the world of the plantation and separates the foregrounded actions of the white characters from problems of labor and economics: "To the ears of the three on the porch [Tarleton brothers and Scarlett] came the sound of hooves, the jingling of harness chains and the shrill careless laughter of negro voices, as the field hands and mules came in from the fields."[26] The latter creates a clear separation of white concerns over marriage, courtship, and pending war from the concerns of the black characters, who appear as appendages to the objects they use in serving white people.[27] For example, the Tarleton twins' playful verbal exchanges with their slavehand Jeems serves to poke fun at the twins all the while maintaining their status as young, bold, and brash gentleman concerned with the important problems of courtship. After the twins command Jeems to tell them what he knows because "darkies know everything that goes on," Jeems gives the correct explanation and the "twins looked at each other and nodded, but without comprehension" (12). This extended conversation solidifies the narrative function of racial divisions, where the twins take on their expected roles as naïve and carping but ultimately benevolent lawgivers, and black characters take on their expected roles as sly, subservient, knowing, and the voice of a more realistic understanding of motives and behavior.

Similarly, the scene where Mammy tries to get Scarlett to eat before she leaves for the barbecue shows Scarlett's petulance and ability to get her way as well as Mammy's nurturing, rigid role. As both Tara McPherson and Richardson show, the Mammy character is constructed via a contrast between black nonfemininity and white femininity.[28] When Mammy's agency and character are foregrounded, however, the descriptions are explicitly animalistic: "Mammy emerged from the hall, a huge old woman with the small shrewd eyes of an elephant" (22–23).[29] In both this scene and the one above, Jeems can know more than the twins and Mammy can assert her agency because they do so within plantation slavery conventions in which racial divisions are clear. Thus, the twins chastise Jeems for calling Able Wynders "po'w'ite trash," easily asserting the distinctions among "real white trash like the Slatterys," whites who "just ain't rich," and "darkies" (17).

After the Civil War has ended and the politics of Reconstruction becomes the setting for the characters' actions, the clear racial distinctions of master-servant relations no longer structure the playfulness of those earlier scenes. While black characters are still largely in the background and white characters are still foregrounded, the increased use of blackness as simile reveals the uncertainties around the racial rules that previously established whiteness and its association with a certain set of actions and behaviors. For example, after putting out a fire in the kitchen, Scarlett tells Melanie that she "look[s] like a nigger," to which Melanie responds, "And you look like the end man in a minstrel show"; Rhett says that Scarlett has been "working like a nigger" (469, 579); Will Benteen is aligned at times with Mammy and Pork.[30] The placement of these descriptions after the end of the Civil War expresses the anxiety that whiteness is no longer guaranteed or stabilized through the distinction of master and slave.

While these descriptions are sometimes occasions for comedy within the storyworld, they also become the markers for the new set of rules that unsettle Melanie and Scarlett's social positions. The new racial rules undergirding their actions are described in the novel as a background dictating a different set of constraints, expectations, and responses. On one level, "The thing to do was to work like the devil and stop worrying about the Yankee government. . . . Scarlett did not realize that all the rules of the game had been changed and that honest labor could no longer earn its just reward" (521). On another level, "There never was anything to those folks but money and darkies, and now that the money and darkies are gone, those folks will be Cracker in another generation" (717–18). These sentences posit a world in which the past is retrospectively constructed as a time of "honest labor" and "just rewards." This representation of slavery, of course, erases the role of slaves as laborers in order to create this equivalence between white labor and white reward. Nevertheless, this picture provides the field of judgments against which the present actions and choices of the characters in the novel are measured. Moreover, it is a world in which whiteness is exposed as depending on "money and darkies" and it becomes harder to tell the difference between poor whites and "quality." Scarlett regards Cathleen, a woman who marries a carpetbagger, poorly: "There was nothing of quality folks about Cathleen now. She looked Cracker, even worse. She looked poor white, shiftless, slovenly, trifling. . . . She shuddered, turning her eyes from Cathleen as she realized how narrow was the chasm between quality folk and poor whites" (707).

This new world is one in which the racist term "darky" is not just a stereotypical representation or a convention of plantation manners, but a role into which multiple people can fit across race lines. It dictates a new landscape of economic valuation. By landscape, I do not refer merely to setting, geographical background, or the historical period in which the action of a plot takes place. Rather, it is the narrative and linguistic conditions that shape that action.[31] Landscape in this sense affords the white reader and the white characters in the novel certain pleasures that hitherto were not available to them in the earlier part of the novel—namely, a gritty realism and an unbridled character that constitutes the appeal of characters such as Rhett and Scarlett. Ashley even gets into the act when he explains to Scarlett that he loves her "so much that a moment ago I would have outraged the hospitality of the house which has sheltered me and my family, forgotten the best wife any man ever had—enough to take you here in the mud like a—" (425). The missing epithet there is, of course, "nigger." By becoming figurative (embedded in a simile) at this moment of transition to a postbellum world in the novel, the racist epithet provides whiteness with the flexibility to adapt to the rules of a new order. This is one in which "getting down and dirty" becomes a valorized principle of white individuality. Mitchell refigures the narrative functions and associations of blackness and whiteness in relation to these new racial "rules of the game." She deploys racial significance specifically as *simile* in order to shift the background assumptions for evaluating character. In doing so, she constructs and valorizes new ways of inhabiting the changed racial landscape of Reconstruction as presented in her novel.

These ways of inhabiting the world are articulated through the characters of Will Benteen, Scarlett O'Hara, and Rhett Butler and how their actions are justified within the narrative. Will is initially introduced as one of the dying soldiers for which "Tara" served as a way station after the war:

> He had the sallow malarial face of the south Georgia Cracker, pale pinkish hair and washed-out blue eyes which even in delirium were patient and mild. . . . He was obviously a Cracker, just as the boy they had buried so short a while ago was obviously a planter's son. Just how the girls knew this they could not say. Certainly Will was no dirtier, no more hairy, no more lice infested than many fine gentlemen who came to Tara. Certainly the language he used in his delirium was no less grammatical than that of the Tarleton twins. But they knew instinctively, as they knew thoroughbred horses from scrubs, that he was not of their class. But this knowledge did not keep them from laboring to save him. (509)

While the old distinctions carry on in a certain instinctive, ineffable knowledge, they have also whittled away in the face of war. Will overcomes the old, petty divisions fostered in the previous landed planter class. He does so by showing an unstinting capacity to work and an ability to look squarely at reality. He answers two specific questions that emerge after the war: "Who will southern women marry?" and "What defines white respectability?" While some southern women go the way of marrying Yankee overseers, Will specifically saves Scarlett's sister, Suellen, the "neighborhood pariah," from ignominy and ruin by marrying her (710). As Grandma Fontaine puts it, "it's good for Suellen to marry Will—to marry anybody for that matter, because she needs a husband bad. And where else could she get one? And where else could you get as good a manager for Tara?" (716). In marrying Suellen instead of Careen (Scarlett's other sister to whom he was devoted), he establishes a kind of whiteness built on selfless actions, self-sacrifice and the act of responding to necessity. He does so while being pliant enough to be a field hand when he has to be. Will is white not so much because of property or money but because he responds to the exigencies forced by the politics of Reconstruction.[32] Even as Will is likened to a field hand, thus blurring distinctions between white and black, the motivations and actions of his character are re-evaluated through the narrative in ways that articulate whiteness with the "rules of the game": "He's got the right instincts," Grandma Fontaine goes on, "Nobody but a born gentleman could have put his finger on what is wrong with us as accurately as he just did" (716).

This re-evaluation of whiteness dictates a more worried outlook toward the prospect of becoming "lower": "Look at Cathleen Calvert. You can see what she's come to. Poor white! And a heap lower than the man she married" (717). At the same time, it creates a new historical possibility for a whiteness that responds to the rules of this world: "Look at the McRae family. Flat to the ground, helpless, don't know what to do, don't know how to do anything. . . . The rest have gone under because they didn't have any sap in them, because they didn't have the gumption to rise up again" (717). This "sap" and "gumption" afforded white folks is embodied by Rhett and Scarlett: a rapaciousness born out of necessity. This ethos of necessity marks a particular shift in Scarlett's character that begins after the end of the Civil War. In the beginning of the novel, Scarlett is someone acting solely on her desires for her own private world, and certainly not in response to necessity. Her actions do not change throughout the novel (marrying Frank for utilitarian purposes is no different than marrying Charles for ulterior and utilitarian purposes), but the world around her does. Within the new moral framework of Reconstruction, Scarlett's actions are revalorized as expressing not a *capricious* attitude toward life but an *unrelenting* one.

Mitchell articulates this way of inhabiting the world by utilizing the particular pleasures of the romance genre. Janice Radway shows how believable the heroes and heroines of romance are because they are "distinguished clearly in the readers' minds by the peculiarity of their circumstances and by the specificity of their responses to events"; they are realistic in the sense that readers "are convinced by the narrative's display of their individual particularity."[33] The romance gets the reader to participate in its meaning-making structures by involving us in the evaluation of how individual characters respond to crises: we are dazzled, sometimes shocked, at how Scarlett responds, but, above all, we are involved in the calculus of her situation. As Thomas Roberts argues, one of the things that "junk fiction" provides for readers are models of deportment: "What it presents is not a series of ethically neutral incidents but an exemplary type of reaction, a repertory of normative attitudes in the supreme crises of life."[34] The deployment of racial salience is crucial in valorizing Scarlett's responses to crisis.

Scarlett's sharpened individuality as a "repertory of normative attitudes" is staged in the famous "almost-rape" scene when Scarlett rides through the shantytown and is saved by Big Sam from the clutches of both a white and black man.[35] After the almost-rape, Scarlett gets sent to Melanie's house, while the husbands go off, as far as Scarlett knows, to a political meeting. Scarlett is upset that there has not been more of a to-do made of this attempted rape. Everybody's reactions, including her husband, Frank, are stolid, and to her mind they seemingly do not care that she was attacked. What she does not know is that Frank, Ashley Wilkes, and others have actually gone off as members of the Ku Klux Klan in order to avenge this attempted rape, thus risking their lives and risking capture by the Yankees. This sequence operates through a narrative technique of shared and unshared knowledge in which characters and readers are differentiated in terms of what they know. Melanie and India share knowledge about what is really going on, while Scarlett and Aunt Pitts are left in the dark. Melanie knows that their husbands are risking their lives but keeps it a secret from Scarlett. Meanwhile, Scarlett stews over the lack of attention paid to this event. The reader is placed in Scarlett's position, though the reader knows and guesses more quickly and clearly what is going on than Scarlett does. Like Scarlett, the reader is searching for the correct causal explanation for Melanie's and India's anxiety. We go from thinking along with Scarlett that the stock racial scene is not important enough in the novel, to then knowing that it plays an important role in representing the Klan. Finally, this sequence becomes an important narrative turning point for the novel. In their attack on the black shantytown, Frank is shot and dies. Rhett emerges heroically as someone whose quick thinking protects Ashley Wilkes and others, shielding their actions from the scrutiny of Yankee patrols.

Mitchell turns this conventional motif of the plantation romance—the rape or attempted rape of a white woman—into a crucial narrative turning point in which the meanings of whiteness and blackness are reconfigured in relation to a new racial organization. As Melanie says in explaining this chain of events, "It's not her fault. She only did—did what she felt she had to do. And our men did what they felt they had to do. People must do what they must do. We don't all think alike or act alike and it's wrong to—to judge others by ourselves. How can you and India say such cruel things when her husband as well as mine may be—may be—" (798). In exonerating Scarlett for her actions that possibly lead their husbands to disaster and by protecting Scarlett from the vitriol of those who wish to blame her, Melanie uses an ethos of necessity to explain everybody's actions. Scarlett echoes Melanie's explanation a bit later: "Oh, it's all my fault! . . . India and Archie spoke the truth. It's all my fault. But I never thought either of them was foolish enough to join the Klan! And I never thought anything would really happen to me! But I couldn't have done otherwise. Melly spoke the truth. People have to do what they have to do. And I had to keep the mills going! I had to have money! And now I'll probably lose it all and somehow it's all my fault!" (801). In this narrative sequence, racial significance is virtually never foregrounded, except in the mention of the Klan.[36] Rather, all of the conventional representations of race in the plantation romance (potential black rapists, black shantytown, struggle for white supremacy via violent reprisals) get submerged into the background and operate as the horizon for the re-evaluation of Scarlett's and the mens' actions as born out of necessity.[37] The response to raid the largely black shantytown is rendered into a normative response to the crises that the landscape itself institutes. As being just part of the way things are, race becomes an invisible cause that frames the judgment that "people have to do what they have to do." Racism becomes embedded into the logics of narrative necessity.

Counterintuitively, racial conflict is placed in the background of the scene in order to link race *all the more* to the necessity of the characters' actions. We can contrast this placing of racial significance in the background with the use of race in the famous scene where Rhett drunkenly attacks Scarlett.[38] Several critics have noted the proliferation of racial imagery in this scene.[39] No longer relegated to the background of the action, racial associations linking primitivism, savagery, and darkness to brownness and Indianness are deployed in the foreground. As such, racial difference itself becomes part of the sexual play: "He pressed her back into her chair with large brown hands and leaned over her. 'Observe my hands, my dear,' he said, flexing them before her eyes" (937); "As she stopped to kick it loose frantically, Rhett, running lightly as an Indian, was beside her in the dark. . . . Up the stairs, he went in the utter darkness, up, up, and she was wild with fear. He was a mad stranger and this was a black darkness she did not know. . . . She was darkness and he was darkness . . . only darkness and his lips upon her" (939–40). As if the reference to skin color by the narrator were not enough, the direct speech must also call attention to his "brown" hands. Scarlett's immersion into darkness relies on the expression of racial difference. In this scene, she is imagined as the victim of a figurative racial attack. These are associations that the historical romance wants the reader to have but also wants the reader to deploy in a particular way. As foreground, as specific objects of attention, the racial associations are played up to such a degree as to overemphasize their figural capacities to render a narrative of brute, pleasurable sexuality.

But note how, in doing so, the narrative has again shifted the entire set of attitudes and qualities that the reader is expected to have. Unlike the beginning of the novel, where racial descriptions are meant to be read as literal and quite central for organizing relations between Scarlett and Mammy or the Tarleton twins and their domestic servant, here the expectation is that race will be read as figurative. In the depiction of Rhett, the reader is allowed to use this imagery toward the narrative pleasure of this scene as opposed to using this imagery and figurativeness (as in the earlier "like a—" statements) in order to mark the changed status of whiteness and blackness after the Civil War. There is no danger here of Rhett or Scarlett losing their racial status precisely because the figurative expression of race is so over the top.

This juxtaposition of the shantytown scene and Rhett's attack on Scarlett thus illuminates two particular uses of race. Unlike the use of race in the shantytown raid scene, the racial associations here are specifically foregrounded in ways that create metaphoric links that are not part of a causal sequence necessary for the reader to understand what is going on in the plot. Instead, these color associations are at the level of stage-setting and at the level of affect: setting the scene of "darkness," setting the scene of being cornered, creating the landscape by which terror and pleasure can mingle. Racial imagery moves from foregrounding specific bodily marks of skin tone (brown hands) to bodily gestures (moving "lightly as an Indian") to similes and metaphors that figure persons themselves as "darkness." The writing moves from locating race on the body to locating race in the scene as a whole. The effect of this deployment is to make race most visible only as an imagistic overlay in the sexual pleasures and tension of the scene, thus displacing it from any thinking about narrative causality.

In the former scene, the narrative dynamics place race into the background assumptions of the world. But in doing so, race becomes *more* important as forming the unstated horizon against which individual actions and choices are evaluated. Indeed, the almost-rape is preceded by a great deal of conversation concerning causality: Scarlett is deliberately putting herself in danger; she knows that the road between Atlanta and her mill are crisscrossed with "dangerous" blacks. Just before the almost-rape she crosses the town and is frightened. The white and black men who attack her are scripted into a causal sequence whereby the "freedom" afforded by Reconstruction allows for this violent action. Race located in the background becomes particularly useful for articulating an individuality based on an ethos of necessity. When Scarlett explains why she hires Johnnie and gives him a "free hand" to deal with convict labor, she captures this ethos of "necessity" in relation to constructions of whiteness and blackness: "Johnnie was indeed her man. He was tough and hard and there was no nonsense about him. 'Shanty Irish on the make,' Frank had contemptuously called him, but for that very reason Scarlett valued him. She knew that an Irishman with a determination to get somewhere was a valuable man to have, regardless of what his personal characteristics might be. And she felt a closer kinship with him than with many men of her own class, for Johnnie knew the value of money" (760). Here, racial and class lines are redrawn around this ethic of rapacious individuality.[40] Scarlett's actions take on a different moral framework within the exigencies of necessity.

This articulation of race and individuality within a new economic landscape of Reconstruction is what separates Ashley's past constructions of whiteness from Scarlett's, Will's, and Rhett's rearticulations of whiteness. The ambiguity of the ending shows this separation: on the one hand, Rhett and Scarlett exemplify characters that respond to the harshness of necessity; on the other hand, Ashley exemplifies the firmer, more secure deformations of the past. For Ashley's world, the backgrounding of black lives and foregrounding of white actions cleanly and neatly create a landscape of noblesse oblige. In Scarlett's and Rhett's world, blackness and whiteness are reconfigured (sometimes as simile; sometimes as foreground; sometimes as background) in ways that create both the conditions for the calculations of economic individuality and the figurative pleasures of appropriating blackness. Judging Ashley from the standpoint of the new rules of the game, we lament Ashley's incapacity to respond to a new world but nostalgically feel for the supposed verities of the old, more "honest" rules. In Scarlett and Rhett's world, we relish the excitement of characters that break all the rules even as antiblack racism becomes narratively rooted in economic and moral necessity.

This ambivalence between two worlds persists through the figure of Mammy. For Mammy again takes on a prominent role near the end of the novel, unchanged in terms of her narrative function but very much read differently in this newly configured landscape. For she is the one who sees the diabolical depths of Scarlett's and Rhett's relationship, and she embodies the moral framework through which the reader can evaluate this relationship. She marks a retreat from the use of race in terms of economic calculation and necessity back to the role of race in terms of sentimental smoothing-over. But ultimately, all of the characters' actions take on a different moral framework precisely because of the exigencies of necessity ushered in by Reconstruction. It is necessity that lessens distinctions between poor whites and gentlemen in the case of Will Benteen's marriage to Scarlett's sister. It is necessity that leaves Ashley apart from new constructions of whiteness even as he embodies past constructions of whiteness. It is this rationale of acting out of necessity that ultimately valorizes Scarlett's individual response to Reconstruction.

CHAPTER 4

Reconstructing Racial Perception

C. L. R. James puts his finger on the valorization of a different kind of individuality in both *Gone with the Wind* and Frank Yerby's plantation romances:

> Yerby is characteristic of something entirely new in fiction sold to the millions. His characters break every accepted rule of society. They are out for what they want and get it how they can. They cheat, lie, scheme, plot, are brutal, cruel, lustful, expressing their free individuality. They are also successful . . . Yerby's books are a primitive elemental response to some of the deepest needs of the American people in their reaction against society. . . . The great success of the main characters in Margaret Mitchell's *Gone with the Wind* shows the same response to characters who let nothing stand in their way."[1]

This construction of "characters who let nothing stand in their way" is the sign of something new in the genre of the plantation romance, as James suggests. But as I have argued so far, this "something entirely new" depends on instituting new modes of racial perception. Mitchell uses racial markers in unlikely places—via the strategic use of simile, backgrounded when we expect it to be foregrounded, foregrounded when we expect it to be backgrounded—as a way to constitute the economic and moral landscape of her storyworld against which this new (white) individuality can be valorized and antiblack racism can be reproduced. Frank Yerby, writing on the heels of Mitchell's success, turns out a novel that has all the trappings of Mitchell's revival of the southern plantation romance. But there is one crucial difference. Yerby, I argue, is alert to this placement of racial significance within the fictional diegesis and its multiple cognitive and affective uses. With his own relocation of race, he critiques the way in which race is used to construct supposedly race-neutral formations of individuality. In doing so, he forces readers and characters alike to confront how much their successes and pleasures depend on a racialized context.

Yerby published *Foxes of Harrow* in 1946 and the novel immediately became a best-seller and was quickly turned into a movie. Contemporaneous reviewers writing for the African American literary establishment as well as for mainstream newspapers and magazines situated the novel squarely within the tradition of popular southern romance. Blyden Jackson writes that Frank Yerby is "another American bargaining in the same free fashion for the public taste as Margaret Mitchell in *Gone with the Wind* or Kathleen Winsor in *Forever Amber*."[2] He characterizes the novel in terms of its "great fidelity" to the reproduction of the antebellum South and the "standardized plotting," "piling on of period atmosphere," and "exclusion of racism as a theme" that is characteristic of these romances.[3] Jackson, like other reviewers, either bemoans the lack of serious treatment of racial issues or reads it as just another historical romance repeating the racial clichés of its genre.[4] But far from being an "unserious" treatment of race or simply repeating racial clichés, the novel engages with the specific techniques of deploying racial signification in *Gone with the Wind*, in particular by rearranging when race appears in the background and when it is foregrounded. In doing so, it highlights all the more clearly the narrative strategies that make *Gone with the Wind* such a powerful engine of racial worldmaking.

The similarities between *Gone with the Wind* and *Foxes* go beyond their repetition of the plantation romance's stock characteristics. *Foxes* can be seen as a prequel to *Gone with the Wind* that centers on the Gerald O'Hara figure and tracks his rise to the status of a landed slaveholder. Stephen Fox, the hero of *Foxes*, is, like Gerald O'Hara, an Irishman who is in exile from his country for some nameless, antiauthoritarian deed, and who comes to the South with very little besides some smarts and a penchant for gambling. He rises to landowner status through some shrewd deals and immediately sets his sights on breaking through certain aristocratic codes and their implicit exclusions—again, much like Gerald O'Hara. The novel tracks Fox's fortunes and misfortunes through the Civil War and to the beginning of Reconstruction, but unlike *Gone with the Wind*, the majority of the novel stages the years leading up to the Civil War. This shift in historical emphasis helps Yerby foreground racial significance in the antebellum social and political landscape in ways that specifically reframe his white hero's actions. This foregrounding takes place through two mechanisms. First, Yerby renders race conspicuous both in the background rules by which we understand characters' actions and in the narrative pleasures of the romance as a genre. Second, Yerby reframes the relationship between primary and secondary characters so as to show the dependence of Stephen Fox's brand of white individuality on particular racial rules.

The novel immediately immerses Stephen Fox in the specific forms of seeing and cognizing race that are necessary in New Orleans. Early in the novel, Fox takes a walk with his friend Andre Le Blanc, an aristocratic creole, through the streets of New Orleans. This tour of New Orleans becomes the occasion to educate Stephen (and the reader by extension) into the importance of racial signification in inhabiting the storyworld. Stephen and Andre are already an unusual sight according to the racial and social codes of the region: "There were not, in that day, many men so tall as Stephen, and his coppery red hair was like a beacon among the dark Creoles. It was surprising, too, to see a *'Mericain coquina*, a despited Kaintock on so friendly terms with an aristocratic young Creole."[5] Thus their social and political positions are conditioned by the particular way in which racial meanings are seen to articulate with class and nationality. In this sense, racial significations are the conditions through which one makes sense of and enters this world.

In buying street food, Stephen is introduced to the various racial associations that permeate this world:

> An old Negro woman called out as they passed: "*Estomac mulatre! Belly of mulatto! Estomac mulatre! Achetez!* Buy! *Venez vous et mangez!* Come and eat! *Estomac mulatre!*" "Are ye cannibals too, in this country?" Stephen asked. "And what do ye do with the rest of the Nigra, if ye eat only his belly?" "One moment," Andre said, turning to the old woman. "Tante! Give me eight pieces of mulatto's belly!" He gave her a coin. The old woman put her hand inside the basket and came out with eight small round cakes. . . . "What a name to give gingercake! Now I know ye French are crazy!" "Perhaps—but there is another of our products—look!" . . . A group of young girls, afoot, and dressed in bright colors was slipping through the throngs like gayly chattering

> songbirds. They carried no parasols, and their lovely young faces were bared to the sun. But strangest of all they wore on their heads instead of the bonnets of the Creole ladies, the bright tignons of the slaves. (32–33)

The racist joke of calling "gingercake" by the name "mulatto's belly" renders perspicuous the ways in which racially othered bodies are consumed and cannibalized. Moreover, it mirrors the incongruity of the "mulatto," whose beautiful appearance and dress do not match her status as slave. Being "bared to the sun" and wearing "bright tignons" on their heads are the markers of slave status that require a socialized eye to discern.

A running joke about how one likes one's coffee further exemplifies the ways in which racial attributions enter into and permeate what one sees and how one sees it:

> "*Black coffee*, Delphine," he said. "*Ma foi*, but you are a very pretty girl!"
> "M'sieu makes a pleasantry," the girl murmured, turning to Stephen.
> "*Café au lait*," Stephen said, "and a piece of coffee cake."
> Andre was watching Delphine pour the café au lait. The dark and light streams arched out of the graceful necks of the pitchers at the same time, combining in the cups in just the right proportions. He liked the way her hands moved, pouring.[6] (57)

In making explicit the relationship between what they drink and racial composition, Yerby shows how intertwined the materiality of one relies on the other. That the examples hinge on the racialized appearance of women is not an accident. The quadroon women operate at the precise intersection between particular modes of seeing and the moral and economic landscape of slavery.

Beginning the novel in this way, Yerby conspicuously foregrounds how certain rules of seeing race structure the pathways that Fox must navigate in order to rise in the world. Like Scarlett O'Hara, Stephen Fox breaks all the rules in order to strive and achieve status. But unlike Scarlett, Stephen's breaking of the rules in order to achieve status as a "gentleman planter" renders visible the unstated rules around race. When he is establishing his sugarcane crop, "Stephen worked in the fields like a Negro," repeating Scarlett's act of working in the fields for her survival (102).[7] This phrase does not appear in the middle of the novel as in *Gone with the Wind* when, as I discussed earlier, race became figurative in the novel's textual world. When Mitchell deploys the simile, it functions to displace anxieties around white status. The reader is invited to both deploy and disavow the racist simile of "working like a nigger" in order to see Scarlett's gritty individuality. Yerby's use of the phrase appears at the beginning of the novel and is part of Stephen's attempts to realize his private world within and against the racially stratified world of New Orleans creole society. As his friend Andre makes clear, "working like a Negro" places him outside the pale of civilization among the aristocratic set: "They have discovered you are mad. . . . They say you live in a hovel, and work in the fields with the blacks" (100). Here, though, the reader is made to participate in Fox's breaking of racial rules and identify with the racial association. In order for the reader to take Stephen as a model of deportment, to enjoy his single-minded purpose against the stratified social structures, they must see "working like a Negro" as part of his construction of character. Whereas in *Gone with the Wind* the association with blackness figures the tragedy of Scarlett's and Melanie's new position after the Civil War, here the narrative makes clear how Stephen is explicitly brooking the conventions of aristocratic creole life. The context of Yerby's simile reframes the way in which race is used to evaluate Fox's actions.

Yerby's strategies of foregrounding race similarly reverse Mitchell's articulation of racial imagery and sexuality in the Rhett-Scarlett scene analyzed above. As if responding to the scene in which Scarlett descends into a figuratively titillating darkness and savagery, Yerby gives us the climactic sex scene between Stephen Fox and his cold, sexless wife, Odalie, only via the highly racialized spectacle of primitivist sexuality. Odalie, in order to win back her husband from the seductions of a quadroon mistress, witnesses the spectacle of a black man named Hercules undulating with a beautiful quadroon girl. Through this means, Odalie transforms herself into a savage presence. In response to being seduced, Stephen says, "So," he whispered. "Ye came to me at last! Ye came and loved like a hot-blooded young savage and there was no reserve in ye, none at all" (226–27). Hyperbolizing the conventional associations, Yerby calls attention to the function of race in generating the sexual pleasure necessary for romance reading. Indeed, unlike *Gone with the Wind*, the reader is required to participate in the associations of race and sexuality in order to simply comprehend the sexual needs and disappointments of the hero and heroine of the first 250 pages of the novel. If the "savagery" of Rhett Butler and the "darkness" of Scarlett can remain metaphorical elements, Odalie's "savagery" cannot, being explicitly linked to the spectacular display of black sexuality.[8] The reader is prompted to traverse actual black bodies in order to participate in the pleasures of the romance, thus making explicit the instrumental use of sexualized blackness.

Taken out of context, the use of racial imagery, stereotypes, and language looks very similar across *Gone with the Wind* and *Foxes*. They include various stereotypes of both domestic and field slaves: Achille in *Foxes* parallels Big Sam in *Gone with the Wind* as they are both large, strong, black field hands; the imagery of a "dark" sexuality pervades sex scenes in both books; both novels even use the same or similar racist similes—"working like a nigger"—in order to describe their protagonist's actions. But when we read the uses of race in the context of their narratological functions and the contouring of foreground and background, we see that Yerby flips Mitchell's narrative strategies. As we saw above, *Gone with the Wind* either places its black characters in a static background or as an absent cause to sharpen and justify the choices that Scarlett makes, thus embedding racism in the narrative logic of necessity. Yerby instead foregrounds the salience of race in the relationship between Stephen's social positioning and his actions. This restructuring of foreground and background can be seen further in Yerby's secondary black characters and the ways in which they do not stay in the background. Indeed, Yerby's secondary characters instruct the reader in seeing a whole set of racial meanings embedded in the economic and social landscape that provides the context for judging Stephen's actions.

For example, Fox takes on a quadroon mistress, Desiree, a plot device used to steam up the sex element of the fiction, but also to sharpen the ethical dilemmas regarding Fox's unhappy marriage. Desiree's desirability as a beautiful quadroon girl reiterates stereotypes and arouses titillation in the reader. But Stephen's position as an outsider to New Orleans society enables Yerby to introduce Desiree in terms of her proper, racialized context. That is, a racially hierarchical world that makes quadroon women into objects of satisfaction for men like Stephen who are disappointed in marriage and lusting for enjoyment. This understanding of race-as-context is never afforded a character like Big Sam in *Gone with the Wind.* When Stephen wishes to make Desiree his mistress, he must work through the financial arrangements first with her mother: "'This gentleman wishes a word with you, *Maman*,' Desiree said. The woman turned her gaze to Stephen, waiting like a queen for him to speak. Stephen found her gaze disconcerting. To be looked at like this by a Negress—even an almost white Negress—was, to say the least, a new sensation. He hesitated" (262).

The financial arrangements are a way of evaluating Stephen, and the use of free, indirect discourse that merges the narrator's and Stephen's perspective ("To be looked at like this") immediately makes the disconcerting look more general. That is to say, the reader too is disconcerted. The narration mixes the pleasures of a specifically masculinist sexual titillation with the uneasy visibility of the racial codes that produce Desiree in the first place. Stephen attests to his uneasiness with the explicit nature of these proceedings: "But this was a new thing: this shameless willingness to sell a daughter into concubinage" (263). After the arrangements are made, Stephen expresses surprise at Desiree's young age, but she reassures him: "Don't let it. We are never young. We cannot afford youth. This wisdom, as you call it, is a thing handed down from mother to daughter for generations. This is what I was born for, monsieur" (269). Her explanation makes clear her straitened circumstances by reframing what Stephen calls Desiree's "wisdom" for pleasing men. Not a "natural" trait developed over time, her wisdom is a "thing handed down from mother to daughter for generations." Desiree thus makes clear the ways in which she has been made through the genealogy of slavery in order to serve Stephen's private world.

As the novel progresses, moreover, Desiree takes on a greater and greater role that exceeds her status as a minor character. In another subplot, Desiree's brother, Aupre, feels deeply humiliated when Stephen forces him to shake his hand. When Stephen registers his inability to understand Aupre's reaction, Desiree says, "Put yourself in his place, monsieur. Suppose you returned to find your sister, flown, unmarried, to the arms of a lover—and that lover a man of another race. What would you do?" (273). Lest the reader get too involved in Stephen's heroic individuality and forget the racialized context that enables his position, Desiree reminds both him and us. This point is driven home by the narrative discourse. For Desiree's explanations interrupt a scene that would otherwise be solely focalized through Stephen's perspective. Because the reader's understanding relies on Stephen's, we would have blithely followed Stephen's incomprehension, learning to ignore or explain away Aupre's reactions. Instead, Desiree's enlarged understanding shows the dependence of Stephen's private world of achievement, land ownership, and lust on the specific racial determinations of the storyworld.

In a final twist, Desiree returns at the very end of the novel to again ironize Stephen's life and career. After the Civil War, Stephen's former slave, Inch, has now become lieutenant governor of Louisiana. Stephen is shocked when Inch brings Desiree out as his mistress and introduces his son, who looks eerily like Stephen himself. The insinuation is that Desiree had a son by Stephen, who is now being raised by Inch. With this scene, Yerby replaces the popular narrative of Reconstruction as a world in which corrupt and ignorant black citizens take over the government with a scene that instead exposes Stephen's position, his adultery, and the sexual privilege afforded the white aristocrat. Unlike *Gone with the Wind* and the particular framing of Scarlett's actions, the reader is never allowed to take pleasure in Stephen's individuality apart from the way in which it has been enabled by racist structures.

Yerby's reconstructions of readerly perception thus work on two planes. On one level, he gives us all the stereotypical trappings of the plantation romance: grinning "field Negroes" happily doing their work; hypersexualized black women and men; characters, including Fox, who inhabit racist rhetoric of "African brutes," and so on. At the same time, these stereotypes and conventional racism of the plantation romance genre are contextualized by making clear the economic, social, and political infrastructure that they support and facilitate. Even as Stephen makes use of racial hierarchies with his own ruthless, drive-oriented principles and desires in order to realize his private world and create excitement and pleasure for the reader, his actions can never be read apart from the racial order that he deploys. For example, after his first wife's death, Stephen Fox marries her sister, Aurore, who attempts to wipe the slate clean with her love: "Whatever you did—your carelessness, your mockery, your quadroon wench, your loving Odalie—I forgave you, Stephen. I could forgive you anything. I lived only for the precious minutes when I should see you, and between them only in the hope of seeing you again" (246). But these associations and contexts remain present: the "quadroon wench"—Desiree—returns, as we have observed, at the end of the novel.

To reconstruct racial perception is to open up historical possibilities for characters like Desiree. It is also to reconfigure the relationship between past and future worlds. Stephen seems to change in his attitudes toward the end of the novel: he voices various arguments against slavery and constructs a complex understanding of the social and economic world through which the evils of slavery are maintained. In arguing with his best friend, Andre, Stephen has the following discussion:

> "How I envy ye your Louisiana faculty for self-delusion!" he chuckled. "Slavery is a very convenient and pleasant system—for us. But I've often had qualms over the rightness of a system which permits me to sell a man as though he were a mule. Still, I have my leisure, which I haven't earned, and my wealth, which I don't work for—so I cannot complain really."
>
> "Stephen!" Andre's voice was thick with shock. "You talk like an abolitionist!"
>
> "Forgive me, my lad," Stephen smiled. "I couldn't resist needling ye. We'll talk no more of this."

> "But we will," Andre declared. "And you may tell your Yankee friends that if they interfere we shall leave them and continue on alone in our own way."
>
> Stephen was no longer smiling. (230)

This is a reflection on what a racist system affords "for us." Fox recognizes the dependence of his own historical possibility on a racist context.[9] Near the end of the novel, after the Civil War, Fox's plantation is completely burned down to the ground and Reconstruction has begun. Yerby hints at the iconic narrative of Reconstruction, familiar to us from Thomas Dixon's romances, in which black people insolently revel in their newfound authority. But he interrupts that story with the reflection on another kind of future:

> Now I must begin again, Stephen thought, and I am old. It must be left to the young men—'Tienne and the rest. And I fear that they will look forever backward to what was. Ye can't turn the world back again, ye must go forward. If they try to shape the world again in the image of the past, they'll waste generations and mountains of blood and treasure in something that cannot succeed because of its very nature. If there is any one thing upon the face of the earth that is unconquerable 'tis human freedom. And if they try to take it away again from the blacks they will end by losing it themselves. (530)

Stephen Fox is poised at a moment of transition. But in critiquing this need to "shape the world again in the image of the past," Yerby challenges the racial worldmaking practices of the plantation romance that he himself inhabits. Scarlett O'Hara is similarly poised at the end of *Gone with the Wind* between two worlds, but in both worlds—whether the world of Tara or the world of economic necessity—antiblack racism shapes her "free individuality." The difference between the two worlds is one that ultimately does not make a difference.

In Scarlett O'Hara and Stephen Fox, both Mitchell and Yerby create models of a ruthless, driven, heroic, and "free individuality" that remake the plantation romance genre. Molly Haskell suggests part of the reason for *Gone with the Wind*'s amazing success is the presentation of Scarlett's gritty economic success, one that played well for an audience that had just experienced the Great Depression.[10] Stephen, too, plays out for the reader's imagination the pathways by which his industry allows him to manipulate markets in building his landed economic empire. Ideologies of individualism—especially of the atomistic variety—have long served to disavow the problem of racial injustice.[11] But instead of reiterating the usual counterargument of showing how structural constraints of race still do exist and persist, my analysis of *Gone with the Wind* and *Foxes* shows the mutually constitutive relationship between the shaping of economic and moral landscapes through racial attribution and the sharpening of certain individual actions and choices. Both novels manage the contexts through which we are made to inhabit this individuality and immerse ourselves in their decisions and choices. Mitchell updates ideologies of individuality not simply by asserting the pluckiness of her famous heroine but also by relocating race in ways that reproduce racism while staging the moral and economic necessity of Scarlett's actions. Yerby's novel works differently than Mitchell's not despite the use of the conventions of plantation romance but because of it, not because there is explicit social protest or commentary on slavery but because he makes the landscape of racial associations readable and visible *as* a formative social context.

Conclusion: Black Reconstruction

Yerby's novels have traditionally been critiqued for their lack of response to racial issues at best, and, at worst, for the reiteration of the racist stereotypes and conventions of the genre in which he has written.[12] But his personal papers housed at Boston University contain reams of notes that he kept on his novels. These notes show a deep awareness of the racism embedded in the historiography of Reconstruction, as well as an eye for the various ways in which racial inequality was structured during that time. In detailing a number of massacres of blacks during Reconstruction, Yerby writes that the historian "Lorn [Lonn] is clearly Pro Southern & every other page exhibits anti-Negro prejudice. Check other sources for true cause of this massacre. The feeling that Southern whites need any very valid [reason] to commit hideously sadistic acts against Negroes does not necessarily hold water. Doubt that many if any of the provocations attributed to Negroes occurred. The rape of dead body is pure rot."[13] His files are filled with notes on various histories of Reconstruction, assessing their biases and cross-checking them. Moreover, he points to the relationship between institutional structures and the racist conventions that emerge from them:

> the municipal authorities, proceeding on the absurd and cynical theory that Negroes paid no taxes, had everywhere consistently ignored them and their claim to the ordinary municipal services. Thus they had quickly got to be the worst slums in Amer. Long rows of crazy

> shacks or shambling rookeries, packed as close as might be along fetid brooks & creeks, railroad tracks, alleys, or unpaved red gullies. . . . Though the segregation of these slum areas served in some part to reduce friction between races, yet in other ways it served to feed the white man's fears. There they stood, behind the white man's houses, half-hidden in daytime, dark, mysterious, & ominous in nighttime. Out of them the jungle beat of drums; the wild chanting gibberish of nameless congregations packed in unlighted halls.[14]

In these notes, Yerby details the relationship between the formation of specific perceptions—"white man's fears"—and the specific structures of taxation and city building that facilitate those pathways of meaning. As I have argued above, Yerby's deployment of racial signification in *Foxes* articulates his sense of the relationship between social structures and epistemologies of racial attribution. His use of the plantation romance genre, moreover, keys in on its role in producing popular, antiblack histories of Reconstruction.

As we have seen, plantation romance is a form of historiography, of narrating Reconstruction and the transition between an antebellum and postbellum world. My analyses of the peculiar historiography and narrative strategies of the plantation romance show how its authors are keenly aware of how race is deployed in the making of the modern world. In both parts 1 and 2 so far, I have shown how race and genre interact, constituting and shaping the built-in knowledges through which moments of change come to be experienced. I have traced textual strategies that relocate racial meanings from bodies into the fictional diegesis that allow it to have *more* explanatory power. More explanatory power on a larger scale and at a level of structure because race gets relocated into the very process of historical explanation as "climate" and "context." This enlargement of textual strategies for making race "mean" occurs even as the explanatory force of biology- and anatomy-based scientific racism and political racism is being challenged. With the critique of Jim Crow and scientific racism already afoot, popular fictions embed race at other levels of meaning by drawing on the energies of anticipation and retrospection. They often do so with the effect of producing new modes of racism. Yerby's novel stands as a challenge to these strategies.

In the next two parts, the importance of historical explanation remains, but we also see other domains embedding race into its modes of knowledge formation: economics and the law. With the critique of scientific racism virtually finished in the UNESCO declarations of 1956[15]—both in the sense of arriving at its final formulations and in the sense of reaching the ends of its usefulness—new modes of apprehending and deploying race to build worlds were already being established and disseminated. The mid-century legislative changes enacted during and after the civil rights movement, including but not limited to the Civil Rights Act of 1964 and the Equal Employment Opportunity Act of 1972 occasioned these practices of racial worldmaking. Part III introduces the domains of cultural anthropology and economic thinking that emerged alongside the popular genre of sword and sorcery. Part IV focuses on the domain of legal thinking and in particular the emergence of anti–affirmative action and reverse racism lawsuits in relation to the storytelling modes of alternate history.

PART III

Sword and Sorcery

CHAPTER 5

The "Facts" of Blackness and Anthropological Worlds

Perhaps no other popular genre relies as much on embedding and relocating race in its worlds than the subgenre of fantasy known as sword and sorcery. "Sword and sorcery," or "S&S" as it is called by fans, was developed by Robert Howard as a series of adventure tales set in ancient worlds "on the brink of civilization" through pulp magazines such as *Weird Tales*, *Oriental Tales*, and *Magic Carpet*. Howard's "Conan the Barbarian" stories had a cultlike appeal in the 1930s and he was retrospectively dubbed the founder of "sword and sorcery" by fantasy writers Michael Moorcock and Fritz Lieber. Most famously, Lieber writes in a July 1961 issue of *AMRA*, a fanzine devoted to Robert Howard's work: "I feel more certain than ever [that this field] should be called the sword-and-sorcery story. This accurately describes the points of culture-level and supernatural element and also immediately distinguishes it from the cloak-and-sword (historical adventure) story."[1] L. Sprague de Camp edited and reissued Howard's Conan stories from the 1950s through the 1970s, thus paving the way for the wider popularization and circulation of Conan via both comic books and major Hollywood movies.

To say that S&S relies on race is at one level unsurprising. Anyone familiar with Howard's stories knows their reliance on stereotypes of primitivism and the ease with which the stories refer to dark-skinned peoples in animalistic terms. Indeed, as I will go into further detail below, de Camp took pains to expurgate Howard's racist language in his controversial heavy edits of Howard's short stories. However, as I have demonstrated in the first two parts, racial worldmaking is not simply the deployment of stereotypes and racist language to build worlds. It is the instruction of the reader in specific modes of noticing race so as to make available certain knowledges about the world. It is the interaction of genre and race in the formation of a work's cognitive effects. In these senses, S&S has both shaped racial attributions and been shaped by the relocation of race. These processes are particularly clear in the case of S&S for two reasons. First, because of S&S's roots in the pulps and fanzines devoted to Howard's work, we have at our disposal rich debates about world-building and the relationship between the secondary worlds created in fantasy and our primary worlds. Second, the origins and development of S&S coincide with major developments in the discursive relocation of race in the twentieth century: from biology to culture on the one hand and from society to the market on the other.

I begin by situating S&S in its relationship to epic fantasy. I put them together to delineate their shared modes of storytelling. But I also want to figure out why they seem to invite the same kinds of interpretive assumptions when it comes to reading race. I diagnose the intractability of such protocols of racial reading and critique their limitations. By going to the roots of S&S in the fanzines, we find a way to complicate this relationship between fantasy genre and racial formation because the debates there detail a fascinating process whereby writers and readers alike embed race at multiple levels and across the imagining of both secondary and primary worlds. This expanded understanding of the interactions between genre and race helps us identify the textual strategies of relocating race found in the fiction, first in Howard's Conan stories and then in Samuel Delany's Nevèrÿon series. This trajectory from Howard to Delany heightens attention to one of S&S's main sites of racial worldmaking: atmosphere. Atmosphere is at a basic level the general mood of a narrative established by highly associative language or imagery. As I will detail below, atmosphere invites a high level of narrative attention to background and involves the reader in the activity of deciphering with particular implications for how race is used to construct meaning.

I put these textual strategies in dialogue with the two major developments in racial discourse noted above: first, the shifts in race-thinking within anthropology and the "scientific critique" of racism put forward by UNESCO in the 1950s, and second, the reimagination of the marketplace and race by economists during and after the civil rights movement. The links between S&S and the midcentury *critique* of racism is surprising because S&S is usually associated with typological understandings of race and its accompanying overt racism. I argue that there is actually a convergence between S&S and cultural anthropology as they both relocate race to the level of a fundamental principle. The links among S&S, race, and economics are less explored. Racial discrimination in relation to the idea of the free market emerged as a central area of concern in the 1960s and 1970s among influential economists such as Gary Becker and Milton Friedman. Though their paradigms and arguments did not prevent antidiscrimination laws from being passed, they did create new representational strategies for locating race so as to frame and shape decision-making practices. Sword and sorcery (as seen through the intertextual relationship between Howard and Delany) and popular economic thought, I argue, both negotiate the problem of how and where to notice race in order to produce the governing ideals of market exchanges.

S&S and Epic Fantasy: Challenging the Conventions of Race Critique

Within the larger field of research on the fantasy genre, S&S gets relatively little attention.[2] Perhaps this is because of its reputation as an "infantile" genre focused largely on "swashbuckling adventure."[3] But it shares modes of storytelling with its more famous cousin, Tolkienesque epic fantasy (*Lord of the Rings* and the tradition that it engendered).[4] Moreover, these shared modes invite similar lines of racial critique. Both S&S and epic fantasy often create secondary worlds: detailed, coherent, and complete imaginary worlds set in the deep past. Across Tolkien's Middle-earth, Howard's Hyborian Age, Fritz Leiber's Nehwon, Delany's Nevèrÿon, and George Martin's Westeros, among many others, much of the pleasure is in the imagination of ancient peoples, lost races, and lost civilizations. One of the signatures of secondary-world fantasy is its map of the world, along with detailed explanations of its peoples and different species ranging from primitive to civilized. As Mark Bould writes, "Recognising its status, fantasy disavows the very possibility of a territory which is not its map."[5] This map often bears some similarities to sources in ancient history in terms of names and movements of peoples, but it disavows any straight correlation by producing its own system and describing its own historical or evolutionary forces.

Because of these tendencies to map the world and generate species populating worlds set off in deep time, both S&S and epic fantasy often draw on anthropology for building knowledge of the secondary world. The spatial distribution of species across the world on a map plots them historically such that the physical and cultural traits of the species can be separated, isolated, and mapped in relation to one another. Elves are different than orcs because of their varying physical and cultural traits but also because they are plotted into different times and spaces. Secondary-world fantasy thus utilizes the same technique that Johannes Fabian says anthropologists do when they prevent the possibility of understanding two distinct cultures as occupying the same time. He calls this the denial of historical coevalness. This mode of producing cultural "others" distances different peoples spatially while constructing them as living in a different *time*—that is, they are developmentally "behind," they are still living in the past. Fabian even isolates the function of the map in ordering these relations. He points out, "distribution maps on which culture historians and folklorists locate variants in the hope of translating spatial relations into historical sequences are just that—maps. Maps are devices to classify data. Like tables and diagrams they are taxonomic ways of ordering cultural isolates with the help of categories of contrast and opposition: source vs. variant, center vs. periphery, pure form vs. mixed variant, displaying criteria of quality vs. those of quantity, or whatever else diffusionists use to map the traits of cultures."[6] Like those anthropologists, the map in secondary world fantasy "translates spatial relations into historical sequences." In this sense, the distribution of peoples across the secondary world might be said to be one of the crucial building blocks for worlds like Middle-earth and the Hyborian Age, constructing the backdrop against which actions and events take on significance.[7]

Given this description of how important the mapping and classifications of peoples and species are to the world-building process, it is not surprising that arguments about race and racism are rampant when discussing works across the S&S and epic fantasy spectrum. On one side stand numerous observations about racial coding: for example, Tolkien's Middle-earth was read early and often in terms of a nostalgic desire for the orderly hierarchy of races with the fairest (the elves) on top in terms of wisdom, longevity, and civilization, and the darkest (the orcs), who were vicious and expendable. On the other side are arguments that these conspicuous racial codings are themselves unstable and/or contingent in ways that undermine these critiques of racism.[8] The most recent version of these arguments about racial coding can be seen in commentary on the hit HBO show *Game of Thrones* based on George R. R. Martin's best-selling series.[9] After a critique of one episode in which Daenerys becomes a savior by freeing people of color, Martin wrote that slavery in his books is not based on race and has much more in common with the Roman and Greek world.[10] The critique of racial representation relies on stabilizing the relationship between racial coding in the TV series and a specific corresponding world—the world of racial slavery in the transatlantic history of the United States, Britain, and West Africa. Martin's response denying racism relies on displacing that correspondence to a different one—the Greco-Roman world.

This dead-end interpretive dilemma of the inability to decide whether these correspondences are racially motivated or not should be a familiar one: its assumptions have organized debates over racial representation with regard to many popular works of fantasy and science fiction. The starting point for these arguments is a reading practice based on a classical account of allegory in which the reader interprets the text by recognizing all points of correspondence between it and another structure of meaning. In presupposing a system of multiple articulated levels, such readings are more or less convincing depending on how well it can show the authenticity with which the two coordinating poles speak to each other.[11] Thus, the arguments about race proceed by constructing correspondences between representations of species in the secondary world with racial stereotypes or racist ideologies from the real world. Within this interpretive structure, works of fantasy are judged to the extent that they either reflect familiar racist tropes or complicate them. Complicating them most often consists in (a) not portraying a "direct" correspondence, (b) creating narrative trajectories that operate against the representations, or (c) the degree to which their racist representations can be seen as deliberate choices. Nevertheless, the framework for this reading remains guided by the activity of measuring how the secondary world corresponds to the "real" world in some allegorical mode.

Now it might be easy to just abandon allegorical reading, say that we have more sophisticated interpretive tools at our disposal—historicist, contextualist—and resolve the relationship between secondary-world fantasy and racial ideology that way.[12] But these strategies for interpreting race in fantasy are so long-standing because the development of secondary worlds invites *the desire for allegorical interpretation*. Its quasi-fantastical lands, names, and peoples involve readers in the process of trying to find proper referents through which to order its historical universe within a set of moral values. This "desire for allegory," I argue, engenders a process of building in knowledge. This differs from traditional uses of allegory and especially Darko Suvin's critique of allegory. For Suvin, "orthodox allegory" with its "one-to-one correspondence between its elements and elements from the author's reality" lacks any cognitive component and thereby any critical potential; it is just a "straightforward fantasy or moral allegory."[13] But for me, allegory is characterized precisely by the instability of these two poles, and it is this instability that sets off a process of cognition. When recognized as such in the context of racial reading, we can see that racial representations in fantasy worlds do not simply correspond to given representations from the author's world. Fantasy world-building entails more than relating race (as some known, albeit coded, representation) in the secondary world back to an already understood given. Rather, the allegorical instability between secondary world and reader's world in both S&S and epic fantasy produces a process whereby reader's knowledge of the primary world is built into knowledge of the secondary world. As we shall see, this process happens in reverse, too: knowledge built in to inhabiting the secondary world frames the reader's knowledge of the primary world. The critical habit of reading race allegorically misses the mark not because of its concentration on allegory as such, but because it does not concentrate *enough* on the desire for allegory. Instead of a method that traces racial representations *back* to their foundational rationales in the "real" world, however complexly conceived, an analysis of our desire for allegory reveals disturbing connections between racial reference and interpretation itself.

Sword and sorcery and epic fantasy overlap both in their construction of secondary worlds and in the allegorical interpretive techniques thereby invited. But what makes S&S distinctive is its relatively closer relationship between the secondary world and the ancient history of our own primary world. Indeed, this simultaneous historical and ahistorical status of the secondary world itself is a famous point of consternation when it comes to Robert Howard's Hyborian Age. H. P. Lovecraft writes in a letter, "The only flaw in this stuff is R. E. H.'s [Robert E. Howard] incurable tendency to devise names too closely resembling actual names of ancient history—names which, for us, have a very different set of associations. In many cases he does this designedly—on the theory that the familiar names descend from the fabulous realms he describes—but such a design is invalidated by the fact that we clearly know the etymology of many of the historic terms, hence cannot accept the pedigree he suggests."[14] Lovecraft sees this closeness to "actual" ancient history as a major flaw. For me, it points to the cognitive effects such similarity and dissimilarity engenders.

I am not interested in carving out hard-and-fast distinctions between S&S and epic fantasy. Rather, I borrow from Farah Mendlesohn's approach to fantasy by concentrating on the differing ways in which fantasy texts both position the fantastic within their narrated worlds and fashion different reader relationships to their fictional worlds. In other words, Mendlesohn is less interested in particular rules that kinds of fantasy would obey and more interested in how the reader is positioned in relation to the world-building strategies of the text.[15] I concentrate in particular on one aspect of this readerly position: how do the knowledges built into making the narrative secondary world interact with the reader's knowledges of the primary world? It is here that S&S activates a different kind of interaction. While Tolkien developed a cosmology around elves in *The Silmarillion* that provided the historical and creaturely depth for Middle-earth, Howard's sources are in the annals of human civilizations. The closeness of Howard's world-building to the work of historians and ethnographers of ancient history means that readers and fans can more easily relate to and compare the imagination of ancient history and all of its geographical and social elements to the Hyborian Age and vice-versa. Howard scholar Jeffrey Shanks writes, "Howard would breathe life into these Hyborian Age kingdoms . . . by describing a particular nation with features similar to an appropriately analogous culture from 'real' history."[16] Various comparisons can be used to supplement knowledge across primary and secondary worlds: the knowledge and imagination of population movements; of technological developments in the use of bronze, stone, and iron; of social relations; of ways of governing; of economic trade; and so on. This closeness, too, reflects the heightened attention that S&S pays to the imagination of social transactions: a trade of a precious artifact for a promise; the payoff of a mercenary; a run-in with palace guards. Rarely, if ever, is the mundane activity of trading represented in Tolkien since every action there is imbued with larger political significance.

The roots of developing S&S as a genre are in the pulp magazine letter pages and the fanzines. That is where the genre—in my sense of making available certain knowledges of the world—gets built. By turning to these roots, we can first of all see the ways in which S&S stages a process of world-building distinct from epic fantasy despite their many similarities. Moreover, seeing this imaginative process unfold reveals interpretive strategies for producing race that have hitherto been missed. Indeed, the development of S&S and strategies for relocating race go hand in hand. If the greater distance between Middle-earth and Earth invites allegorical interpretation at the level of racial ideologies and broad correspondences between its fantastical species and racial groupings, then the closer relationship between the Hyborian Age and the imagination of ancient history invites a process whereby race takes on the greater function of building in knowledge of the world.

Building S&S and Relocating Race

H. P. Lovecraft's identification of the close resemblance of Howard's worlds to ancient history is mirrored by many other early readers and writers. It becomes the starting point for the process of building worlds staged by Howard's stories. The letters pages in *Weird Tales* and the commentary and essays published in fanzines such as the *Hyborian Age*, *AMRA*, and *REH* generally contain a great deal of praise for how Howard brings ancient times and civilizations to life. The majority of the attention is paid to the relationship between Howard's world and ancient histories, legendry, and myth, leading to a great deal of discussion of the anthropology and ethnography of ancient peoples. The activity of tracing Howard's place names to historical fact or legend is prominent. For example, de Camp alphabetically catalogs Howard's world and its "sources" in "Exegeses of Hyborian Age." One entry reads—"'Wadai'—In (SZ), a Negro country. A part of the Chad Colony of French Equatorial Africa; also, a powerful Negro kingdom in that region, conquered by France in 1908–1912. (In view of the unsettled state of the British and French possessions and former possessions in Africa, I have not tried to bring my geographical references to those regions up to date.)"[17] Here "SZ" is an abbreviation for the Howard story in which this place name was found. De Camp traces it to its modern geographical location, acknowledging the "unsettled state" of British and French colonialism in Africa. Other sources are literary or mythological. Justin Kidd in a letter in *AMRA* traces Howard's use of the name "Jhil" to a name in Rudyard Kipling's *Jungle Book*.[18]

But this academic exercise is just a part of the larger desire to both discover and imagine the referents of Howard's narratives. In various articles, readers build worlds from Howard's "Hyborian Age," supplementing details about peoples, customs, and ways of life, using logics derived from histories of ancient civilizations.[19] Readers fill the gaps of fictional worlds, rendering them more coherent by using their own knowledge or hypotheses about historical and social processes. For example, in "Ocean Trade in the Hyborian Age," John Boardman states, "we know from both Viking and West Indian history of the Sixth Age that pirates found shore raids far more profitable than ventures against commercial shipping. The coastal lands of Zingara and Kush were frequently raided, and under bolder and abler leaders Shem and even Stygia did not escape these marauders. Probably the black corsairs obtained the bulk of their plunder from the coasts of Kush and the other mainland Negro kingdoms."[20] The first statement about Viking and West Indian history draws a conclusion about piracy that is then applied to Howard's world in order to produce suppositions about different geopolitical conflicts ("even Stygia did not escape these marauders"). Moreover, they are used to manufacture characterizations of people that would fit this scenario—"under bolder and abler leaders"; "probably the black corsairs obtained the bulk of their plunder." In another essay titled "Hyborian Technology," de Camp imagines the Hyborian Age at the material, infrastructural level, detailing entries on "leather goods," "mining and metallurgy," "houses & furniture," all of which take knowledges from "real history" in order to support suppositions about Hyboria. Thus the sentence: "Hyborian houses are furnished with good, substantial chairs, tables, and desks, which was the case with ancient Chinese houses but not with those of other parts of the world before the European Middle Ages."[21]

At the same time, these fictional worlds provide structures of belief that are taken up by readers as true, believable, and probable, and used to construct generalized statements and judgments about real histories and peoples. Lin Carter's article, "The Real Hyborian Age," for example, brings the imagination of sword and sorcery to bear on the prehistory of the world: "Since the time when Howard wrote, we have learned enormously more about prehistory than was known in his day. In fact, we have *discovered a genuine Hyborian Age!* . . . The map of Europe was considerably different, *but not as different as you might suppose from a look at Sprague's map* in the front of the Lancer Conan editions."[22] Likewise, P. Schuyler Miller relates Geoffrey Bibby's 1961 book, *Four Thousand Years Ago*, an archaeologist's account of what it is like to live in the Bronze Age, through the conventional "truths" built into the Hyborian Age. After stating that Conan's world is irrevocably lost to us, Miller writes, "And yet, in our own world and long ago, there have been times when shining kingdoms grew and bickered and met in the market places. . . . There was one time in particular when laden mules plodded behind their masters across the mountain passes that separated the cities of the Midland Sea from the black forest of the North."[23] Writing of Bibby's nonfiction account in particular, Miller states that "he [Bibby] has his own mirror of Tuzun Thune, and he is not afraid to report what he sees in it. He hears the drum of hoofs as the first horses charge down out of the steppes beyond the Caspian."[24] Tuzun Thune is a wizard character in Howard's short story "The Mirrors of Tuzun Thune." In both these statements, it is the truths and beliefs founded within Howard's fiction that builds in knowledge of "real" ancient history.

As Michael Saler writes in *As If: Modern Enchantment and the Literary Prehistory of Virtual Reality*, a commonplace of much of the pulp fiction of the early twentieth century is this emphasis on creating rigorously rational, detailed, coherent worlds extrapolated from the invented worlds of fiction and fantasy.[25] These worlds, like the Hyborian Age, are fully inhabitable. They are, in Saler's terms, "virtual worlds": "acknowledged imaginary spaces that are communally inhabited for prolonged periods of time by rational individuals."[26] This fully inhabitable, virtual world, though, becomes the medium through which to generate "facts." The process enacted in building S&S supplements Saler's account: across these articles, there is a two-way process whereby the coherence of Howard's world is used to generate facts of ancient history and the coherence of the ancient world is used to generate "facts" in Howard's worlds. As can be seen from some of the examples above, moreover, this process of discovering and imagining the "facts" of these worlds relies primarily on race.

The evocation of race plays a crucial role in this double movement of world-building in which Howard's readers enthusiastically engage. While there is little direct discussion of racism in terms of derogatory language, race is everywhere disseminated in these discussions as a way to build in knowledge. Readers acknowledged this aspect of Howard's world-building. In a letter in a 1960 issue of *AMRA*, Mrs. T. A. Burns writes, "Mr. Howard usually approaches his stories from the racial standpoint, if one may call it that. That is, human races, and especially those of long ago, are often the subject of his stories."[27] In Marion Zimmer Bradley's comment, "Some Strange-Sounding Names," she writes, "The very familiarity of these names in an alien setting suggests that the 'dark world' has some tenacious and meaningful tie with our own world of legendry and myth. For the 'dark world,' of course, is the dark human mind . . . filled with shifting racial images."[28] These insights cast in broad form what occurs at the level of specific interpretive strategies used to produce race and worlds together. For example, in "Who Were the Aesir," Poul Anderson supplements aspects of Howard's fantasy world by reimagining the ebbs and flows of colonization and large-scale evolutionary patterns: "Their trek was long and eventful, doubtless taking years and involving much incidental warfare; but at last they conquered a large part of the North, divided it among their chiefs, and settled down. Their numbers were not enormous—racially speaking, they were soon absorbed, just as the English in India have left no genetic trace."[29] This article mixes assumptions about peoples and histories from the real world (the absorption of the English in India) with that of Howard's fiction in producing a "fact"-based inquiry about who were the historical peoples known as the "Aesir." The rather oblique or indirect reference to race is not uncommon. Here, race is used to signal and verify these processes of population absorption and dispersion. It secures believable assumptions about population movements and wars through the vanishing point of something that leaves no trace.

If Anderson uses race to teach us something about what really happened in ancient history, the coherence of the fantasy world is also used to generate "facts" about race in the more immediate past and present of our world. In "Balthus of Cross Plains," George Scithers takes up one of Howard's most controversial and debated representations—the imagination of the Picts. The Picts are a people whose existence is debated by ancient historians and archaeologists. As represented by Howard, they are often thought to allegorize Native Americans. Scithers's statements acknowledge the allegorical reading of the Picts, but they then extend the instability of the allegorical reading of the Picts as Native Americans to build in racial knowledge of these peoples, as if this knowledge were true on their own terms: "There are the 'Picts,' the bloodthirsty wild men of eastern Hyborea (*whom some people will see as cognates of the Amerinds, although in fact some of the Amerinds went in for far more diabolical tortures than anything Howard ever wrote*), implacable enemies of the more civilized Aquilonians."[30] The desire to imagine the referents for the Picts is used to generate a further structure of belief about Native Americans—that they "went in for far more diabolical tortures than anything Howard ever wrote"—as if it were fact. De Camp, the famous popularizer of Conan stories after Howard's death, explains this logic very well without critiquing it. He writes, "several widespread beliefs about well-established historical matters can easily be confuted. But people believe them anyway; Robert Howard embraced several."[31] Upon listing several of these beliefs—such as the "Aryans . . . were tall, blond, blue-eyed Nordics, who won by superior courage and other moral virtues"—he then traces the origins of these ideas through different sources ranging from historiography to fiction. The accumulation of these beliefs as they build in knowledge of the world takes on the function of "truth" and "reality" endowed through collective beliefs.[32] De Camp calls this "pseudohistory." Though de Camp presents "evidence" that contradicts some of these beliefs, he shows the tenacity of these beliefs as they get sustained through the world-building strategies of both fictional writers and their readers.

These debates concerning Howard's fiction and its relationships to ancient history were not just the esoteric musings of fans. As you may have noticed already, many of the writers cited above were fantasy writers in their own right and played instrumental roles in constructing the genre tradition of S&S to this day. As writers, they debated the craft of world-building. One debate concerns whether or not elements from distinct "worlds" should be mixed in the same fantasy world. De Camp calls this the "trouble" with "combin[ing] two incompatible elements." For example, blending elements from antiquity and from the technological present would produce a "fictional milieu" that is "technologically incongruous." Here we again find the central role that race plays in organizing interpretation, for within this debate, the identification of distinct worlds occurs via the examples of race. De Camp goes on: "True, such incongruities do exist in the real world. Today you can see a Peruvian Indian jogging along on his mule and holding a transistor to his ear. But a mixture of the technics of different eras is always an unstable and rapidly changing state of affairs, because people compelled to mix with those of a technically more advanced culture soon adopt the gadgets of the others, as far as they can do so without disturbing their basic cultural attitudes, social organizations, and traditional way of life."[33] Anderson argues against de Camp, but uses the same line of reasoning: "Cold steel in modern warfare? The Viet Cong people use it a lot, such as disemboweling village headmen as a sort of primitive election campaign. The Nips quite often charged people who had loaded M1s. I think I have a few of their swords, by way of various souvenir dealers."[34] Leigh Brackett clarifies this faulty logic of conflating "world" with our assumptions about what is incongruous, but does so only to reinforce those assumptions around a notion of homogeneous cultures: "I would agree with him [de Camp] completely, except for one word, which is basic to the whole argument. That word is *world*. If he had said *culture*, there could be very small argument." Brackett goes on to argue for the possibility of mixing technologies, for it is not at all unusual for peoples to adopt technologies available to them. But the separation of cultures must remain in order for a world to be coherent: "There was Rome, and there were the barbarians. On one hemisphere, among a population all of the same rootstock, there were the Eskimo, the Cherokee, the Dacotah, the Digger, the Maya, Aztec, and Peruvian, the Jivaro, and the people of Tierra del Fuego. Today there is industrial, atomic-age Western culture, and there is the

Stone Age culture of New Guinea where an airplane means only the basis of a new religion."[35] To be sure, this is cultural essentialism 101, culture being used as a proxy for race to produce the same separation, hierarchization, and discrimination. But the larger point is that these are the examples on which the coherence of the imaginary world rests. The example of racial incongruity is used to project, indeed, create worlds. Brackett makes explicit its function as the organizing logic of world-building.

This commentary shows the deep connections between the imagination of secondary worlds and how race is located in the making of ancient and modern worlds. Robert Howard's own essay, "The Hyborian Age," both encapsulates these interpretive strategies and shows how they lead to a set of narrative strategies. Howard wrote his essay in the 1930s. As he states in a preface to the essay,

> I prepared this history of [Conan's] age and the peoples of that age, in order to lend him and his sagas a greater aspect of realness. And I found that by adhering to the "facts" and spirit of that history, in writing the stories, it was easier to visualize (and therefore to present) him as a real flesh-and-blood character rather than a ready-made product. . . . I have never violated the "facts" or spirit of the "history" here set down, but have followed the lines of that history as closely as the writer of actual historical fiction follows the lines of actual history.[36]

This world is given the status of "fact" and "actual history" in the sense that it models a set of geographies and nomenclatures to be followed by the stories. Once we read "The Hyborian Age" history, we can then, for example, take the depiction of the Aquilonians in one story and relate it to the structure established in his essay.

As in the commentaries, race emerges in the essay to organize knowledge as the reader is made to move back and forth between imagining the real world and imagining the secondary world. Howard uses an allegorical structure not in the sense of creating a one-to-one correspondence between elements from the Hyborian Age and elements from our reality but rather as an organization of desire and interpretation. If allegory "elicits continual interpretation as its primary aesthetic effect, giving us the feeling that we are moving at once inward and upward toward the transcendental 'other,'"[37] then Howard taps into this effect by making race the vehicle and effect of continual interpretation. As the essay makes clear, because of the long history of civilizations, tribes, and peoples recounted there, it is virtually impossible to keep track of distinct races: "Absorbing the blood of conquered races, already the descendants of the older drifts have begun to show modified racial traits, and these mixed races are attacked fiercely by new, purer-blooded drifts, and swept before them, as a broom sweeps debris impartially, to become even more mixed and mingled in the tangled debris of races and tag-ends of races."[38] Classification by skin color and "blood" is present, but these signifiers do not separate barbarism from civilization. Nor do they necessarily serve to "relate" people: "Zamora lies to the East, and Zingara to the southwest of these kingdoms—peoples alike in darkness of complexion and exotic habits, *but otherwise unrelated.*"[39]

And yet, racial markers continue to be mentioned, especially prefaced by remarks such as "Look at the world" or "Glance briefly at the peoples of that age."[40] With these remarks, race as a verifiable category is reintroduced and used to track the formation of peoples: "The dominant Hyborians are no longer uniformly tawny-haired and grey-eyed. They have mixed with other races. . . . The eastern Brythunians have inter-married with the dark-skinned Zamorians, and the people of southern Aquilonia have mixed with the brown Zingarans until black hair and brown eyes are the dominant type in Poitain, the southern-most province."[41] In producing knowledge of the world, race occupies a double position. On one level, when considering the long history of the world, race is disconnected from being able to produce any meaningful relations among peoples. On another level, when prefaced with statements like "Look" or "Glance briefly," racial attributions afford a new coherence through which to organize the world. In this way, race floats as an open organizing framework *to be* configured by future arrangements. Howard's Hyborian Age does not make clear correspondences between the Picts and savages or between Westerners and civilization. Rather, it uses race as a principle that is ultimately unknowable but that still provides the vanishing point through which all other relations in the world can be understood. As Teskey describes the process of reading allegory, "the intelligence behind the veil of allegory is always withdrawing to more remote ground, leaving behind the sense that our aggressive attention has failed to grasp what is there."[42] As used by Howard, race organizes the desire for interpretation.

The critical tradition on race and fantasy has relied on excavating writers' racist attitudes and on allegorical readings of fixed correspondences between stereotype and fictional representation.[43] But what we have seen above is not a simple process of racial allegory. Through commentaries on the processes of building S&S secondary worlds, we see the development of interpretive and narrative strategies that embed race "beyond" the realm of mere biological groupings. Race assumes this knowledge-building force because of the allegorical instability between primary and secondary worlds, an allegorical instability that relocates race to other levels of narrative diegesis. Within a tradition of SF criticism influenced by Frederic Jameson, allegory is exactly why we cannot imagine the future, that is, we can only ever allegorize our present. Allegory in S&S is comparatively successful: "We have discovered a genuine Hyborian Age!" Such a pronouncement is made possible through the use of race to imagine the facts of the world. In the next section, we turn to Howard's stories themselves in order to see the development of these narrative strategies of racial attribution. Howard's storytelling techniques provide powerful examples of how a popular genre like S&S does not just reflect racial ideologies but also produces new ways of apprehending race. Race as a built-in knowledge is its cognitive effect. Moreover, it is a cognitive effect that converges with other major disciplinary frameworks for producing knowledge about race from the 1930s through the 1980s: cultural anthropology and economics. As civil rights legislation and the language of formal equality was being codified, modes of racial thinking were being reconfigured. Sword and sorcery, cultural anthropology, and economics were at the center of this reconfiguration.

Blackness as Atmosphere

To read Howard's stories is to be immersed in blackness. Literally. Figuratively. And every expressive register in between. It is arguably the single most recognizable trait of his prose, from his story titles to his language to the shape and direction of his narratives. Fritz Lieber, the writer who helped coin "sword and sorcery" and who would go on to make his own mark in the genre through the Fafhrd and Gray Mouser series, discusses Howard's style, in particular the proliferation of words like "dark" and "black":

> He knew the words and phrases of power and sought to use them as soon and often as possible, the words and phrases that the writer with literary aspirations usually avoids (sometimes quite mechanically) because they're clichés or near-clichés, words and phrases like (I select from "The Moon of Skulls") black, dark, death, volcanic, ghost, great black shadow, symbol of death and horror, menace brooding and terrible, shrubs which crouched like short dark ghosts, outposts of the kingdom of fear, black spires of wizards' castles, ju-ju city, grim black crags of the fetish hills, henchmen of death, the Tower of Death, the Black Altar. . . . These aren't bad words and phrases really. In fact, they are the same general sort that still make some Americans embarrassed

> about Edgar Allen Poe and his European reputation and influence. . . . There is no worry at all how it intersects the real world. It is an inner world for a boy's solemn adventuring. . . . Although it was one of his first long stories, "Red Shadows" is a wonderful compendium of Howard . . . there is a magnificent hymn to the jungle running through the prose, the African witchcraft is superb, and even the Giant Ape (which appears so often as a stock menace in Howard's subsequent tales) is handled with sympathy as well as power.[44]

Lieber's catalog of the many uses of "dark" and "black" points to Howard's own narrative strategies and the ways in which Howard significantly expands the domain of racial attribution. Far from being a homogeneous group, Lieber's catalog testifies to the great range with which images of "black" and "dark" signify, from literal and concrete descriptive registers to metaphorical, abstract registers and everything in between; from descriptions of natural features to human-made architecture to surface reflections to metaphysical essences. In Howard, "black" becomes an all-purpose adjective, referring variously to a coast, a river, persons, a heart, and so on. The accumulation of instances creates a dizzying effect in which one is not sure just how literal or just how metaphoric to take the word, and whether or not it is functioning catachrestically—being applied "to a thing which it does not *properly* denote"—or not. In fact, one might say that the descriptor pushes the limits of catachresis itself: what are the limits of applying "black" to things, if any? When is it improper or proper to use "black"? Far from there being "no worry at all how it intersects with the real world," the very proliferation of uses maximizes the possibilities of intersections with the real world. In the list above, "ju-ju city" stands out as having associations with real-world primitivist representations, while "black crags" might be taken to conjure a certain atmosphere, and "Black Altar" calls forth something more of the metaphysical aspects of good and evil, especially in a religious framework.

"Black" and "dark" thus function within what the philosopher Nelson Goodman calls "routes of reference": "various relationships that may obtain between a term or other sign or symbol and what it refers to."[45] These relationships include verbal denotation (naming, predication, description), exemplification (reference by a sample to a feature of the sample), and expression (exemplification of a label or feature that metaphorically rather than literally denotes).[46] These species of reference often interact, or may work through "chains of reference" that move from a verbal description to an instance denoted to a feature exemplified. Goodman gives this example:

"a picture of a bald eagle denotes a bird that may exemplify a label such as 'bold and free' that in turn denotes and is exemplified by a given country."[47] To take the example of the "Black Altar" above, the verbal label "Black Altar" may apply to an actual material altar that in turn exemplifies a species of the Antichrist that in turn expresses terror and foreboding. Each of these relationships is a link in a chain of reference that marks the organization of reality constructed through the label "Black Altar." As Goodman points out, "the same object may simultaneously rotate in opposite directions, dance madly, and remain at rest, depending upon the frame of reference—or, better, the world-version—in question . . . such organization of discourse participates notably in the organization of a reality."[48] Whether we take "Black Altar" as a basic description of an object ("an altar that is black"), as an exemplification of a metaphor to religion, or as an expression of foreboding and terror, it organizes reality differently.

The use of a variety of relationships that obtain between "black" and what it refers to plays a large role in Howard's Conan stories. Take, for example, the first paragraph of *The Hour of the Dragon*, which begins as many of these tales do with a scene of sorcery: "The long tapers flickered, sending the black shadows wavering along the walls, and the velvet tapestries rippled. . . . In the upraised right hand of each man a curious black candle burned with a weird greenish light. Outside was night and a lost wind moaning among the black trees."[49] Couple these instances of "black shadows," "black candle," and "black trees" with the title of section 2, "A Black Wind Blows" and the verbal term of "black plague" evoked at the beginning of the chapter, and the reader not only has a set of associations but a set of routes of reference. "Black wind" operates at a metaphorical level to refer to portent through the operation of a cliché; "black candle" refers to an object, but an object that is curious precisely because it is black—its blackness being an unusual feature that runs through a reference to black magic; "black trees" is not quite literal as it is the effect of darkness, directing the reader to another source for the blackness. The proliferation of blackness across a variety of routes of reference raises the issue of how it relates to its possible or potential racial signification. It suggests a mobilization of blackness across the range of literal and metaphorical, and across distinct entities as they fluidly move to the expression of moods, feelings, or even a sense of the ineffable. It develops a cluster of objects to which it refers, often indirectly through other world-versions: fear; terror, darkness, the invisible, the obscure, the metaphysically evil, the evil that is beyond the bounds of religious belief. It produces a world of possible routes of reference where anything can be black and thereby transformed into a linkage between the referent and something mysterious, portentous, dark, and so on.

In Lieber's quote above, he defends Howard against charges of racism: "these aren't bad words and phrases really." Lieber frames Howard's penchant for "dark" and "black" as a value-neutral expressive style. But Howard himself is aware of the potential racial denotations. The narrative strategy that he develops is not to simply divorce these words from the potential of racial signification. It is to relocate race to other narrative levels where they can then construct different cognitive effects of building in knowledge. Roland Barthes introduces a distinction between indices and informants, with indices "involving an activity of deciphering" by which the reader learns more about a character or the atmosphere, and informants serving to locate in time and space with "immediate signification."[50] As Barthes explains, "Indices imply a deciphering activeness and consequence, what-comes-*after* being read in a narrative with a character or an atmosphere; informants bring with them a ready-made knowledge."[51] It is worth noting just how often the imagery of "dark" and "black" work at the level of the indice—involving the reader in the activity of deciphering, integrating other elements that come after it, and becoming a part of the atmosphere such that all the narrative energies of hesitation, suspicion, expectancy, and fear are involved in the word "black." Rather than performing any kind of "immediate signification," "black" and "dark" extend through the narrative in order to become a constitutive part of the narrative dynamics through which the reader enters into and navigates the world of the Hyborian Age.

This strategy of manipulating when "black" and "dark" have and do not have racial signification is present in "Iron Shadows of the Moon." In this story, Conan saves a woman named Olivia from her former master and they flee to an apparently deserted island, where they spend the rest of the story fighting off and escaping from both pirates and various dark figures. But at the center of this story is a sequence where Conan and Olivia camp among a set of statues. Encountering this set of lifelike statues, Conan inquired of the world at large, "What manner of men were these copied from? . . . These figures are black, yet they are not like negroes. I have never seen their like."[52] Here, blackness is explicitly decoupled from a historical referent of racial classification. Earlier, the narrative description of these statues goes like this: "They were statues, apparently of iron, black and shining as if continually polished. They were life-size, depicting tall, lithely powerful men, with cruel hawk-like faces. They were naked, and every swell, depression and contour of joint and sinew was represented with incredible realism. But the most life-like feature was their proud, intolerant faces. These features were not cast in the same mold. Each face possessed its own individual characteristics, though there was a tribal likeness between them all. There was none of the monotonous uniformity of decorative art, in the faces at least."[53]

Despite explicitly saying that the statues are "not like negroes," the statues' blackness ushers in the atmosphere of a "dark" threat. While sleeping among the statues, Olivia has a dream in which a "slender white-skinned youth" is murdered by these "black-skinned warriors." In the narration of the dream, the decoupling of blackness from racial classification is stated again: "the hall was thronged with black-skinned, hawk-faced warriors. They were not negroes. . . . The black warriors laughed at him [the slender white youth]. . . . A dagger in an ebon hand cut short his cry, and the golden head rolled on the ivory breast."[54] But as can be seen from the registers of blackness in the quote, its racial meanings are relocated from racial correspondence to being a part of a general atmosphere in which white bodies are threatened. Not surprisingly, the black statues do indeed come to life and slaughter the pirate crew. Being divorced from one route of reference ("They were not negroes") arguably lends more narrative power to the racial significations of blackness as it organizes the fears and threats embedded in the story.

This relocation of race to elements of the narrative diegesis is carried out in "Queen of the Black Coast." Similar to "Iron Shadows," Conan finds himself on a haunted island in which he and his ship's crew are threatened by unknown creatures. The creatures are sometimes thought of as "winged birds," "apes," or "monster bats." As the foes in this story become more and more supernatural, they are increasingly distanced from real-world referents. And yet the unstable relationship between these creatures and their potential references to blackness is continually evoked through different mistakes of perception. Conan, for example, has trouble discerning his ally, N'Gora: "At first Conan thought it to be a great black gorilla. Then he saw that it was a giant black man that crouched ape-like, long arms dangling, froth dripping from the loose lips. It was not until, with a sobbing cry, the creature lifted huge hands and rushed towards him, that Conan recognized N'Gora."[55] At first, "black" is a value-neutral description "great black gorilla." Then "black" integrates racial associations shaping perception in order to articulate "black" with "ape-like" ("giant black man that crouched ape-like"). Finally, blackness disappears from perception and we are left with the proper name of "N'Gora" even as the racial valuation remains via the noun "creature" ("the creature lifted huge hands

. . . Conan recognized N'Gora"). This movement of Conan's perceptions captures the embedding and incorporation of race into the features of the world. Blackness leaves the perceptual field and is instead embedded in the valuations themselves through a series of mistaken perceptions. Blackness has effectively been removed from direct correspondence to a black person while gaining even more narrative power as it immerses the reader into a world of supernatural foes.

"Black," then, is not just one of Howard's favorite storytelling words. It is a narrative strategy that produces race at levels other than biological differences. As a narrative strategy, "black" signals a beyond, ultimately pushing the reader further and further out of the world in order to locate the proper referent for blackness. It makes the reader identify blackness at further removes and in nonvisible registers. "Beyond the Black River" is a great example of this narrative strategy. In the story, Conan tries to defend a colonial settlement by pursuing the Picts and in particular defeating a Pictish wizard. Throughout the story, Conan is either chasing the Picts or they are chasing him, a narrative structure that mirrors the story's set-up of a geographical relationship between civilization and barbarism. As Howard describes it, "Fort Tuscelan was the last outpost of a civilized world."[56] But this story does not make a simple identification between the savage, racialized Picts and the conflict over civilization. "Beyond the Black River" hinges on the odd referential status of the Picts. In this story, the Picts, who are repeatedly referenced in terms of their dark skins, their horde-like mentality, and their rapaciousness, are explicitly qualified as being a white race. At an early point in the novella, Conan picks up a dead body to make sure that the Picts do not defame it: "We'll carry the body into the fort. It isn't more than three miles. I never liked the fat bastard, but we can't have Pictish devils making so cursed free with white men's heads." Directly after Conan's statement, though, the narrative inserts: "*The Picts were a white race*, though swarthy, but the border men never spoke of them as such."[57]

These statements are not just contradictory representations that show the arbitrariness of racial attributions. This move instructs the reader toward following one chain of meaning rather than another, one that *does not move* from the present action of targeting Picts for destruction back to distinctions between civilization and savagery and then back to racial classification. That chain would lead to an identification of whiteness. Rather than follow that route of reference back into ethnography, the route of reference that the readers are made to follow is a chain of metaphors about darkness, animality, and savagery—various indices that establish character, mood, and emotion. Readers are directed in a movement inward further into the text, always locating the Picts somewhere "beyond." In "Beyond the Black River," the plot continually pushes the reader to further geographic extremes. As one character describes the horrors of what lies "beyond," "Who knows what gods are worshipped under the shadows of that heathen forest, or what devils crawl out of the black ooze of the swamps? Who can be sure that all the inhabitants of that black country are natural?" "Black ooze" and "black country" do not identify the Picts in terms of race as a people. They are indices in Barthes's sense of implying a "what-comes-*after* being read in a narrative." In following the plot, the reader deciphers the identification of blackness at the level of atmosphere, and then geography, and then the whole architectonics of the plot. It is certain that Conan *will* encounter the Picts as dark and menacing peoples in his pursuits "beyond the black river." Once the reader thinks that they have reached the depths of blackness, there is another plunge, another further remove. This narrative movement makes the identification of blackness not a visual component but a visceral one, one that is indeed necessary for accessing the pleasures of suspense. Howard creates a cognitive effect of sorting the Picts as dark even though they are of the white race.

Howard's stories consistently appeal to blackness. But racial meanings are not merely there in the form of racist imagery, stereotypes, and connotations that associate certain peoples and populations with racist ideologies. Nor does its racism consist mainly in the Manichean allegory of associating black with evil and white with good. His narrative strategies displace racial meanings from one order (the order of stereotype, classification) into another order (atmosphere, narrative causality, integration of story). The tip-offs are lines such as "they were not negroes" or "the Picts were a white race . . . but the border men never spoke of them as such." These moments of negating racial classification pave the way for other routes of reference. Howard thereby redeploys racial signs at other narrative levels that become a part of the reader's very comprehension and construction of sequence, or "what-comes *after*." Howard's characteristic prose embeds race such that it permeates the atmosphere of the world itself.

Howard and Cultural Anthropology

Howard is not alone in producing these cognitive effects. From the time of Howard's writing in the 1930s through the 1990s, we see the development of the scientific critique of racism produced through dialogues between anthropologists, population geneticists, and biologists as contained in the

1950 and 1951 UNESCO statements on race. Historical periodizations of racism generally track a movement from biological racism (nineteenth and twentieth centuries) to culturalist racism (twentieth and twenty-first centuries), with the critique of scientific racism operating as a hinge between the two. But as we have seen already, while the building of S&S secondary worlds seems to mirror the way in which culture substitutes for race in producing the same racist effects, it also relocates race so that it functions as an interpretive structure of upward-moving meanings. These interpretive strategies converge with the midcentury scientific critique of racism and the role of cultural anthropology.

To put Howard's narrative strategies in dialogue with cultural anthropology and its influence on scientific critiques of racism seems outlandish at first glance. Cultural anthropology in the vein of Franz Boas from the 1900s on is well known to have combated, even discredited, evolutionary racism and "biological interpretations of history and civilization."[58] It enshrined the concept of culture as being more important than race. Most Howard scholars link Howard's work not with cultural anthropology but with racialist theories of physical anthropology. Jeffrey Shanks writes, "Now-discredited racialist theories dominated the study of physical anthropology. . . . So 'The Hyborian Age,' even with all of its antiquated concepts, would have carried a greater sense of veracity in the early 1930s than it does today."[59] But a closer look at one aspect of racial discourse shows a shared textual strategy from Howard through the UNESCO statements and the influence of cultural anthropology.

As Jenny Reardon argues in *Race to the Finish*, the historical narratives, popular understandings, and critical race theories that locate the demise of the biological concept of race in the 1950s are all wrong. They are wrong because there was never a wholesale rejection of the scientific study of race nor was there ever a stable, consistent concept of race on which everyone could be said to have agreed or disagreed. Rather, there was a rejection of some uses of race and the transformation of other uses and meanings of race. These debates, which were both part of the UNESCO statements and part of the discourse after the first statement in 1950, have been overlooked. For example, historians of race and science will often distinguish between the supposedly rejected approach to race that involves an emphasis on phenotypic differences, static taxonomies, and typologies versus the supposedly favored approach to race that involves genotypic differences, dynamic populations, and fluid cultural and biological processes. But, as Reardon demonstrates, even the differences between these approaches lose coherence when debates within the scientific community are carefully considered.

I do not have time to go over all of Reardon's excellent history here. For my purposes, I find strong evidence for the doubt that Reardon casts on the conventional historical narrative that race was deemed a biologically meaningless category in the 1950s. Rather than any consensus on the biological meaninglessness of race, Reardon establishes that the most prominent critical move at this time was the argument that "biological concepts of race . . . did not have any inherent fixed social meaning."[60] This is very different. The lack of consensus is particularly clear when we remember that UNESCO had to issue not one but two statements on race, first in 1950 and then in 1951. The second statement was necessary because the first was challenged by biologists and population geneticists. The statements were then further revised and updated in 1964 and then again in 1967. The 1950 UNESCO statement on race is widely credited with the scientific critique of racism, and its rhetoric shows the impact of cultural anthropology's main definitional moves. Across points 3 and 4 of the statement, Montagu writes, "A race, from the biological standpoint, may therefore be defined as one of the group of populations constituting the species *homo sapiens* . . . the term 'race' designates a group or population characterized by some concentrations, relative as to frequency and distribution, of hereditary particles (genes) or physical characters, which appear, fluctuate, and often disappear in the course of time by reason of geographic and or cultural isolation."[61] Then in point 14, in what was the most controversial sentence, Montagu states that "the biological fact of race and the myth of 'race' should be distinguished. For all practical social purposes 'race' is not so much a biological phenomenon as a social myth."[62]

The statements together are unclear: is race a "biological fact" or a "social myth"? The implication that race itself is a "social myth" is specifically challenged by subsequent statements. But what gets carried forward is the distinction between race as a given (anthropological, biological, evolutionary) and the improper use of race in the form of racial prejudice, racialism, or racism. L. C. Dunn writes in the heading for the statement of 1951,

> We were careful to avoid dogmatic definitions of race, since, as a product of evolutionary factors, it is a dynamic rather than a static concept. We were equally careful to avoid saying that, because races were all variable and many of them graded into each other, therefore races did not exist. The physical anthropologists and the man in the street both know that races exist; the former, from the scientifically recognizable and measurable congeries of traits which he uses in classifying the

> varieties of man; the latter from the immediate evidence of his senses when he sees an African, a European, an Asiatic and an American Indian together.[63]

The 1951 statement was aimed precisely at the ambiguities left open by Montagu in 1950, reasserting that "the word 'race' should be reserved for groups of mankind possessing well-developed and primarily heritable physical differences from other groups" and distinguishing the *analysis* of these differences from "popular notions of any general 'superiority' or 'inferiority' which are sometimes implied in referring to these groups."

As if to make the province of "race" as a biological matter even clearer, the 1964 Moscow statement is titled "Proposals on the Biological Aspects of Race" and the 1967 statement focuses almost exclusively on the historical roots of race prejudice and racism. Improper uses of race are decried throughout the 1964 document, and race is divorced from connections in language, geography, nation, and so on *in order to assert that* "the concept of race is purely biological."[64] As Kamala Visweswaran puts it, despite or because of the controversies over the 1950 statement, "'race defined from the biological standpoint' remained intact," and "race is assigned to biology."[65] I point this move out not in order to suggest that we have yet to fully critique biological notions of race. The important words in Montagu's statements above are "standpoint" and "fact," not "biological." As such, race remains a given, an ordering principle—produced through many evolutionary processes, to be sure, but produced as received knowledge nonetheless. Racism is separated from race and constituted as a "universal myth or prejudice that has affected human history in different forms."[66] Simultaneously producing an interdiction against the use of race and the preservation of a domain of racial facts elevates race to another level of meaning, one that does not so much classify as it creates the potential for other combinatory logics.

This cognitive separation of race and racism enables race to persist as a built-in knowledge for organizing meaning. One sees this effect most clearly in a work as significant as Ruth Benedict's *Race and Racism*. First published in 1942, Benedict sets out to systematically answer the question, "Does racism have a biological basis?" in the negative. Her work is cultural anthropology's answer to scientific racism and the physical anthropology on which much of it rests. It is also a precursor to the 1950 and 1951 UNESCO statements on the meaning and use of the notion of race. What we see in the movement of this text is not so much just a scientific refutation of biological racism, but a refutation and embedding of race at a further remove. Each chapter proceeds systematically in terms of its unraveling of biological racism. Benedict demonstrates in various ways how racial classifications collapse because there are no pure races; racial classifications themselves have nothing to do with psychological or moral criteria; race does not correlate with superiority or inferiority. With each chapter, though, the importance of race for understanding the history of humankind is continually reinscribed. In showing how there is only "negative evidence" against the relationship between race and superiority or inferiority, Benedict writes, "The scientific study of race tells us many important facts which have nothing to do with the question of the superiority or inferiority of given races. It tells us unrecorded and forgotten facts of early history and of the movement of peoples; it tells us what combinations of traits occur upon the mixture of two racial types, it distinguishes between a group of people who constitute a nation and a group of people who constitute a biological type (race)."[67] A similar move is made in preserving and redeploying the significance of race while refuting biological racism in two key chapters—"Man's Efforts to Classify Himself" and "Migration and the Mingling of Peoples." In each of these chapters, Benedict shows that racial classifications collapse and that because of historical migration and intermarriage there is no such thing as a pure race. At the same time, she repeats racial classifications as a historical fact: "No one doubts that the groups called Caucasoid, Mongoloid, and Negroid each represent a long history of anatomical specialization in different areas of the world. . . . It is clear also that no scientific purpose is served by speculating about the allocation of doubtful peoples to one or another primary stock. It only happens that Caucasian, Mongoloid, and Negro have the widest distribution in the world and the most definite anatomical traits."[68]

The crucial aspect here is not that Benedict still preserves the significance of race even as she critiques biological racism. Rather, it is that Benedict, in doing so, redeploys the significance of race and arguably expands its significance in giving us "facts of early history," a "combination of traits," and the capacity to distinguish between biological type and nation-group. In this vein, race can now afford various conceptual connections and relationships among geography, people, nation, history, and migration—connections that we have already seen utilized by historians and political scientists (in Chapter 1) and again in the fanzines around Robert Howard's fiction in this chapter. Her book follows a similar rhetorical trajectory as Robert Howard's "The Hyborian Age" and his stories. Recall how in "The Hyborian Age" Howard acknowledges the impurity of races and race as an effect of long evolutionary processes, but he then produces race as a given from which to build in knowledge about what is going to happen geopolitically. Recall, too, Howard's signature use of "black" as a racial ordering device even as he divorces its use from any "racist" correspondences to racial groups classified as "Negroes." In being taken off the table as a legitimate means of exercising racial prejudice, race has been submerged into the history of humankind, and authors then take up the task of instructing us how to see it *again*.

In this way, "racial worldmaking" is a set of textual strategies that demonstrates a reconfiguration of race and racism. Not because racial categories simply continue to be used in racist ways but rather because race is reconfigured as a given used to connect disparate phenomena and thereby shape outcomes in racist ways. This is not the same as arguing that racism has migrated from biological to cultural discrimination. Rather, it is to say that racism has progressed into speculative modes of thought that have not been fully understood. This *extension* of race and racism into our modal imagination and in the constitution of social reality is the unlikely place where S&S and cultural anthropology meet. In the next chapter, I outline relationships between S&S and the domain of knowledge production that has principally been associated with the possibilities of prediction: economics.

CHAPTER 6

Fantasies of Blackness and Racial Capitalism

Editing Blackness

One of the peculiarities in the publishing history of Robert Howard is that his work was reissued in the 1950s by Gnome Press and then in a series of Lancer/Ace paperback editions from 1967 to 1977. Both series, especially the Lancer/Ace editions, popularized Conan the Barbarian for a wide readership and established the franchise. Both series, moreover, bore the imprint of L. Sprague de Camp's editing and rewriting. Indeed, de Camp's editorship is one of the central controversies within Howard fandom: How much did de Camp rewrite? What is the effect of those changes? Did de Camp ruin Howard? One line of argument uses de Camp's editorship to argue the ethics of his interventions. But less remarked upon as an important context for understanding de Camp's edits is the fact that he reissued, repackaged, and rewrote Conan the Barbarian in the 1950s, 1960s, and 1970s during the civil rights movement, the Vietnam War, and worldwide attention to decolonization movements. Not only that, de Camp was well aware of the effects of a changed racial climate on the Conan publications.

After de Camp, the politics of race were further registered in the sword and sorcery genre by writers such as Charles Saunders and Samuel Delany. Charles Saunders self-consciously constructed his hero, Imaro, along the lines of Conan, staging him against the backdrop of African history and storytelling.[1] Samuel Delany's *Nevèrÿon* series, published between 1979 and 1987, stages S&S as a series of interventions in discourses of race, economics, sexuality, and slavery, among others. This chapter takes up S&S's publication history and development from Howard to Delany to show how it shapes and is shaped by another reconfiguration of racial discourse: the critique of societal discrimination and the relocation of race from society to the market. De Camp, Howard, and Delany are all part of a larger landscape of interpretive strategies that emerged at the same time "intentional" or "de jure" discrimination was being delegitimized through the political activism and international critique of the civil rights movement. In the previous chapter, S&S articulated the merging of anthropological thinking and popular world-building and the relocation of race into atmosphere and object of interpretive desire. In this chapter, Delany's extension of S&S both recognizes the relationship between social and market transactions and constructs alternative routes for noticing race.

The influence of the critique of social discrimination on S&S first occurs through the heavy hand of de Camp. In his article, "Editing Conan," de Camp notes how in editing Howard he had to remove some of the ethnic and racial signifiers in order to make his work more palatable to the current world:

> I thought I should pay some heed to Howard's tendency to bruise ethnic feelings and to step on ethnic toes, particularly Negroid ones. While I do not claim to be the world's most compassionate man, I feel that, since the purpose of the Conan saga is escapist entertainment and not the revelation of profound truths, there is no point in unnecessarily spitting in anyone's soup. If by a little tinkering that does not change the essential Howardness of a story, I can make it more enjoyable to an ethnic reader, I have no compunction about doing so. It is all very well for black fan Elliott Shorter to say *he* likes Conan and is not bothered by Howard's cracks at Negroes; not everybody is so objective about his digs at one's own ethnos. . . . I have therefore made a few small adjustments to take the edge off Howard's most cutting ethnic remarks. These changes have been very slight, since it would be ridiculous to try to turn Howard posthumously into a civil-rights activist. In *Conan the Conqueror*, for instance, Howard spoke of Negroes' "apelike speech." This term was not only abrasive but also absurd to any-

> one who knows about the complex, often musical African languages. When Wollheim edited *Conan the Conqueror* for the Ace edition of 1953, he changed "ape-like speech" to "strange dialect." When I did likewise for the Lancer (now Ace) edition, I changed "ape-like" to "guttural." That is not perfect, either, since most African tongues are not in fact guttural. But Howard seemed to think that they were.[2]

Far from just making Howard's stories more palatable within a climate in which explicit racism is not tolerated to the same degree, though, these editing procedures are themselves an instance of textual and interpretive strategies concerning when, where, and how to notice race. In substituting "guttural" for "ape-like," de Camp's framework becomes an ethnohistorical one, replacing the association of African peoples with apes with the question of its accuracy or inaccuracy to the "complex, often musical African languages." De Camp says that he is trying to take the edge off of what he perceives as Howard's more explicit racism. What he is actually doing is producing a different route through which to embed racial judgments in a world understood in ethnohistorical terms. This is not replacing biological racism with cultural racism, exactly. It is a textual strategy that, in fact, mirrors Howard's own as I described them in the previous chapter. Replacing "ape-like" with "strange dialect" or "guttural" displaces racial meanings from the order of common stereotype to the order of atmosphere such that "strangeness" and "gutturalness" carry moments of fear and the expectation of danger. Moreover, de Camp's textual strategy effectively narrows the notion of racism to just those instances where there is some direct, conventional correspondence between word and racist association.

This assumption of a narrow definition of racism that is divorced from the supposedly neutral description of race as an anthropological fact—however *dynamic* it is—becomes a principle that guides the edits of the Conan stories. In discussing the long revision history of Howard's "The Black Stranger" story, de Camp discusses the title change back and forth between "The Black Stranger" (Howard's title and Lester de Rey's preference) and "The Treasure of Tranicos" (de Camp's preference): "Thinking that too many of Howard's titles had 'black' in them, I changed the title to 'The Treasure of Tranicos." . . . I kept my title, 'The Treasure of Tranicos,' not only because of Howard's *excessive fondness for 'black,'* but also because the 'stranger' was now not a demon but the Stygian he-witch, Thoth-Amon, who was brown rather than black."[3] De Camp links "black" primarily to skin color and therefore eliminates the title because it no longer references a black character. In displacing "blackness" and replacing the black figure with now a "brown" enemy, de Camp does not get rid of racial associations but rather elevates them and embeds them into the story itself, now no longer marked by any specificity of skin color but in the more integrated elements of a fight against an enemy. In this way, he misreads the function of blackness in Howard—for Howard as analyzed above, blackness never simply had a one-to-one correspondence with the skin color of specific characters. Moreover, in his editing, he does not get rid of racial connotations; he extends the function that blackness already plays in Howard's fiction, which is to signal and integrate a variety of elements within a set of correspondences that broaden the meaningfulness of race in organizing experience.

As I quoted in the previous chapter, fantasy writer Fritz Lieber notes the heavy use of "black" and "dark" in Howard's style. But in making this observation he is careful to divorce these words from their "intersection with the real world": "*These aren't bad words and phrases really. . . . There is no worry at all how it intersects the real world.*" Writing this essay in 1961, he is using a similar interpretive strategy as de Camp. Lieber narrows what counts as racism by expanding and universalizing the domain of nonracial meanings: uses of "dark," "black," "African witchcraft," "ju-ju city" are "words and phrases of power," not ones that "intersect with the real world." Lieber takes things like "African witchcraft" and the heavy use of black as dark and menacing as givens, as conventions whose utility within the storyworlds in which they are embedded is not questioned.

Although de Camp and Lieber are hardly exemplars of antiracism, their writings evince a sensitivity and recognition regarding the unpalatability of conventional racist statements and representations. Their interpretive strategies for handling race, though, divide the proliferation of "blackness" into racial and nonracial meanings, radically narrowing racial attribution to just versions of biological racism or political stereotyping while missing the crucial racial modes of thought perpetuated at the level of narrative. Some might see their rhetoric as participating in an ethos of colorblindness, race neutrality, or cultural diversity. But what they more precisely share is the simultaneous denigration of explicit racism and the relocation of race to other registers of meaning. For example, embedded in the idea of "ju-ju city," the racial connotation serves readers' preferences for associating black magic with foreign or primeval settings. In this relocation, racial meanings produce other "utilities"—in the economic sense, the satisfactions or usefulness one gets from any action. Shaped as it is by the racial climate of the 1950s, 1960s, and 1970s, this publishing history indexes how S&S extends the utilities of blackness even within a world increasingly characterized by the disavowal of racism.

One finds a similar interpretive strategy in an unlikely place: economic thinking. I do not claim that economists were reading S&S nor that S&S writers were immersed in economic thought. Rather, they are two parallel responses to the discourse of societal discrimination. Just as de Camp sought to identify and root out intentional, social discrimination from Howard's works, economists at the time were framing methodologies for determining if racism was present or not in the workplace and in schools. I turn in this part, then, to the literature on the "economics of discrimination" in order to illustrate the convergence of these modes of racial world-making across S&S and economic thinking.

The Economics of Discrimination

Economic thinking has had an underappreciated role in shaping racial discourse. Within critical race studies in the humanities or social sciences, rarely will one find an engagement with Gary Becker's *Economics of Discrimination* or even Glenn Loury's *Anatomy of Racial Inequality*. Perhaps this is because racial discrimination is generally framed as a moral dilemma that has or should have nothing to do with the "rational" workings of market behavior. After all, Gunnar Myrdal was an economist who turned away from economic thinking in order to address U.S. race relations. His famous and deeply influential 1944 work, *The American Dilemma: The Negro Problem and Modern Democracy*, emphasized a moral contradiction between stated American values of freedom, equality, and individualism and the prevalence of discrimination. As Jean-Baptiste Fleury puts it in characterizing Myrdal's approach, "Disappointed with neo-classical economics because it had not offered solutions to the depression of the 1930s, Myrdal resorted primarily to psychology, sociology and social psychology to study this moral dilemma. Discrimination followed a vicious circle pattern by maintaining African Americans in poor living conditions which fueled prejudice among whites and eventually led to discrimination."[4]

But in the wake of civil rights legislation and racial discrimination as a major Cold War issue, and in the wake of the 1954 *Brown v. Board of Education* decision and the increasing role that government seemed to play, economists addressed racial discrimination in economic terms. Much of the early work was oriented toward producing models for measuring racial discrimination, its effects, and its interaction with market behavior. Some of this early work used discrimination as a test case for defending free market practices and arguing *against* government intervention, such as fair employment practice commissions tasked with preventing discrimination. For example, the question of discrimination plays a large role in Milton Friedman's influential 1962 treatise, *Capitalism and Freedom*. Friedman sees the market as a natural corrective to societal discrimination because it is, according to Friedman, a paragon of impersonal exchange. Vigorously attacking equal employment opportunity legislation and defending capitalism, Friedman states, "It is a striking historical fact that the development of capitalism has been accompanied by a major *reduction* in the extent to which particular religious, racial, or social groups have operated under special handicaps in respect of their economic activities; have, as the saying goes, been discriminated against."[5] According to Friedman, capitalism accomplishes this reduction in discrimination because the "free market separates economic efficiency from irrelevant characteristics . . . the purchaser of bread does not know whether it was made from wheat grown by a white man or a Negro, by a Christian or a Jew."[6]

Though with a very different conceptual framework, Friedrich Hayek, the so-called father of neoliberal economics came to similar conclusions. In a larger attack on "social and distributive justice" that is explicitly in dialogue with John Rawls's 1971 *Theory of Justice*,[7] Hayek characterizes the market as a game of "catallaxy," a word that he derives from its Greek meanings "to exchange" but also "to admit into the community" and "to change from enemy to friend."[8] In such a market order, Hayek argues, "nobody 'treats' people differently and it is entirely consistent with respecting all people equally that the outcome of the game for different people is very different."[9] Hayek very rarely directly references race relations: his language is more often the general language of "treating people differently" that he uses above. Or that of tribalism versus civilization, as in "we are relapsing rapidly into the conceptions of the tribal society from which we had been slowly emerging."[10] For sure a longer analysis of the direct and indirect uses of race in Hayek and Friedman, among others, is needed. My purpose here is to notice that prominent economists such as Friedman and Hayek are writing in specific dialogue with the political changes and legislation concerning midcentury civil rights movements. More strongly, their defenses and even definitions of the market order are shaped by their engagement with practices of racial discrimination.

For Hayek, Friedman, and others, the theoretical picture of the market as one of impersonal exchange is sharpened in contrast to the excluded domain of personal exchanges and racial discrimination. My claim here is that these early models are examples of interpretive strategies that do not merely take up racial discrimination as a phenomenon to be explained. Rather, they encode and build in certain ways of noticing race that expand its effectiveness in forming our background knowledge and expectations. I thus read influential, post-1950s economic analyses for the ways in which race is denoted, deployed, and distributed so as to produce new utilities and new frameworks of value-creation. Foremost among these early models was the work of Nobel Prize–winning economist Gary Becker, whose dissertation was published as the 1957 *The Economics of Discrimination.* Though Becker is well known now for his development of human capital theory, the development of his "economic approach to life" began with the question of race. Becker writes in his preface, "no single domestic issue has occupied more space in our newspaper in the postwar period than discrimination against minorities, especially against Negroes."[11] Written after Myrdal's *American Dilemma, Economics of Discrimination* moved away from the prevailing use of sociological and psychological paradigms in analyzing the economics of discrimination and focused more centrally on the economic as a principle mode. Instead of seeing noneconomic discrimination as the primary engine of economic discrimination, Becker prioritizes what he would later call the "economic approach to life."

One of the innovations of Gary Becker's economic theory is to factor such difficult, unruly things as tastes and preferences into economic thought and to show the powerful way in which economic decisions are made to build such things as consumption capital and social income. As he describes his work, "Along with others, I have tried to pry economists away from narrow assumptions about self interest. Behavior is driven by a much richer set of values and preferences. The analysis assumes that individuals maximize welfare *as they conceive it*, whether they be selfish, altruistic, loyal, spiteful, or masochistic. Their behavior is forward-looking, and it is also consistent over time. In particular, they try as best they can to anticipate the uncertain consequences of their actions. Forward-looking behavior, however, may still be rooted in the past, for the past can exert a long shadow on attitudes and values."[12] As he recounts, Becker's approach began with his work on discrimination in the market: "In college I was attracted by the problems studied by sociologists and the analytical techniques used by economists. These interests began to merge in my doctoral study, which used economic analysis to understand racial discrimination. Subsequently, I applied the economic approach to fertility, education, the uses of time, crime, marriage, social interactions, and other 'sociological,' 'legal,' and 'political' problems."[13] He blurs the boundaries between economics and the social in order to show the way in which nonpecuniary motives enter into market transactions. He created models for the proliferation of economic reasoning into various domains of human behavior (economic behavior of family relationships and parenting; the economic reasoning used to explain criminal behavior).

For Becker, this redefinition of *homo economicus* widens the way in which discrimination is thought of and conceived as playing a factor in economic decisions: not just a prejudice based on stereotypes, it is a factor in future decision making with regard to what can be anticipated and expected in the future. For this reason, he suggests that his theory allows for a widening of our measures of discrimination:

> Instead of making the common assumptions that employers only consider the productivity of employees, that workers ignore the characteristics of those with whom they work, and that customers only care about the qualities of the goods and services provided, discrimination coefficients incorporate the influence of race, gender, and other personal characteristics on tastes and attitudes. Employees may refuse to work under a woman or a black even when they are well paid to do so, or a customer may prefer not to deal with a black car salesman. It is only through *widening* of the usual assumptions that it is possible to begin to understand the obstacles to advancement encountered by minorities.[14]

In this way, Becker provides a methodology for how race might permeate the market itself and structure decision making in particular ways. In doing so, he incorporates race at the levels of taste, utility, and preferences and thereby builds race into the formation of value. He shows how race is embedded in the market as such in order to generate certain expectations and future calculations.

Given my analysis above, it would seem that Becker's methodology has the potential to uncover exactly the modes of thought that I detail through Howard and to powerfully widen our understanding of how race makes worlds. However, in *The Economics of Discrimination*, Becker's procedure and his particular definition of the "discrimination co-efficient" produces the contrary effect of narrowing the definition of race. For one, his discrimination coefficient always has a positive value in his equations: in other words, it is always computed as a cost imposed on doing business, never as a utility for the production of more profit or for a desired gain of the employer, employee, or company: "Discrimination is commonly associated with *dis*utility caused by contact with some individuals, and this interpretation is followed here. Since this implies that *di*, *dj*, and *dk* are all greater than zero, to the employer this coefficient represents a non-monetary cost of production, to the employee a non-monetary cost of employment, and to the consumer a non-monetary cost of consumption."[15] Becker defines discrimination as always incurring a cost to the discriminator, since it always involves a deviation from acting within a pure paradigm of economic efficiency: "Money, commonly used as a measuring rod, will also serve as a measure of discrimination. If an individual has a 'taste for discrimination,' he must act *as if* he were willing to pay something, either directly or in the form of a reduced income, to be associated with some persons instead of others. When actual discrimination occurs, he must, in fact, either pay or forfeit income for this privilege. This simple way of looking at the matter gets at the essence of prejudice and discrimination."[16]

Second, in an approach followed by legal thinking in different ways, as we will see in the following chapter, the procedure for measuring discrimination is to create an equation for wages, or prices, or some other economic unit of analysis *with* discrimination and then one *without* discrimination and to compare the two results. The paradigm of nondiscrimination as a "base" state is incorporated into the equation that calculates what Becker calls the "market discrimination coefficient." This method isolates race as a factor that can be put in or out, assuming that mechanisms like rent control, the setting of prices, and so on *can* be determined along principles of maximum economic efficiency that exist apart from race. For example, in order to get at the essence of prejudice, Becker treats blacks and whites as "perfect substitutes" in the labor market in order to isolate the effect of discriminatory behavior defined purely as a cost—the difference in wages paid to blacks and whites. In this way, the effects of race on mechanisms of efficiency—competition, distribution, the formation of certain markets—are rendered invisible and incorporated into the equations themselves as their given apparatus for determining whether or not discrimination exists. Thus, while Becker opens up the domains of the economic and the social in many ways, he forecloses the implications of that opening by both defining discrimination in particular ways and by incorporating the effects of race on some of his unquestioned variables—such as utility—into the equations themselves.

The economist Kenneth Arrow registers these limitations of how one frames economic units of analysis such as "productivity" and "efficiency," when he writes, "I have spoken of personal characteristics that are 'unrelated to productivity' and not 'properly relevant.' These terms imply definitions of product and of relevancy which are themselves value judgments or at any rate decisions by the scholar. *The black steel worker may be thought of as producing blackness as well as steel, both evaluated in the market*" (my italics).[17] Here, Arrow touches on—without pursuing the interesting possibility of thinking—how the black steelworker is producing blackness as well as steel, both of which are open to be utilized in market evaluations. Arrow thus points out the way in which the many debates about the economics of discrimination embed certain assumptions about when and where race is salient into its equations and analyses. In Becker's framing of discrimination, the black worker and white worker are initially "perfect substitutes": only a calculation of disequilibrium registers the effect of discrimination. In assuming efficiency as the governing ideal for the market, Becker rules out the possibility that discrimination or the production of blackness is economically efficient and profitable for some but not others. In other words, he rules out the possibility that blackness and whiteness are themselves utilities in the formation of exchange.

Despite the promise of "widening the usual assumptions" of the relationship between discrimination and economic behavior, Becker's method for locating race at the level of preferences inoculates practices of exchange and economic expectations from being marked by racial signification. Friedman specifically cites and draws on Becker's methods (Becker was Friedman's student at the University of Chicago) to popularize the conception of market transactions as naturally working against the activity of racial attribution. Here, I underscore the way in which this method both displaces race from the workings of the market proper *and* embeds it everywhere in the form of expectations and utility based in race. Indeed, if the subprime mortgage crisis from the 1990s through to the Great Recession showed us anything, it is that it became highly profitable for banks to utilize and incorporate race as a sign to control loss and profit.

In "Race, Power, and the Subprime Mortgage/Foreclosure Crisis," Gary Dymski, Jesus Hernandez, and Lisa Mohanty critique prevailing sociological and economic analyses that emerged in the wake of the 2006 recession. On the one hand, the sociological analyses locate the cause of the crisis in a history of housing segregation and racialized lending practices (racial targeting, for example): "So home-loan lending over the years amplified spatial racial disparities, subprime lending exploited them, and consequently the foreclosure crisis has disproportionately affected minority homeowners."[18] The economic analyses, on the other hand, find little empirical evidence of disparate treatment, and disparate impact indicators are limited by the conceptual need to narrow the effects to ones caused "*solely*" by race: "Economists have grounded their explanations instead in the incentives and behaviors of the institutions and markets that generated and distributed subprime credit. This has led them to trace the subprime crisis to human fallibility: over-optimistic assessments of housing-price trajectories; and the inability of financial authorities to either prevent unwise lending or to compel borrowers to repay. The disproportionately minority and female subprime borrowers were less victims than they were either myopic or overly greedy and over-reaching (or both)."[19] Sociological analyses have blind spots because without an analysis of the market mechanisms they can only move tentatively toward a correlation between racial impact and these mechanisms. Economic analyses do not include the "structure of social relations that shape the risk and return that provide the raw material for instruments with different risk/return combinations."[20]

In critiquing these perspectives, Dymski, Hernandez, and Mohanty show the intertwined relationship between the construction of these social relations and the development of market mechanisms to take advantage of them. It is not, as the economists would have it, that race cannot be pinpointed as a factor, nor is it accurate to say that this crisis is simply the extension of past inequities and discriminations. Mortgage lending became structured and incentivized around the extraction of fees and credit from disadvantaged communities of color at the same time that race became a piece of information to be used in order to create the conditions for profitability. As Dymski, Hernandez, and Mohanty show, the mortgage market moved from one of exclusion to exploitative inclusion when markets were retooled to maximize profitability from racial conditions. This is both more and less than racial "targeting": it did not affect only people of color, but being a person of color became a market index, or to use narratological terms, an indice that integrated a set of practices of extraction (balloon payments, extremely volatile adjustable rate mortgages, pricing of mortgage insurance) that leveraged short-term gains.

These practices are perfectly in line with the mechanisms of embedding race in the world that I have been tracking through Becker. Dymski, Hernandez and Mohanty leave us with the phenomenon of race being "ever-present and absent in the play of market forces; some will see the effects of disparate racial treatment and outcomes everywhere; others will deny the importance of race in social and economic outcomes."[21] However, the analysis of racial salience and its mechanisms of attribution gets us out of this indeterminate perceptual dilemma and probes further into the relationship between relocating race and building in knowledge. As we saw from Howard's strategies in which the specific racial denotation is removed as a way to enable the broader, less-targeted, but more integrative quality of blackness to come through, a similar process can be seen in banking practices. Race as an integrative sign across multiple levels of meaning plays a crucial role in the link between exchange and value, and thus does not appear simply as a stereotype or form of racial inferiority and superiority at the level of psychology or society. Patricia Williams details her own experiences with mortgage lending where race is rendered invisible not simply because it has been erased or not mentioned, but because it has been incorporated into the very processes that generate values and the calculation of utility: "the reason they gave was that property values in that neighbourhood were suddenly falling. They wanted more money to cover the increased risk. . . . And even though I work with this sort of thing all the time, I really hadn't gotten it: for of course, *I* was the reason the prices were in peril. The bank was proceeding according to demographic data that show any time black people move into a neighborhood in the States, whites are overwhelmingly likely to move out. . . . Pulling every imaginable resource with them, from school funding to garbage collection to social workers who don't want to work in black neighbourhoods. . . . It's called a tipping point."[22] The explanation that Williams is given—"property values in that neighborhood were suddenly falling"—shows the way in which economic exchanges already incorporate forward-looking determinations into their calculations, producing specific inequalities. Williams goes on to analyze this example as part of the new "rhetoric of racism" in which race is not mentioned and it is displaced onto the domain of class discrimination as a way to get around civil rights legislation.[23] This displacement, however, accomplishes one additional function: it embeds race into the perceptual framework for market mechanisms, a set of expectations that can be performed and actualized in the future: "*I* was the reason the prices were in peril." Blackness *as a source of certainty and economic expectations* is used to create the *uncertainty* through which profit is calculated and generated. In order to "cover" the uncertainty caused by the "certainty" of blackness, the bank needed more money.

Since Becker's 1957 publication, economic analyses have of course produced different models for thinking about race discrimination, but Becker's methods remain influential.[24] Most importantly, there has been increased attention to social interactions as places where racial discrimination can enter into economic processes. Glenn Loury provides a very useful corrective and critique of Becker's approach to discrimination by re-emphasizing the social as the domain for the production of race *prior to* market transactions.[25] As Kenneth Arrow writes in "What Has Economics to Say about Racial Discrimination," "personal interactions occur throughout this process, and therefore there is plenty of room for discriminatory beliefs and preferences to play a role which would be much less likely in a market subject to competitive pressures . . . each transaction is a social event. At each stage, direct social transactions unmediated by a market play a role. Even the market manifestations will be altered by these direct social influences."[26] Racial discrimination influences and frames the market via these personal interactions. But even as these formulations show, both Loury and Arrow hold on to the idea that these social transactions are unmediated by or set off from the market. They have thrown out Becker's model, even the good stuff: Becker's recognition that social interactions *are* market processes. If, as Arrow writes, "racial discrimination pervades every aspect of a society in which it is found," then it is not just that social interactions provide a place for racial discrimination to enter into the market.[27] Rather, it is that market processes themselves depend on the circulation of racial meanings.

In Becker's model, race is only ever present as "disutility," a cost to the discriminator. As we have seen, this interpretive strategy both obfuscates and proliferates the multiple functions of race as integral to the market. By analyzing the "economics of discrimination" and S&S together, I identify the expansion of race as *utility* in the latter half of the twentieth century. I use "utility" in the sense developed by economics, first as an ordering of preferences and satisfactions obtained from a given good; second as a measure of an individual's willingness to take risks. The sword and sorcery genre vividly illustrates the crucial function of race in both these senses of economic utility. It develops a richer vocabulary for understanding the varied functions of race as signs and explanations that are not beyond market transactions but rather constitutive of the very activity of exchange itself. It explores Lindon Barrett's foundational insight that the "abstract entities 'value' and 'race' keenly reflect one another. . . . At its simplest, value is a configuration of privilege, and at its crudest, race is the same." As such, Barrett argues, the process of valorization operates through a network of exchanges with racial blackness, promoting certain forms forcefully over others.[28] As I explain below, sword and sorcery explores the doubling of value and race because the idea that social transactions are always *mediated* by a market is an important part of the genre itself. This aspect of the genre is specifically taken up by Samuel Delany's Nevèrÿon series, four S&S novels published from 1979 to 1987. The next section juxtaposes Delany's S&S series and Howard's stories with particular attention to their "market scenes." Reading these scenes with the developments of race and economics outlined above in mind, race ceases to be mere representation judged in terms of whether or not it is discriminatory.

Instead, the activities of noticing race become ways of building in knowledge that constitute economic expectations.

Fashioning New Utilities of Blackness

In distinguishing S&S from epic fantasy above, I mentioned S&S's heightened attention to the activity of mundane social transactions. The hero is not the prince or the king but rather the barbarian, outcast, or mercenary. The tradition developed from Conan the Barbarian to Fritz Lieber's pairing of a tall barbarian (Fafhrd) and a short thief (Gray Mouser) through Joanna Russ's female barbarian/thief/mercenary Alyx. As such the background of the story is not the domain of high politics but rather the smaller social events that mark the adventures of someone just making their way through the world: Alyx is approached by a man who pretends to be a magician in the market; Conan escapes from some guards and steals his way onto a merchant ship. Rarely would one find a chapter detailing the high politics of the world among various political representatives, such as Tolkien's famous "Council of Elrond," in an S&S tale. Instead, deals are made in the dark between the "high" and the "low": thief and princess, rogue and desperate man or woman.

It is within these narratives of adventure and roguery that Samuel Delany emphasizes the centrality of the market scene for S&S:

> When, as a child, I first read *The Hour of the Dragon* and the other of Howard's Conan stories, certainly the market scenes fascinated me most. . . . Thieves went slipping through it. People dashed up to other people in it, whispered mysterious or menacing messages, then dashed off again to be absorbed in the crowd. How many quarrels there erupted into vicious, bloody sword fights? Rumors had lives there as complex as the lives of human beings. There the high met the low, to discuss quickly and quietly their secret off-stage (i.e., obscene) relations. The market gave you a vision, not of the average citizen, but of the range of specific economic individuals, beggar and student, housewife and horse-dealer, farmer and potter, acrobat and army man, barmaid and baron, the vendor hustling belt buckles and the farmgirl on her day off looking for entertainment, from which the average is drawn.[29]

Delany was the first to point out the central role of economic transactions in the plots and actions of S&S. He suggests that the larger abiding concern of S&S is in narrating the social and psychic shifts that accompany the transition from a barter economy to a money economy. The market "scene" in S&S often plays a stage-setting or transitional role in these stories: a stranger enters the city and is struck by the motley populations and activities of the marketplace, a fight springs up in the market, something suspicious is going on there, a thief steals something that pops up later, a crowd forms. It is a site that is so central for S&S because it is the place where people go to satisfy their desires for money or power. It is the site where objects circulate within different regimes of value. As George Simmel writes, the economy consists "not only in exchanging *values* but in the *exchange* of values."[30] Value is not simply a property of goods found in the marketplace that are then exchanged. Value is formed through the process of exchange that is already shaped by desire and systems of signification. For Delany, the market in S&S is so fascinating precisely because it stages this mediation of social relations and market processes. What Delany does not mention explicitly in his commentary are the textual strategies of racial attribution that are an integral part of social and economic exchange. I return to Robert Howard in order to explicate the popular market logics that are embedded in some of Conan's adventures. Howard's textual strategies that I analyzed earlier are seen here in a different light, showing the important ordering role that race plays in the imagination of the market itself.

In Howard's scenes of economic exchange, race is not referenced at the level of the exploitation of labor and use of bodies. It serves as the arbiter of value itself: the narrative uses race in order to produce the reader's assent with a set of racial assumptions that allows value to be rendered stable and certain. "The Man-Eaters of Zamboula" could not begin in a more mundane way: Conan the Barbarian needs a place to rest so he visits an inn. This scenario is a classic horror story: things are not what they seem and Conan must figure out an explanation for the horrors going on in this strange town. But the story is both framed and given shape through the relationship between race and economic expectations. At first, race confuses relationships between social and economic value. In discussing the inn whose guests mysteriously disappear, Conan talks about the difficulties of figuring out who is an honest or dishonest proprietor through the racial composition of the city: "in this accursed city which Stygians built and which Hyrkanians rule—where white, brown and black folk mingle together to produce hybrids of all unholy hues and breeds—who can tell who is a man, and who a demon in disguise."[31] In this marketplace, racial signs interfere with the proper delivery of economic expectations.

And yet, this confusion and uncertainty is overturned, not by excluding racial considerations due to their unreliability, but by endowing race with a clearer utility. Once Conan understands that race is tightly linked to the satisfactions and pleasures one gets from goods, then everything in the town makes sense. The disappearance of the inn's guests is not a supernatural occurrence. It is part of an economic racial order, one that mixes the expectation of profit at all costs with the expectations and desires of specific racial traits:

> He understood now the mystery of the strangers who had disappeared from the house of Aram Baksh; the riddle of the black drum thrumming out there beyond the palm groves, and of that pit of charred bones—that pit where strange meat might be roasted under the stars, while black beasts squatted about to glut a hideous hunger. The man on the floor was a cannibal slave from Darfar. . . . Cannibalism was not tolerated openly in Zamboula. But Conan knew now why people locked themselves in so securely at night, and why even beggars shunned the open alleys and doorless ruins. He grunted in disgust as he visualized brutish black shadows skulking up and down the knighted streets, seeking human prey—and such men as Aram Baksh to open the doors to them. The inn-keeper was not a demon, he was worse. The slaves from Darfar were notorious thieves; there was no doubt that some of their pilfered loot found its way into the hands of Aram Baksh. And in return he sold them human flesh.[32]

Aram Baksh "was worse" than a "demon": he is a businessman who trades human flesh to cannibals. Conan's understanding of this economic order hinges on the use of race to accurately index desire. Much like the Howard stories analyzed earlier, the proliferation of references to "black"—"black drum," "black beasts," "black shadows"—displace blackness into the "atmosphere." As such, though, it creates reinforcing levels of knowledge of the market to satisfy cannibalistic desire. The terms of exchange are often dictated by what one knows of the other, and the ultimate knowledge in producing these expectations and profits are built around race. What can be absolutely counted on are the blood lust of the cannibal slaves and the lasciviousness of black women. This built-in knowledge of blackness produces a certainty around which a whole set of economic expectations, choices, exchanges, and profit—in short, a market—can revolve. When Conan asks the girl whom he saves, "Why don't the citizens clean out these black dogs?," again an economic explanation is given: "'They are valuable slaves,' murmured the girl. 'There are so many of them they might revolt if they were denied the flesh for which they lust.'"[33]

Howard scholars might object that "The Man-Eaters of Zamboula" is easy pickings as his most racist story. But as I hope to have demonstrated, its strategies of racial representation are not different from many of his other stories. The framework I am using is not one in which we judge which story is more or less explicitly racist. What is different is the way in which it builds racial knowledge into economic expectations as a way to solve the narrative mystery of the story. In Howard's "The Vale of Lost Women," the exchange of services via racial codes again takes center stage. A woman enslaved by a black tribe sees Conan and attempts a trade of services with him:

> "How can you stand there like a dumb brute?" she screamed in a ghastly whisper. "Are you but a beast like these others? Ah, Mitra, once I thought there was honor in men. Now I know each has his price. You—what do you know of honor—or of mercy or decency? You are a barbarian like these others—only your skin is white, your soul is black as theirs.
>
> "You care naught that a man of your own color has been foully done to death by these black dogs—that a white woman is their slave! . . .
>
> "I will give you a price!" she raved, tearing away her tunic from her ivory breasts. "Am I not fair? Am I not more desireable than these soot-colored wenches? . . . Kill that black dog Bajujh! . . . Then take me and do as you wish with me. I will be your slave!"[34]

She imagines a clear exchange between two free agents—her current captor and Conan. Her valuation comes as a direct result of putting herself in contrast with black women, trading on the value of whiteness over blackness.

What Conan imagines, though, is the larger order of exchanges that devalue her and make her one (similar) object among many: "'You speak as if you were free to give yourself at your pleasure,' he said. 'As if the gift of your body had power to swing kingdoms. Why should I kill Bajujh to obtain you? Women are cheap as plantains in this land, and their willingness or unwillingness matters little. You value yourself too highly. If I wanted you, I wouldn't have to fight Bajujh to take you. He would rather give you to me than to fight me.'"[35] And yet, this economic explanation only forestalls the ultimate explanation, which is to reassert, even more strongly, the value of race to set the terms of this economic exchange: "If you were old and ugly as the devil's pet vulture, I'd take you away from Bajujh, simply because of the color of your hide. But you are young and beautiful, and I have looked at black sluts until I am sick at the guts. I'll play this game your way, simply because some of your instincts correspond with some of mine."[36] The rhetoric of these sentences suggests that race is *not* being used in this valuation: *if* she were old and ugly, *then* he would save her on account of her race; *but* she is young and beautiful. The racist comparison to "black sluts" reasserts the utility of race in reordering the expectations of economic behavior. Conan's ultimate explanation rests on the seemingly race-neutral language of instincts, but it is these instincts that have already been shaped by the givens of racist valuation. Market processes of setting a price are themselves shaped by the embedding of racial signification.

In "Man-Eaters," the narrative explanation of the mystery depends on a market logic. In "Vale of Lost Women," Conan's economic decision depends on a narrative explanation. Both rely on race to create certainties on which the determinations of value and exchange rely. Both produce blackness in order to make Conan's explanation or decision converge with a larger landscape of profit, satisfaction, and desire. In following Howard's thematization of the market, Delany, I argue, is quite cognizant of these textual strategies deploying blackness. For both Howard and Delany, race does not function primarily as an operation for classifying and categorizing individuals. It produces utilities through which narrative *and* economic expectations are shaped. Delany, however, critiques the links between race as it is used to construct the "atmosphere" of a story and the formation of utility. In doing so, he practices an *antiracist racial worldmaking*: the deployment of race in ways that do not necessarily build in racist structures of exchange.

Delany's Nevèrÿon and the Reimagination of the Market

That Delany is a crucial source for a project investigating genre and race together is not surprising. First heralded as a science fiction writer in the mid-1960s, punctuated by Nebula Awards in 1966 and 1967, and Hugo Award nominations in 1967, 1968, and 1969, Delany has written in and through the language and protocols of science fiction, S&S, pornography, autobiography, among others. Delany describes genre as a structuration of readerly response: "A genre is constituted of a way of reading . . . a set of texts produces a way of responding to these texts that is different from the way we respond to texts we might say belong to other genres."[37] Thus Delany participates in genre not as a constraint but as a set of continual possibilities in order to produce new ways of reading: "What I am doing in almost all my books is the genre equivalent of 'gender bending.' That's how all genres expand, progress, survive."[38] As scholars such as Carl Freedman and Madhu Dubey have made clear, Delany's SF writings build worlds in ways that construct new epistemologies as well as ways of being in the world.[39] Further, as a black, gay writer, Delany's work has invited commentary on the relationship between his writing and themes of race and sexuality. At the same time, it has resisted attempts to analyze its literary representations as direct "treatments" of marginalized identities.[40] This is likely because the participation in genre already complicates any easy mimetic relationship between representation and social content, but also because Delany places racial references in unlikely places in order to create new ways of perceiving the world.[41]

The *Nevèrÿon* series exemplifies this generation of new readerly responses. Delany writes: "The *Nevérÿon* enterprise . . . is to articulate for adults the hidden and subterranean currents that are forever at play in the largely infantile genre of sword-and-sorcery: to make explicit—and use the tale as a stage radically to explore—the sadomasochistic and homoerotic elements without which Howard's *Conan the Conqueror* would never have survived, nor proliferated into a subgenre of its own."[42] It is in this deconstructive spirit that Delany explores, among other things, the origins of reading and writing and the history of sexuality, wearing his references to poststructuralist thought on his sleeve.[43] The series mixes literary criticism, S&S, and slave narrative in redeploying the economic and sexual motifs in S&S toward meditations on slavery and freedom. It concerns the life and career of Gorgik the Liberator, a former slave who leads raids to free slaves and who eventually spearheads the end of slavery in Nevèrÿon as a politician. This transition from slavery to freedom is narrated as a particular economic upheaval, sweeping up the lives of various characters: the young girl Pryn; Madame Keyne (an obvious play on the economist John Maynard Keynes); Small Sarg, Gorgik's lover; Clodon, a thief and bandit; among many others. It is a decentered narrative, to say the least, because it follows the movements of desire, social organization, and capital:

> Once fear of slavers was gone from the highways and backroads of Nevérÿon, more and more folk from the southern forests and the northern mountains and the western deserts had begun to make their way to the cities. And those in the cities with money, imagination, and industry had begun to take their primitive industrial knowledge out into the country to see what profit and speculation were to be had. Motion from margin to center, from center to margin was constant—till, in a handful of years, it had altered Nevérÿon's whole notion of margin and center. New margins had been created.[44]

These "new margins" signal a meditation on the Reagan-era economic landscape during which Delany wrote, one in which race is being reconfigured toward various capitalist ends.[45] As such, he shines a powerful light on the processes of "racial capitalism" in which it is not just the labor and bodies of people of color that are incorporated into capitalist circuits of meaning.[46] It is the very utility of race as expectation that is incorporated.

I thus place Delany's intervention in relation to the economics of discrimination and racialized market logics analyzed above. But the critical potential of his text goes beyond rendering visible these dynamics. He opens up alternative worldmaking practices by constructing different routes of reference and social exchange. I focus on one narrative technique of world-building in particular: reordering racial perception so as to make other kinds of economic and social utility possible. As we saw above, for Howard race rises above the contingencies of value in order to provide the ultimate narrative explanation that stabilizes economic exchange. But for Delany, the appearance of racial markers is always an exercise in reordering perceptions of value. In Delany's S&S, there is none of the overdetermination of darkness, shadowy, black, and so on that constitutes the landscape of the typical Conan story. In this way, race ceases to be the "atmosphere" through which readerly desire, fear, and comprehension is necessarily routed. Instead, racial denotations tend to be details introduced after the reader has already had some interaction with and knowledge of the character.[47] They likely may be details about skin color in relation to someone else, as opposed to just a defining attribute of the character that stands alone. Even when given as such, they tend to be qualified by some other element or circumstance.

In Delany's Nevèrÿon, the ruling class is largely black or brown, and the barbarian and slave classes are predominantly white. The world thereby reverses the expected racial hierarchies of identifying slaves with blackness inherited from U.S. history. In Nevèrÿon, though, slavery is also not exclusively race-based. Gorgik himself was a slave and has brown skin. Having dark skin does not render one immune from enslavement as is apparent in various instances. Without a "pure" reversal, readers must continually attend to context, circumstances, and other signs in order to determine what functions racial markers might have. This shift in attention demanded by the narrative has been acknowledged, but its implications have not been fully explored. In one of the central readings of the Nevèrÿon series attending to the dynamics of race and slavery, Jeffrey Tucker notes that the series "is by no means a transparent allegory of race-based slavery that occurred in antebellum America. Slavery in Nevèrÿon, as just noted, is not exclusively race-based as it was in America."[48] But he goes on to analyze various correspondences between the depiction of slavery in Delany's novel and depictions and themes of slavery in the slave narrative tradition, a critical move that restabilizes this perceptual shift back to an understood historical given.[49] The narrative discourse of the Nevèrÿon series makes it difficult to attach racial descriptions to any corresponding historical context. The confusion of perception seems to be something that Delany counts on precisely in order to question the false dichotomy between a race-based slavery and a non-race-based form of economic organization based on contract and the market.[50]

For example, in "The Tale of Dragons and Dreamers," two male lovers (Gorgik and Small Sarg) meet a masked woman and her female companion (Raven and Norema). Gorgik and Small Sarg fight to end slavery even as Gorgik wears a slave collar and Small Sarg calls him "master." Raven and Norema are similarly engaged in freeing slaves, specifically female slaves. But Raven and Norema cannot figure out who is who because while Gorgik wears the slave collar, he is also dark-skinned, which *does not,* in this world, denote slavery. When Small Sarg declares, "My master and I are free," Raven responds, "You both claim to be free, yet one of you bears the title 'master' and wears a slave collar at the same time? Surely you are two jesters."[51] The conversation continues in further misunderstanding:

> "We are lovers," said Gorgik, "and for one of us the symbolic distinction between slave and master is necessary to desire's consummation."
>
> "We are avengers who fight the institution of slavery wherever we find it," said Small Sarg. . . .
>
> The redheaded Norema said: "You love as master and slave and you fight the institution of slavery? The contradiction seems as sad to me as it seemed amusing to my friend."[52]

It is clear from the confusion of perceptions that what slavery *is* is not simply a preunderstood given. In highlighting this uncertainty, Delany points to the multiple organizations of desire and capital and the narrative expectations for race and sexuality that attend them. What matters here is not just the initial confusion but the routes through which this confusion becomes resolved—leading as they potentially could to different organizations of meaning.

This confusion is played out at the micro-level as well. For example, we get details about Gorgik's appearance via his act of looking at another person: "Thin. That's the first thing he thought, looking at those knobbly shoulders, those sharp knees. Gorgik walked nearer. The boy's skin had begun the same brown as his own. But it was as if some black wash of street dirt and gutterwater had been splashed over him, heels to ears."[53] Here, Delany highlights the interaction between the identification of brown skin and the "black wash of street dirt and gutterwater," not the transcendence of one sign over the other. In other words, Delany gives us a notion of race in which the various specific mentions of race and racial identity are rendered less "in the logical sense" and more as "contingent metonymic associations that other situations and other discourses can reassign."[54] Howard always gives us "blackness" *first*—the "black river," "black coast," "black pirate"—even before we enter the narrative and before we know what is black about these objects. This procedure enlists the reader in using race to form primary ways of organizing spatio-temporal experience. This is why in Howard's stories it becomes comprehensible to run away before you know what is chasing you, to hack your way through darkness or fog even though you can't see what you are killing. This is how the allegorical desire activated by Howard "draws its readers into deeper ideological commitments" and how it forms the infrastructures of an antiblack world.[55] Delany plays on the same associational logics in order to show the process of assigning meaning. The "same brown" and the "black wash of street dirt" combine in producing a perception of the change that circumstances make on the boy's appearance. It alters expectations that would otherwise just stop at the racial identification of skin that is the "same brown as his own." For Gorgik, it engenders desire and fascination.

Delany instructs readers toward a distinct mode of perception, one that does not rely on imposing an upward-trajectory of meanings but rather one that forces the reader to think about the relationship between a racial marker like "brown skin" and a social transaction. This shift in perception takes on particular critical potential in Delany's imagination of the market. Gorgik's plot to end slavery is transfigured by several other narrative elements. Gorgik is often juxtaposed with Madame Keyne and situated within an emerging capitalist order of the market that further complicates the dynamics of slavery, labor, and exchange. Delany conceptualizes the New Market as operating within these logics: "The New Market, for which a whole, impoverished neighborhood of Kolhari has had to be torn down, is constructed in Nevèrÿon because Madame Keyne and people like her have noticed ways in which the Old Market works—and are trying to abstract those principles, to improve on them, and to set them to work at greater intensity, over a greater range, at a manufactured site, in order to control loss, profit, capital in particular, and power in general."[56]

Delany meditates on the signs of race, class, and sex in a capitalist construction of value and exchange in the marketplace primarily through narratives of the surplus population that shadow the larger narrative arc of slavery and freedom. At the same time that Gorgik moves from slave to liberator to politician, characters such as Udrog, Clodon, and Pryn are dispossessed in many ways by new structures of capitalism, often moving back and forth between country and city in order to make their way.[57] Those "new margins" driven by profit and speculation took Udrog "from country to city. They took him from desert to forest. They took him from great breweries to share-cropping combines to tanning troughs to construction sites—seldom as a worker, at least for more than a day or so, but as someone who lived off what spilled into the marginal track—now in the fields and woods, now in the cities and villages."[58]

These figures are part of what Karl Marx would have called the "lumpenproletariat," "vagabonds, criminals, prostitutes,"[59] those outcasts from even the working-class surplus population. For Marx, this group can never gain class consciousness and thus may even be an impediment to revolutionary struggle. For Delany, this also seems to be the case. Udrog is a blonde barbarian who lacks understanding of how his position has been historically formed. Clodon is a character who parallels Gorgik but eschews the possibility of fighting for the enslaved. But also for Delany, these characters display operations of racial capitalism, especially in the construction of new utilities of race that exist apart from labor exploitation as traditionally conceived. This is not just the legacy of slavery on the operations of the New Market, for it is not as if slavery constituted something "whole" to be imported into new organizations. Rather, it is a continual reorganization of social relations and economic processes built on racialized and sexualized exchange.[60] Delany's troping of sword and sorcery's market scenes displays a keen awareness of the ways in which modes of racial perception build *fantasies* of blackness that are used to form economic expectations of profit and speculation.

I explore Clodon in particular as one example of the lumpenproletariat because his story so clearly shadows Gorgik's. They both have brown skin. They both bear scars. He is in fact the young man whom Gorgik observes as a boy in the passage quoted above. His story, told in "The Tale of Rumor and Desire," is placed in between two stories that tell the story of Gorgik's life in different ways. All three stories are found in the final volume of the Nevèrÿon series, *Return to Nevèrÿon*. But while Gorgik goes on to become a liberator, Clodon becomes a petty criminal, rapist, and vagabond. Most crucially, Clodon is at the center of a market exchange that utilizes racial signification in an unusual way. His story most clearly indexes the resignifications and productions of race in their evaluations by a market. Everywhere he goes, we see the organizing forces of narrative desire, race, and economic expectations.

"The Tale of Rumor and Desire" traces the meanderings of Clodon, who travels from country to city and back again, making do via occasional foreman work, sex work, and thievery, bearing the flogging marks from his criminal past on his back. These flogging marks are shown to operate on several registers, working in conjunction with other signs and within an economics of visibility that organizes desire and exchange. On one level, these flogging marks organize a moral structure of visibility that articulates work to debt: "'Flogging marks on a man only mean he once took out a debt he's paid back since. Work hard, Clodon, and they won't stand against you here.' Clodon had heard it before and knew how far it went."[61] The moral narrative here is one of forgiveness: work hard and one's debt to society will be paid. But Clodon knows better. Though the flogging marks are not supposed to stand between him and a proper place in society according to this form of worldmaking, Clodon knows that the flogging marks in fact structure a different kind of relation: the inability to get work precisely because of the social signification of a debt paid. Indeed, a merchant points to Clodon's welts, saying, "'There—you see?' . . . You've already gotten yourself in trouble in whatever huddle of hovels you hail from—so I can't take you on.'" The merchant goes on to narrate Clodon's extenuating circumstances for him, that it was probably an "unfair trial," that "no one paid attention to your side of the story."[62] Nevertheless, the relation between the flogging marks and debt cannot be overcome.

The flogging marks appear in a second organization of meaning when Clodon meets a man who takes him to a restaurant in the city. There the waiter draws a curtain between them and the others with the announcement—"Now you'll have your privacy." When Clodon says, referring to the curtain, "That's so the others won't see my—flogging marks, isn't it?," the man responds,

> Well, consider this. You come in here, wearing only a rag of leather about your loins and the signs of a country felon on your back. Most of the clientele you see here arrives in tunics, robes, and capes. Perhaps you never asked yourself why. But if, by some whim of the nameless god of count and accounting, all were suddenly struck naked here, you might be surprised who among us was marked and who was not—not to mention the nature of the marks we bear. . . . And I'm sure you're

> already aware that the biggest criminals are specifically marked by the fact that they have no marks at all.[63]

Clodon responds—"Come on—that's just a story!" The man's explanation, though, describes another economy of visibility, one that allows certain kinds of crimes and behaviors to go hiding in plain sight while others are overrepresented in terms of criminality. That is another way in which Clodon's flogging marks are rendered real for the purposes of economic utility while rendering others' marks unreal. Clodon's response—"that's just a story!"—shows again the way in which economic expectations are given form through narrative expectations: when narratives are not believable, they become dismissed, leaving this economics of visibility intact. The man's story rearranges signs, thus displaying the mechanisms through which real criminality is hidden in plain sight and secured via the overvaluation and fetishism of the flogging marks that are rendered more visible. Clodon himself is thus valued in a certain way—given the privacy to engage in a specific circuit of exchange involving sex—and devalued in relation to other kinds of exchange. In short, his flogging marks are being made economically useful.

This economic utility is made all the more apparent to Clodon in the agreement that Clodon eventually makes with this man. The man tells Clodon to put a fake slave collar around his neck and to stand on the Bridge of Lost Desire (the center of sex work in the city). If Clodon does so, the man tells him, he'll make more money in an hour than he would have otherwise in a week or month. When the man places the collar around Clodon's neck, he remarks on the transformation:

> There: what is it that looks out at you? In his iron collar, with the whip marks scarring his strong, brown body, surely that's no drunken country boy, in trouble because he's stolen some silly tax collector's supper. . . . Don't you see a slave? And not just *any* slave, but an evil one—a slave who once rose up against his master, a slave who pulled down on his careless back all punishment and retribution, and who now carries the welts of his wickedness inscribed on his flesh like a message to all. Can't you see him? Can't you see a slave who has been marked, and in whose markings, there for all who can to read, lie his disdain for all authority, his contempt for all human law. . . . I know that [you're not a slave] very well. . . . But between you and me, we have all the pieces from which to *construct* such a slave. . . . And such a slave, created of craft, artifice, and crime, may be more valuable, finally, than one formed only by the accidents of society and nature. Certainly he may well make more money.[64]

The man as capitalist produces surplus value by arranging signs that tap into certain circuits of desire and exchange. The combination of "strong, brown body," "whip marks scarring," and the collar creates a new economic utility, one that "may be more valuable" and "may well make more money." The new utility or structure of preferences relies on creating a new narrative and a fantasy of slavery and rebellion: "wickedness," "punishment," the "disdain for all authority." This fantasy is held out in the market as potentially realizable through social and economic transaction.

If Howard uses racial reference in order to produce certainty within an uncertain market, Delany uses it to show how surplus value is formed through the circulation and production of social meanings around criminality and race.[65] The new utility of "such a slave, created of craft, artifice, and crime" embeds particular images of criminality and slavery as elements from which to derive profit and speculation. At one level, then, this scene exposes some of the ways in which race and slavery are rearticulated to produce new forms of profit. At another level, though, this rearrangement of signs creates another world of desire and exchange that is suddenly open to Clodon:

> He felt very strange. It was as if the collar both trapped him and, at the same time, freed him into this odd world—freed him, at least, to stand at its edge and, as he listened to one request after another, to gaze out into it. He said no to them all. It was at the end of the second day he began to get the feeling the people he refused were actually taking something away from him. Each one, walking off when he told them, curtly, that, no, he didn't *do* that, left, he was sure, with a little more; and still a bit more. . . . And on the third day, he wandered off it in a kind of daze—actually surprised some barrier was not there to keep him to the place where collar and flogging marks, in combination, alone had the meaning they did.[66]

What is this "more" that prospective buyers leave with? What all of Clodon's potential buyers come away with is the availability of their desire, a desire that structures a set of social norms from which they profit. The combination of collar, flogging marks, and color produces a knowledge of Clodon for others that renders real their desire as well as the potential satisfaction of that desire; it produces a pattern of exchange via the eroticization of criminality, slavery, and color. But Clodon also feels "freed." "Freed," I think, in his understanding of the combination of signs and how new economies of desire and exchange might be fashioned. Clodon, of course, does not take the leap into this other world. But his choice to not enter this world throws into relief Gorgik's attempts to create a new space of liberation. Such a space is one that does not merely remove the chains from the enslaved. It is one that has to refashion the economic utility of race in relation to exchange. These new economies would be built not on the construction of a race-neutral market, but one that deploys signs of race, criminality, and slavery toward different ends.

Conclusion

It might be tempting to characterize Howard's representations of race as explicitly racist in contrast to Delany's more decentered representations of race. This characterization would serve prominent historical accounts that trace a trajectory from overt racism to covert racism, from an earlier moment of formal, legalized inequality in which race was omnipresent in legal and social classifications to a current moment of informal stratification in which race is erased or displaced from explicitness. This story, I hope to have shown, is inaccurate. It does not accurately describe Howard's and Delany's narrative practices. On the one hand, Howard's representations are more complex: they operate via a displacement from one level of meaning to another. On the other, Delany's representations do not merely decenter race. Rather, they confuse and reorder perception.

It is also inaccurate because it does not get at the reconfiguration of race in relation to market logics. Both writers are more usefully analyzed within the long history of racial capitalism. For both Howard and Delany, racial capitalism does not merely lie in the exploitation or exclusion of racialized labor. Nor is it something that ended with the abolition of slavery, as the identification of contractual wage labor with freedom would suggest.[67] Rather it lies in the embedding of racial meanings within economic functions of utility and uncertainty. Howard locates racial reference at the level of causal sequence and certainty in ways that stabilize the uncertainties of the market and control profit. His narrative logics suggest that when in doubt, the differential value of race can always be relied upon. Delany draws attention to this mode of thought at the intersection of economics and S&S when he represents the ways in which contiguous racial associations are incorporated into circuits of exchange.

Delany's engagement does not contest these strategies of referentiality simply by making race visible. He challenges the *ways we notice race*, because he understands that these ways are intimately tied to the construction of value. As he points out,

> People have noted for years how fast racism or sexism or classism reasserts itself as soon as a certain vigilance is allowed to relax. That's because they don't come in from outside. They are a *necessary* underlying factor within the egalitarian behavioral structure itself. Such a behavioral structure is not about ignoring differences. It's about noticing them, valuing them, realizing that there are certain situations, cultural and defined, when these differences are important—and realizing that they are crashingly irrelevant in others. (That's what valuing means.) If the structure of when and where they are relevant and irrelevant gets loose or generalized, you have racism, classism, and sexism all over again.[68]

Delany is not talking about economics per se here. But his S&S brings this sensibility to the domain of economic exchange. The scenes analyzed above point our attention to the processes of noticing race that are constitutive of our mechanisms of value-creation, often though not always linking the creation of surplus value to the production of blackness as utility.

Scholars have challenged the idea of a race-neutral market that operates through the rationalization of choices and serves the contract-based individual. Patricia Williams analyzes the ways in which the market privatizes (racial) preferences in order to structure inequalities. For example, she notes the market for egg donors in which tall, blonde, Ivy-league degree-holding women are particularly valued.[69] Jodi Melamed argues that neoliberalism structures racial inequalities using nonracial discourse: "racism constantly appears to be disappearing according to conventional race categories, even as neoliberal racialization continues to justify inequality using codes that can signify as nonracial or even antiracist. . . . These neoliberal codes, which fix human potentials and justify different social fates, interact with preexisting ethnoracial schemes that 'are reinforced and crosscut by new ways of governing that differentially values populations according to market calculations.'"[70]

Although not mentioned, Becker's human capital theory is precisely this kind of neoliberal racialization, a theory that naturalizes structural inequalities via a race-neutral language of human potential. The trajectory from Howard to Delany deepens our understanding of this relationship between race and market calculations. Indeed, as we have seen in putting Becker in conversation with S&S, the activity of noticing race has been crucial for the reconstruction of market ideals in the face of civil rights challenges.

These challenges were also met within the domain of legal thinking. However, the story is not as simple as positing a set of civil rights gains followed by a reaction or a taking away. Part IV details a longer history of legal thinking in order to track the forms of noticing race and their links to particular narrative explanations: narrative explanations that circumscribe the very possibilities of imagining an antiracist world. It is to legal thinking that we now turn.

PART IV

Alternate History

CHAPTER 7

Racial Counterfactuals and the Uncertain Event of Emancipation

As we saw from Part III, the methodological question of the relationship between racial inequality and market processes turns toward the fashioning of the very tools used to embed race into calculations of profit, utility, exchange, and value. This process of embedding racial phenomena into the generation of our systems of reference similarly permeates the domain of legal thinking. But these textual strategies of racial worldmaking in the law cannot be simply categorized in terms of an era of Jim Crow, de jure discrimination and an era of de facto discrimination. As legal scholars Sora Han and Osagie Obasogie argue, periodizations of the legal history of civil rights reforms and a post–civil rights era are deeply misguided. They wrongly impute some past civil rights success in which formal equality has been established in law.[1] Both Han and Obasogie return to the language and rhetoric of the law in order to analyze how it is animated by structuring racial fantasies. For Han, the law returns again and again to a "fundamental problem slavery posed, and continues to pose." The incoherence of its language in addressing racial inequality registers not the errors or inconsistencies in the rule of law, but its "general condition." She calls the cover story for this structuring role of race in the law the "fantasy of colorblindness."[2]

For Obasogie, the law is structured by assumptions about what it means to "see" race, and these procedures of seeing animate equal protection jurisprudence from *Plessy v. Ferguson* onward.

Such work demonstrates that racial reference has not simply been eliminated at the legal level with the institution of formal equality and a doctrine of colorblindness. Nor has racial reference been displaced onto other categories such as ethnicity, culture, or class. Legal language produces evidence everywhere of the ongoing desires, disavowals, and protocols of seeing used to address racial inequality that forms legal doctrine itself. Part IV follows these insights by focusing on law's textual and interpretive strategies. Chapter 7 takes up the "racial counterfactual"—a scenario that uses the "what if" formulation of the counterfactual and substitutes one race for another, such as, "if Obama were white, he would . . ." I identify the crucial role that the "racial counterfactual" plays in producing legal outcomes, particularly in reverse discrimination cases within the context of U.S. white-black relations. Chapter 8 isolates the perceptual frameworks constructed via the vocabulary of "strict scrutiny" developed in *Korematsu v. United States* (1944) within the context of Asiatic racialization. These two chapters together work through specific narrative logics within the development of equal protection jurisprudence, focusing alternately on a pervasive form of narrative explanation (racial counterfactual) and a landmark doctrinal standard (strict scrutiny).

I also follow Han's and Obasogie's insights in their understanding of the longer histories animating legal writing, a genre that operates through continually looking backward in the form of citation and precedent. I track the strange temporalities used in legal opinion, but these textual strategies are not limited to the domain of law. Rather, they find their most condensed and popular expression in the genre of alternate history, the influences of which date all the way back to early historiography but a genre that finds its formal, novelistic expression in the nineteenth century and then takes off within the U.S. context from the 1950s onward.[3] Alternate histories are built as experiments in counterfactual logic, asking "what if?" In addition, I suggest that a prominent strain of alternate histories utilize the racial counterfactual. Like the legal cases, alternate histories put into place a set of narrative explanations that showcase the use of race as a connective principle. As a connective principle, race is used to shape facts and determine possibilities. In some cases, it is used to reproduce racism as a precondition for thinking about what happens next, which does nothing less than presuppose racism in order to make the world coherent. In other cases, authors inhabit these narrative logics in order to build antiracist worlds. I thus couple analysis of legal cases with an interpretation of alternate histories of the Civil War and World War II—the two most prominently represented themes within the genre.

The prominence of these scenarios indexes their importance as major historical events that have shaped and continue to shape the world. They shape the world in the form of the narrative explanations they put into place—explanations that cut across the domains of law and popular fiction. These events have lodged the contexts of black and Asiatic racialization within legal thinking to the exclusion of other racial groups. Both equal protection jurisprudence and alternate histories are thus examples of ongoing responses to these condensed sites of historic racial inequality—slavery, the Civil War and Reconstruction on the one hand and World War II, Nazism, and Japanese internment on the other hand—and all the fantasies, resentments, disavowals, and projections that attend them. If race here is used as a connective principle that makes worlds, the question remains: do alternate histories imagine alternate worlds? What are the possibilities of embedding not racism but antiracism into our world-building? In order to understand how alternate histories and legal reasoning put into place what Du Bois codifies as the "white world" as well as the efforts to surpass these limits, we must first explore the rhetorical and poetic effects of the racial counterfactual.

Racial Counterfactuals

In the film *A Time to Kill*, lawyer Jake Brigance (Matthew McConaughey) delivers a closing argument that turns on the act of imagining what is not the case. Arguing in defense of Carl Lee Hailey (Samuel L. Jackson), who killed two white men in retribution for their sexual assault and brutalization of his daughter, Tonya (RaéVen Larrymore Kelly), Brigance begins by inviting the jury to listen to a story: "I want to tell you a story. I'm going to ask you all to close your eyes while I tell you the story. I want you to listen to me. I want you to listen to yourselves. Go ahead. Close your eyes, please. This is a story about a little girl walking home from the grocery store one sunny afternoon. I want you to picture this little girl."[4]

He goes on to recount the horrific details of what happens to this little girl, but ends his argument by engaging the jury in an act of counterfactual imagining: "Can you see her? Her raped, beaten, broken body soaked in their urine, soaked in their semen, soaked in her blood, left to die. Can you see her? I want you to picture that little girl. Now imagine she's white."[5] This move uses a racial counterfactual—what if this victim were white and not black—in order to allow the all-white jury to place themselves in the victim's position and by extension into Hailey's position. The defense is successful.

In substituting one race for another, Jake's racial counterfactual argues for equal treatment by creating empathy on the part of the jurors for the situation of the victim and highlighting the racist forms of judgment that evaluate the same action differently based on race. It does so, problematically, by relying on the limitations of empathy and identification on the part of the white jurors: they can only see the victim as a person worthy of respect and humanity if they imagine her as white. Indeed, Hailey implores Jake to make more of an effort in the trial with precisely this argument:

> See Jake, you think just like them, that's why I picked you; you are one of them, don't you see? . . . You are my secret weapon because you are one of the bad guys. You don't mean to be but you are. It's how you was raised. Nigger, negro, black, African-American, no matter how you see me, you see me different, you see me like that jury sees me, you are them. Now throw out your points of law Jake. If you was on that jury, what would it take to convince you to set me free? That's how you save my ass. That's how you save us both.[6]

Hailey explicitly overturns Jake's sense that in order to convince the jury, he needs to "be friends" with Hailey and understand where he's coming from. Instead Hailey insists that Jake will do his best only if he can identify with his own whiteness.

But beyond these politics of identification, racial counterfactuals more crucially show how race is embedded in our modes of explanation and prediction. When Jake says, "Now imagine she's white" right after he says that he wants you to "picture her," he is capitalizing on the projectable effect of race on our narrative explanations—namely, the unstated ground of whiteness as innocence. The shift in perception that the counterfactual introduces at the end relies on an assumed understanding of the sequences of contexts, actions, and judgments that obtain given somebody's race, and the altered set of sequences that would obtain once races are switched. It makes the jurors re-evaluate the entire sequence of the story and forces them to reconsider all the unstated antecedents that they used to explain and/or justify it. Brigance introduces his closing argument by saying that he is "telling a story." He plays on the limits of their imagination by associating "innocence" and "purity" with the victim. He never mentions the skin color or other bodily markers of any of the participants, even as aspects of the incident itself—the use of a noose—immediately code the situation as a racial act of violence. Racial counterfactuals thus do not just enact a reversal or a substitution in order to create empathy or point out the difference that race makes. They usher in an alternate world—replete with its embedded valuations, judgments, and ways of making meaning—so as to shape the direction of our explanations. In constructing an alternate world, the counterfactual illustrates the way in which we organize worlds through race and take the projectability of race as a necessary given.

Nelson Goodman analyzes counterfactuals as exemplifying the larger problem of induction and valid projection: in what ways, he asks, do some predicates become projectable and others do not? According to Goodman, there are two principle philosophical issues that the counterfactual presents. First, every counterfactual presumes our agreement with a set of statements that are asserted without being stated in order for the counterfactual to be true.[7] For example, if I say that "if I were taller, my life would be better," I am assuming as already true a whole set of ideas about the statement "if I were taller," and I am singling out the property of tallness. Second, Goodman notes that the connection between the "if" statement and the "then" statement is not a logical one, but a predictive one: "rather than the law being used for prediction because it describes the causal connection, the meaning of the causal connection is to be interpreted in terms of predictively used laws."[8] Goodman calls these general statements that allow one to connect antecedent and consequent "lawlike." Counterfactuals thus use the idea of a potentiality or a probability to replace a logically necessary relationship. They transform potentiality into something "lawlike" that shapes our sense of the truth of the counterfactual.

Goodman's identification of these "predictively used laws" demonstrates the interrelations of fact, fiction, and forecast as they interpret and make causal connections. The racial counterfactual example above shows how the lawlike predictive rules can be grounded in the projective capacity of race taken as a necessary given. "Now imagine she's white" is used to restart the sequence of what could and should happen given this different state of affairs. It reinterprets the meaning of the connections between the girl's behavior, the harm done to her, and what our response should be. Race as a mode of thought is usually described in terms of the cognitive processes of classification, categorization, and mapping, as well as in its relationship to modern concepts of essence and likeness.[9] But what racial counterfactuals show is race as a mode of thought in terms of the cognitive processes of explanation and prediction. The function of race in this case is not so much to see and hierarchize racialized traits but rather to attribute necessity or contingency in constructing our "pictures of the possible."[10]

Counterfactual thinking has long been a favorite tool in tort law and in the work of fashioning a remedy in law because of its presumed efficacy in isolating causes. The "determination of factual causation" proceeds through the "but-for" test: if *x* had not happened, then *y* would not have happened, thus establishing *x* as a salient and important cause for *y*. As Robert Strassfeld puts it, "Under this test, the defendant's conduct or defective product will only be described as a cause of the injury if, but for that conduct or product, the injury would not have occurred. The test instructs the factfinder to recreate an imaginative past, in which the factfinder eliminates the tortious act and plays out an alternative (counterfactual) history."[11] Counterfactuals are also used as a strategy by litigators to invest meaning in particular facts while ignoring or erasing others.[12] But tort law is not the only place where the counterfactual is used, nor are the filmic tropes of racial melodrama the only place where we see the racial counterfactual. Racial counterfactuals, in fact, have a long history in the rhetoric of racial equality and U.S. equal protection jurisprudence. As Stephen Best demonstrates, counterfactual thinking played a large role in the turn of the century response to the Fourteenth Amendment and in the ruling of *Plessy v. Ferguson*: "Counterfactuals clustered in an unprecedented way in late-nineteenth-century equal protection law. A certain density of counterfactual speculations intruded on constitutional law in response to the Fourteenth Amendment's mandate of 'equality.' Counterfactualism provided the doctrine of equal protection with its logical correlate, with that 'fuzzy logic' that enabled the courts to imagine a separate-but-equal (alternative and parallel) universe."[13] It seems as if the only way to imagine formal equality is to render it through the prism of counterfactualism. Why?

Best identifies counterfactualism as a strategy for preserving racial *inequality*. On the one hand, it can be used to weigh different circumstances in order to make sure that the principles of rights remain constant. On the other hand, in looking for and being guided by the constancy of a principle, it requires the "evacuation of historical consciousness."[14] It is in this way that counterfactualism, according to Best, "made an end run around history" and "improvised a detour around historical causes, around the 'event' of emancipation." Best writes, "The counterfactual's conditional rhetoric . . . flaunted the fictiveness of the law's constructs, and these assertions of fictiveness replaced a more forcefully analytical and pragmatic strategy with a speculative one, abdicating the law's reality principle (the pragmatic adjudication of injury) for an imaginary one to which all parties—and, constitutionally, all citizens—had finally to assent."[15] Here, Best analyzes the way in which black experience of the injury of segregation is replaced by the abstract principle of equality in a way that renders it exchangeable "on the basis of something similar."[16] This exchange effected by the counterfactual, according to Best, mirrors the exchange characteristic of commodification.

The use of the racial counterfactual for equal protection jurisprudence that Best clarifies lives on in the second half of the twentieth century and the twenty-first century most clearly in anti–affirmative action cases and the idea of "reverse racism" as it has been mediated through the law. Much like their counterparts in the late nineteenth and early twentieth century, the racial counterfactual facilitates a detour around historical causes and responsibility. In the late twentieth- and twenty-first-century moment, reverse discrimination lawsuits obviously have rested on an explicitly stated or implicit counterfactual: for example, the prosecution is suing on the basis that, if Alan Bakke were black, he would have gotten into UC-Davis Law School. As Obasogie argues, in *Bakke v. University of California Regents*, Justice Powell erases the context and history of injustice when he declares,

> The guarantees of the Fourteenth Amendment extend to all persons. Its language is explicit: "No State shall . . . deny to any person within its jurisdiction the equal protection of the laws." It is settled beyond question that the "rights created by the first section of the Fourteenth Amendment are, by its terms, guaranteed to the individual. The rights established are personal rights," Shelley v. Kraemer, supra, at 22. Accord, Missouri ex rel. Gaines v. Canada, supra, at 351; McCabe v. Atchison, T. & S. F. R. Co., 235 U.S. 151, 161–162 (1914). The guarantee of equal protection cannot mean one thing when applied to one individual and something else when applied to a person of another color. If both are not accorded the same protection, then it is not equal.[17]

The new descriptive statement here is one in which white persons can be black in order to be accorded the same considerations of potential injury and discrimination. As Stanley Fish writes regarding the idea of "reverse racism" and the equivalence of antiblack and antiwhite racism posited therein, "Only when the actions of the two groups are detached from the historical conditions of their emergence and given a purely abstract description can they be made interchangeable."[18] Patricia Williams takes note of the ahistorical reversal, cogently pointing out that "in the charged context of dismantling a system of favoritism that 'favored' whites and 'disfavored' blacks, the vocabulary of preference has been glibly reversed, so that now presumably it is blacks who are favored and whites who are automatically disfavored. The casual ahistoricism of this reversal implies a causal link between the inclusion of blacks and the oppression of whites."[19]

Racial counterfactuals, however, perform something beyond abstracting and dehistoricizing. They require the listener to agree with a set of conditions that are defined as relevant because of prediction. Best notices these "speculative" and "imaginary" assertions that put conditions into place to which "all parties . . . had finally to assent." Counterfactuals rely on the predictive force of lawlike connections that are used to isolate speculative scenarios as if they were causal facts. Racial counterfactuals in particular mobilize the projectability of race to produce these conditions. As quoted earlier from Goodman, but worth repeating here, "rather than the law being used for prediction because it describes the causal connection, the meaning of the causal connection is to be interpreted in terms of predictively used laws." One crucial aspect of the racial counterfactual, then, is regulating when and how race appears so as to shape narrative explanation. In the following, I turn first to a Supreme Court affirmative action case as one example where we can clearly see the use of the racial counterfactual that goes beyond abstracting or dehistoricizing. Using race as a connective principle, judicial doctrine codifies an alternate world in order to embed racism in this one. I then pursue these aspects of the racial counterfactual in the genre of alternate history, exploring the ways in which individual works both inhabit and contest these textual strategies of racial worldmaking.

In *Ricci v. Destefano* (2009), white and Hispanic firefighters filed a lawsuit against the City of New Haven. The city had administered a test to firefighters and it had a demonstrable disparate impact—a statistically disproportionate number of black firefighters did not meet the cutoff for promotion within the terms and weighting scheme of this test. This test was then thrown out because of its disparate impact and because of the fear of the potential for a disparate impact lawsuit to be filed under Title VII employment antidiscrimination law. This case is already structured by a counterfactual in multiple ways: the city threw out the test results because they thought that *if* they certified them, *then* they would be subject to a discrimination lawsuit from the affected black firefighters. They did not certify them, thus opening them up to a reverse discrimination suit under the Equal Protection Clause from the white and Hispanic firefighters. The majority opinion in the case sided with the white and Hispanic firefighters who, they argued, were personally injured by the city that threw away the results of this test.

Prominent throughout the oral argumentation is the use of counterfactuals, which assist the majority justices in making this argument by rendering antiwhite discrimination more salient and perceptible than antiblack discrimination. Whenever the minority opinion justices attempt to make distinctions within the use of race, Justice Roberts, Scalia, or Kennedy brings up a counterfactual. Justice Souter states, "But you make no distinction between race as an animating discriminating object on the one hand and race consciousness on the other."[20] For Souter and Ginsburg and others, there are appropriate and inappropriate uses of race: one can use it for remedy; one can use it, as in redistricting cases, for setting terms of political organization. Moreover, for Ginsburg, just because racism is unintentional does not mean that it does not exist. But Chief Justice Roberts responds to these distinctions *within* uses of race with a counterfactual: "So, can you assure me that the government's position would be the same if this test—black applicants—firefighters scored highest on this test in disproportionate numbers, and the City said we don't like that result, we think there should be more whites on the fire department, and so we're going to throw the test out? The government of United States would adopt the same position?"[21] This use of the racial reversal counterfactual is used to detach the question of race from an institutional history of racism that is linked to the evidence of disproportionate impact. It replaces the facts of the case with the new speculative scenario and creates a false symmetry. Roberts implies that within this new scenario, they would not adopt the same position, thus showing that the disparate impact criterion does not treat different groups equally.

But the use of this counterfactual does more cognitive work, for it shapes where and how racial discrimination is noticed and thereby what forms of racial discrimination are valued. Roberts goes on to draw out the conclusions of his counterfactual: "That's the part I don't understand. What you're saying is that the department can engage in intentional discrimination to avoid concern that they will be sued under disparate impact. Why doesn't it work the other way around as well? Why don't they say, well, we've got to tolerate the disparate impact because otherwise, if we took steps to avoid it, we would be sued for intentional discrimination?"[22] Note how in the stating of the counterfactual, intentional discrimination gets raised as the problem to be solved, not disparate impact. Roberts uses the counterfactual to render more salient one cause of harm (intentional discrimination against the white and Hispanic firefighters) than another (disparate impact that disproportionately affects black firefighters). In using the counterfactual, Roberts is not substituting white for black simply in order to argue for equal treatment. He produces another asymmetry, one in which intentional discrimination is always weighted more than disparate impact. Justice Scalia returns to Roberts's counterfactual in order to shape this perception even further: "if there had been a disproportionate number of minorities who—who passed the test—you would say that it's neutral to set that test aside? . . . *How you can call that race-neutral I—I do not know.*" Scalia here redefines "race-neutrality" based on the outcome of the racial counterfactual: if a disproportionate number of minorities do not pass the test, then the test is race-neutral; but if a disproportionate number of minorities pass the test, then it is not race-neutral. Because the racial counterfactual performs a reversal of positions, it is never used to imagine the conditions of harm against the black firefighters. Instead, it redescribes the city's actions as intentional discrimination against whites by shaping it as overt and as harming individuals.

Tired of these counterfactuals, Justice Ginsburg repeatedly states the need to get back to the facts: "What—what has New Haven done in fact?"[23] But what she does not quite acknowledge is that the potentiality of the counterfactual scenario has already taken the status of a fact that has shaped the perception of race in this case. Justice Scalia can now redescribe the "facts" of the case as a discriminatory action, proliferating the use of the word "racial" in order to accentuate the harm done: "As the facts of these cases illustrate, Title VII's disparate-impact provisions place a racial thumb on the scales, often requiring employers to evaluate the racial outcomes of their policies, and to make decisions based on (because of) those racial outcomes. That type of racial decisionmaking is, as the Court explains, discriminatory."[24] "Racial thumb," "racial outcomes, "racial decisionmaking": by locating race at the level of intentional discrimination on the part of the city, it is the Title VII laws, which were made to *prohibit* covert discrimination, that are all of the sudden responsible for *producing* racial discrimination—now redefined through the counterfactual as harm to white individuals. Counterfactuals make perceptible only one aspect of race—the instance of whites being treated unequally, not the instance of disparate impact as if the disparate impact is not itself evidence of inequality. Moreover, it singles out this aspect of race as a causal fact. Thus, a scenario can be conjured in which race appears everywhere *except* when it comes to the disparate impact on black populations.

As quoted above, the counterfactual "instructs the factfinder to recreate an imaginative past" and "play out an alternative (counterfactual) history."[25] In *Ricci v. Distefano*, the majority justices use the predictive knowledge of the counterfactual in order to construct a certain way of perceiving and weighing race—imagining intentional discrimination against white people as causal fact; constructing a false symmetry; rendering the disparate impact both invisible and virtually unimaginable. These modes of perception shaped by the counterfactual are taken as necessary givens from which to build a world and project a calculable outcome. The majority-opinion justices have played out their own alternate history. Worse still, they have made their alternate history into a legal reality with binding, meaningful effects.

This example shows the continuing force of the racial counterfactual in rendering certain uses of race projectable. In occupying a terrain that shows the powerful conjoined force of explanation and prediction on what we perceive as the "facts" of the world, the reasoning in the majority opinion of *Ricci v. Destefano* extends beyond legal doctrine. It permeates everyday imaginative acts. These legal developments from *Bakke v. University of California Regents* to the present have their counterparts in the alternate history genre. I do not mean to posit an analogy between the genre of alternate history and the domains of legal thinking. Rather, I point to a convergence in their textual and narrative strategies. The racial counterfactual with all its contortions, twists, and swaps of different kinds of potentiality marks one prominent site of what Han calls "law's inseparability from fantasy."[26] In this case, the inseparability of legal writing and alternate history reimagines a world, the coherence of which depends on antiblack racism. The question I pose to the genre of alternate history below, though, is this: can it be used to imagine otherwise?

The genre of alternate history not only gains its narrative impetus from the counterfactual, but it also often utilizes counterfactual thinking within multiple levels of its narrative discourse. Alternate histories are well known for exploring our modes of historical explanation, what constitutes our notions of causation, and how we determine the necessary conditions for any given event. Long distrusted as a useless thought-experiment by historians, alternate histories have recently been revalued as usefully exploring cutoff possibilities and probabilities in ways that teach us a great deal about what did happen: the relevant facts and conditions that went into a given event and the multiple modes of determination for an event.[27] I am less interested in using alternate histories to rethink historical determinism and more interested in the dynamics of how they generate narrative explanations. Because of the drive to represent something that might have happened but did not, alternate histories often contain a large amount of their narrative discourse in the mode of explanation—passages that "explain, motivate, or justify at least some of the events and situations represented and the mode of their representation."[28] Analyzing the nature and form of these explanations within the narrative discourse, we can learn a great deal about what is knowable, what is presumed to be known, and the "value of different kinds of explanation."[29] As such, alternate histories provide a rich array of strategies in exploring how certain predicates become projectable both backward as explanation and forward as prediction.

In the following, I analyze alternate histories of the U.S. Civil War, a prominently represented theme within the alternate history genre that obsessively rehearses the relationship between race and narrative explanation. Alternate histories of the Civil War—in particular, the imagination of inevitable and eventual emancipation despite the South winning the war—are often seen as ideological critiques of a historical past: an indictment of Reconstruction policies and of an emancipation that is done on Northern terms. But I show how the use of the racial counterfactual introduces a set of conditions for perceiving race that shapes narrative explanation. In this way, its ideological engagement is less with a critique of the historical past and more with constructing certain habits of perception for organizing racial meaning in the present and future. Analyzing their narrative dynamics and the multiple ways in which counterfactual thinking constructs certain ways of knowing I highlight the relationships between the domain of predictive explanatory frameworks and the salience and distribution of race across the narrative. The goal here is not to analyze racial representations as they appear in alternate histories and measure their ideological content. Rather, my argument demonstrates how these alternate histories are powerfully generative racial ways of knowing in their own right. But even as I critique the explanatory and predictive forms used to put into place certain futures, I remain alive to the possibility of using racial counterfactual scenarios to open up different forms of explanation and perception. Can the speculative imagination of the counterfactual actually imagine an alternate world?

Expectations of Emancipation

"What if the South had won the Civil War?" is one of the most popular questions within the alternate history genre.[30] Early examples include F. P. Williams's *Hallie Marshall: A True Daughter of the South* (1900) and Winston Churchill's essay, "If Lee Had Not Won the Battle of Gettysburg" (1931). But ever since Ward Moore's *Bring the Jubilee* (1953) and MacKinlay Kantor's *If the South Had Won the Civil War* (1960), this scenario has been both prominent and popular, ranging from the historical scholarship of Roger Ransom's *The Confederate States of America: What Might Have Been* (2005) to the detailed military analyses found in Peter Tsouras's collection, *Dixie Victorious: An Alternate History of the Civil War* (2004) and to the more imaginative departures of the best-selling writer Harry Turtledove. One of the main interests in imagining this scenario is speculating on the possible futures of slavery and race relations in the United States (or the Confederate States of America these works often posit) and using these possibilities to reflect on contemporary race relations and the historical explanations that undergird them. Interestingly though, prevalent in many Civil War counterfactual histories is the scenario in which emancipation would be voluntary and inevitable because of the progress of society. As Catherine Gallagher notes, "most counterfactualists have maintained our old-time faith that slavery was on the way out."[31] In Moore's *Bring the Jubilee*, the South abolishes slavery on its own after winning the war, but the narration focuses exclusively on the deteriorated conditions for white workers in the North, relegated as they are in this alternate history to indentured servitude and virtual unfreedom. In Kantor's *If the South Had Won the Civil War*, the South also abolishes slavery on its own and the grounds for improved race relations are forged through this more gradual emancipation.

Imagining an emancipation led by an independent South often serves to critique Reconstruction as a misguided policy with disastrous consequences for race relations.[32] But these alternate histories are doing more than just rehearsing a critique well known since historical romances such as Thomas Dixon's *The Leopard's Spots* (1902).[33] For Gallagher, what these alternate histories do is give probabilities "solidity" and construct a "different order of fact—the fact of a potential" that compels belief.[34] She concludes that these counterfactual histories have been successful in shaping the fact in her imagination that slavery is not a "lawful component of an advanced twenty-first-century industrial country, for such a narrative seems to me not only implausible but also untrue to what might have been."[35] However, such a narrative explanation relies not just on the "poetics" of counterfactual histories—statistical modeling, the continuity of character, a deep investment in enlarging the reader's sense of probability—but also on the projectability of racial conditions taken as givens from which to build the narrative world.

Geoffrey Hawthorn usefully describes two modes of reasoning used within alternate histories to open up probabilities and generate their alternative causal explanations. The first he calls "theoretical reasoning," which moves from descriptions of conditions and inductively constructs a set of generalizations. This mode focuses on events and conditions that are independent of human agency. The second he calls "practical reasoning," which opens up the possibilities resulting from the contingency of human deliberation. For example, Robert E. Lee changes his mind about an important decision, thus creating a new outcome. Hawthorn explains: "Practical reasoning is done by particular agents in the light of their particular experiences and the particular circumstances in which they find themselves. This is obviously so if they are reasoning from their desires or their conceptions of themselves. But it is also so if they are reasoning from generalities, from the rules which they take to govern a role or an office, for instance, or from some more abstract precept."[36] As we shall see below, race often plays a crucial role as ground or unstated given for both these processes of "theoretical" and "practical" reasoning.

For example, in *If the South Had Won the Civil War*, unquestioned racial conditions are part of the fabric of generating narrative explanations. In projecting the history of the Confederate States of America forward, Kantor imagines a conflict over the central and Midwest territories emerging between Texas, the United States, and the Confederate States. But he explains that a conflict between the "Texas Rangers" and Kansans was averted because "both parties, it turned out, had more to fear from Indian attack than from each other."[37] Significantly, there is little mention of Native populations before this moment in the narrative: the major agents in the story are the national entities of the Confederate States and the United States. The "Indian attack" appears as an external factor in the world that is posited as a given. It is easily projected as a predictive rule, namely that an "Indian attack" is always more dangerous than another kind of conflict. This assumption of racial dynamics is used to gain readerly assent to the counterfactual. Similarly, in Peter Tsouras's "Confederate Black and Grey" and Harry Turtledove's *Guns of the South* (1992), we can see how certain ways of noticing race produce the predictive knowledge that is at the heart of the alternate history genre. Both, moreover, prompt us to notice race via racial counterfactuals.

Tsouras imagines that if the Confederate army had conscripted slave soldiers in early 1864 and immediately freed them (as opposed to what actually happened, which is they were enrolled in the army with no guarantee of freedom in 1865), the South would have won and universal emancipation would have followed. Tsouras's alternate history hinges on a counterfactual: it presumes as given the idea that "as between the loss of independence and the loss of slavery, we assume that every patriot will freely give up the latter—give up the negro slaves rather than be a slave himself."[38] This statement introduces a set of conditions for perceiving the difference that race makes. It places on the same level the potentiality of white people to become slaves with the actuality of "negro" slaves. In this sense, it makes their statuses symmetrical—both white slave owner and slave have the same relationship to the concepts of freedom and slavery. The racial dynamics of the master-slave relationship are taken out of the equation when inhabiting the narrative logics of this counterfactual scenario. It is a given not only that slaves would fight for their freedom when given the chance, but that even if the South won, the masters would free them upon seeing their valor on the battlefield. Using the fact of a potential—the freeing of conscripted slaves—this counterfactual history creates an equivalence between white and black subjects when it comes to the choice between freedom and slavery. Producing a logic of formal symmetry with respect to the conditions of slavery and freedom abstracts these concepts from particularities and places them into a probable sequence: as a matter of pure choice, who wouldn't fight for freedom and keep from being enslaved?

Turtledove's *Guns of the South* imagines a group of time-traveling South Africans arming the Confederacy with AK-47s as a way to win the Civil War. Ultimately, the new Confederate States of America have to put down the South African group whose antiblack sentiments exceed even their own. This time-travel twist juxtaposes South African Afrikaaner sentiments against the attitudes of U.S. Southerners in order to generate the lawlike predictive force of progress. Once it is revealed that the opinions and attitudes of the Afrikaaners, who are more brutal and hateful to blacks than anyone else in the novel, are those of a retrograde minority of the future world, the on-the-ground perspectives of U.S. Southerners look like they are on the way out. This fact of a potential—the outmodedness of slavery—leads to a narrative based around the Southern, voluntary emancipation of the slaves. These kinds of explanations take on value and generate the expectations for this world: a slow, steady, gradual lifting of former slaves. But *Guns of the South* further embeds certain ways of perceiving race within the practical reasoning of its characters in light of their particular experiences and circumstances. The narrative relies on the racial counterfactual in order to move from the contingencies of individual desires to general descriptions that are taken as necessary givens.

For example, a conversation between Robert E. Lee and his house slave, Julia, becomes a meditation on freedom. He asks her if she "ever thought she would like to be free" and "what she would do if she were free." When Julia responds to his question with "'Wouldn't mind findin' out what free was like,'" Robert E. Lee says, "I thought as much," and then the narrator extends Lee's thoughts with a counterfactual: "It was the answer Lee would have given, were he in Julia's shoes; it was, he thought, the answer anyone with spirit, black or white, man or woman, would give.'"[39] This counterfactual conditional at the end of the dialogue converts Julia's practical reasoning from her own desires and circumstances ("Wouldn't mind findin' out what free was like") into a form of practical reasoning from general descriptions ("it was . . . the answer anyone with spirit, black or white, man or woman, would give"). The world of slavery is rendered continuous with the imagination of a world in which emancipation is a reality via this general description of feeling rather than via Julia's desires. Moreover, the projection of freedom forward takes Julia's immediate conditions of labor as the given from which to calculate outcomes. When Lee's wife protests the freeing of Julia—saying, "but who shall care for me if Julia is set at liberty?"—Robert Lee responds, "I *expect* she will, but for wages."[40] Emancipation is imaginable *only* through the twists and turns of the racial counterfactual, one that uses Lee's generalized feelings toward freedom to interpret the meaning of the causal connection.

Alternative Alternate Histories

Drawing on the distinction the anonymous collective called "uncertain commons" makes between speculative practices that foreclose potentiality (firmative speculation) and those that engage a radical uncertainty (affirmative speculation), we could categorize Tsouras's and Turtledove's alternate histories as exemplifying the former. Firmative speculation is defined by uncertain commons as a speculative mode that "seeks to pin down, delimit, constrain, and enclose—to make things definitive, firm," while affirmative speculation is a mode that "embraces uncertainty and, in so doing, remains responsive to difference, to unanticipated contingencies."[41] In both Tsouras and Turtledove we are instructed to assent to a set of racial givens that allows the narrative to arrive at a lawlike predictive rule (as a matter of pure choice, who wouldn't fight for freedom and keep from being enslaved, and who wouldn't mind knowing what freedom was like?) In doing so, the predictive knowledge that they generate is used to render the possibilities of change into a calculable outcome, establishing the terms of emancipation within well-worn pathways of racial *in*equality. By contrast, Terry Bisson's *Fire on the Mountain* (1988) and Steven Barnes's *Lion's Blood: An Alternate History of Slavery and Freedom* (2002) are examples of alternate histories that "embrace uncertainty" by not taking emancipation as an inevitable given.

Both of these novels move beyond the event horizon of the U.S. Civil War as such. *Fire on the Mountain* speculates on what would have happened if John Brown's raid on Harper's Ferry had been successful, imagining a completely reconfigured world in which socialism is dominant.[42] *Lion's Blood* reimagines a world in which Islamic empires are dominant, Africans are the slaveholders, and white peoples are the slaves. It is set in what we know as the U.S. South but what in the world of the novel is a colony called "New Alexandria," and while there is an imminent war that structurally parallels the U.S. Civil War, emancipation is not an expected given that follows naturally from the war. Alternate histories such as these are often not given as much value when it comes to knowledge formation because of their more speculative, improbable nature. Hawthorn, Gallagher, and Niall Ferguson all emphasize the importance of exploring only *probable* conditions and outcomes in arguing for the cognitive work that the alternate history does as a genre.[43] But instead of *assuming* what counts as probable, for me the more "affirmative" speculation of these works lies in engaging precisely those limits of what is thought to be probable, especially the particular role of racial meanings in this determination. Both works use the racial counterfactual but avoid Best's critiques of the pure "exchangeability" often created by them. They do so because they exploit precisely that which makes the racial counterfactual such an effective narrative strategy: the relationship between race and predictive laws. By relocating race in ways that generate other kinds of predictive laws, these works can embed antiracism into our modes of explanation and thus question the logical connections between race and the inevitability of emancipation. I will give a brief example from Bisson's novel before taking a more extended look at *Lion's Blood*.

Several times in *Fire on the Mountain*, characters contemplate what would have happened if John Brown's raid were *not* successful from the perspective of a world in which the raid *was* successful. In these instances, Bisson engages the counterfactual in order to undermine the probabilistic evaluations that did occur in a world in which Brown's raid was unsuccessful. For example, Bisson reconstructs the speech Frederick Douglass made at Tremont Temple regarding John Brown, only in this alternate world it is spoken in relation to the fact of Brown's *success*. In this fictional speech, however, Douglass reflects on what might have happened if Brown had not succeeded, thus incorporating in our mind real-world historical valuations into the speech: "Think for a moment. What if John Brown had failed? . . . Oh, many a grand speech would then be made! Oh, what fiery denunciations of Virginia's cruelties we would then applaud! Brown and Tubman would be heroes and martyrs."[44]

This construction of Brown as hero and martyr is, of course, largely what happened during the time between his capture and his hanging.[45]

This construction is itself made possible through what Douglass in the speech calls the "familiar factors: the sullen slave owner, the fervent abolitionist, the wavering federal government, the slave groaning under his oppression."[46] This picture of the actors relies on using race to generate some general laws of the situation—the weak and helpless slave to be helped by the abolitionist or hurt by the exploitative forces of the slave owner. According to this narrative explanation, Brown as martyr furthers emancipation because of the way it divided North and South even more. But what Brown's victory in Bisson's alternate history adds is a "new factor," a new formal historical structure built around an "army of abolitionists, black and white; and already, freed African slaves, the heirs of old Nat Turner."[47] Such a "factor" shifts racial perceptions and thereby the possibilities of racial organization: instead of white abolitionists struggling on behalf of slaves, we have "black and white" fighting side by side; instead of the opposition between "slave" and "freedmen" we have slave and "freed African slaves" together. As such, the story creates the grounds for shaping narrative explanations around a different set of racial potentialities, in particular a history of black slave revolts. The counterfactual here is imaginatively used to reconfigure dominant status quo notions of race and the way in which they are embedded into our imagination of what we think will happen.

Near the end of the novel, Bisson engages another moment of contemplating our own world from the perspective of the alternate history. Two characters discuss the book, *John Brown's Body*, which refers to a real book in our world, the epic poem written by Stephen Vincent Benét. As the characters discuss the history presented in *John Brown's Body*, they redescribe our own history in a way that highlights how race is embedded into expectations of temporal progression:

> "The Mericans wipe out the buffalo, string the country together with railroads and barbwire; annihilate, not just defeat, the Sioux, the Crow, the Cheyenne. . . . Settlers run the Mexicans out of California and Texas, or turn them into serfs, and move north to Alaska and south into the Caribbean, eventually seizing the entire continent . . ."
>
> "Gross," says Harriet.
>
> "Ridiculous!" said Yasmin. "The author would have all of history hanging on one strand of rope with poor old Captain Brown."
>
> "Oh, I agree," Grissom said. "It's a white nationalist fantasy, and somewhat overdone. But you must admit, *John Brown's Body* gives food for thought. What if the war had been started not by the abolitionists

> but by the slave owners? . . . What if the war had been fought to hold this nation together, instead of to free yours?'[48]

As Grissom says, "it's a white nationalist fantasy" built on "one strand," but it uncannily describes our own historical and narrative explanations of so-called progress. The technique of engaging the history of our world from the point of view of the alternate world is one that is repeated both in Barnes as well as in Philip K. Dick. Here, such a technique invites readers to take a look at the racist assumptions taken for granted in our storytelling. It defamiliarizes our own history by highlighting the way using race as a predictive law often rationalizes the current world. *Builds* the world would be better, though, because reason has nothing to do with it.

Like Bisson, Barnes uses the counterfactual more "affirmatively." He highlights uncertainties within the counterfactual scenarios in order to reshape the "firm," probable narrative explanations that imagine racial difference in a certain way. For example, Barnes uses the exact same scenario as Tsouras does, imagining a sequence in which the slave owners conscript slaves into fighting and giving them their freedom. In Tsouras, this scenario posits as a given that white people will give up slavery in order to ensure their independence. In Barnes's novel, the counterfactual becomes the occasion to highlight the uncertainties of slave life—the disposability of slaves in relation to the master. This condition, factored out of Tsouras's reasoning, reshapes the relationship between race and narrative explanation. Instead of using one's probable desire for freedom in order to create an equivalence between masters and slaves, Barnes foregrounds the master-slave relationship as the determining factor in what is probable or not. What happens is that the masters train the slaves in ways that ensure their extermination: "The masters are deliberately leaving a vulnerability, for fear that their servants will rise against them. Of course. Dar Kush's had been but a small uprising. There had been a few larger ones, smashed so viciously that slaves were afraid even to dream of freedom for years to come. But in their hearts, the masters knew that men were men."[49] Barnes points to the unequal circumstances of master and slave in order to change the imagination of what is probable. If Tsouras and Turtledove use the inevitability of emancipation in order to organize racial meaning, Barnes uses the master-slave relationship as the predictively used law in order to generate a different sense of how race is used to shape what might happen.

Throughout *Lion's Blood*, Barnes cleverly uses the counterfactual and the way in which it creates a scenario of formal symmetry only to undermine it, showing us the limits of this horizon of expectations for organizing our narrative explanations. For example, the whole novel is an imagination of a reversal—white people are slaves and black people are the slave owners. But rather than use this scenario to create a formal symmetry by which all people are potentially subject to slavery, Barnes uses his reversed descriptions of white slaves and black slave owners in order to give a deeper contextualization of race. In Turtledove and Tsouras, racialized descriptions are rarely present. Little descriptive attention is given to Julia in *Guns of the South*, for example, since any heightened attention to her physical characteristics might seem like drawing more pointed attention to her blackness. Instead, as we saw above, she is taken more in terms of the counterfactual substitution in order to generate a "picture of the possible" when it comes to imagining emancipation. In this way, any valuations of race are embedded into the more abstract argument about slaves' desire for freedom. Barnes, however, does not shy away from racialized descriptions in the same way, rendering either physical characteristics and/or racial categories salient in a variety of ways: "Father and son were sculpted from the same clay: blazing golden hair, crystal blue eyes, clean angled profiles"; the slaveholders and slave traders are first designated as "soot-men," and then as "black men" or "black-skinned" (3). The racism of subjective perceptions is used persistently in these opening pages in order to mark the captors from the captive. Instead of the perception of exchangeability often formed in the racial counterfactual, Barnes foregrounds racist perceptions in order to show how they shape narrative explanations.[50]

For example, the novel is alternately focused through the perceptual experience of a white slave named Aidan and a black slave owner named Kai, switching back and forth between them. Early in the novel, the reader gets a description focalized through Aidan of the black slave owners and slave traders using racist descriptions that are familiar to us not from the alternate world but from our experiential world: "Immediately Aidan and his family were surrounded by black-skinned men, creatures so strange they made the Northmen seem like cousins. And at this range, he could clearly see that they were men, though with dark eyes, thick lips, and blunt noses" (28). The use of racist descriptions that obtain even though the positions are reversed interrupts the counterfactual scenario, reminding readers of the dangers of purely abstracting the terms of slave and slave owner apart from their particular formations. The description above continues: "They did not smell like men, but of flowers and fruit, as if they did not sweat, or perhaps exuded nectar. They smelled like husband-seeking girls at Festival. Such skin! . . . And such clothing! . . . Never had he seen such wealth" (28). Here, conventionally racist associations about smell and skin are revalued within a landscape of social judgments that at first mirror homophobic discourse's feminization of the men and then makes distinctions based on class and money. In this narrativization of the counterfactual paradigm—if white people were slaves and black people were slave owners—Barnes does not simply perform a reversal to show how "anybody" can be a slave and "anybody" with power acts in certain ways. In a "pure" reversal, the white people would be the racialized others while the black people would be the unmarked subjects. The heightened attention to racial descriptions and the strategic use of racist language and homophobic discourse from *our* experiential world interrupts the reader's capacity to merely inhabit Aidan's perspective as the victimized other in this world. These descriptions make it difficult for the reader to rely on a horizon of expectation based in symmetry, substitution, and reversibility.[51]

One further narrative strategy that Barnes uses to avoid the symmetry of inversion diagnosed by Best is "variable focalization,"[52] where the narrative essentially shifts the focal point from which it views the world. The focalization of the narrative from Aidan's point of view shifts in the next part to a focalization of the narrative through Kai. In Aidan's focalization, we are given his racist language, which evokes conventional antiblack racism in the United States. At the same time we are made to feel sympathy for his position as a white person captive. In Kai's focalization, we are given a more nuanced discussion and understanding of black people without the conventional U.S. racism. At the same time, he expresses the excuses and rationales for slavery familiar to us from nineteenth-century pro-slavery tracts. "Variable focalization" can be thought of as a corrective to the abstract, predictive law often instituted through the racial counterfactual. In *Lion's Blood*, it is a narrative technique used to show not the "fuller" knowledge gained from reversing positions, but the blind spots.

For example, the first shift in the novel from Aidan's to Kai's focalization marks an ellipsis, a chronological gap in the plot. Kai sees Aidan and his mother Deidre working in the kitchen, but missing is any account of Aidan and Deidre's introduction to their new surroundings and status as slaves at Dar Kush. While the previous section focalized through Aidan tells of their capture from their homeland, our next encounter with Aidan and Deidre is focalized through Kai at a moment when they have already been placed as slaves:

> He spied a new woman and boy who looked to be mother and son, the woman red-haired, the boy's yellow as the sun. The woman's smile was shy if tired, but the boy seemed less happy. Why? Kai wondered. It *had*

> to be fun to work in the kitchen. Kai wished he could spend time there, stealing *fufu* grits and slices of *bobotie* meat loaf, sharing song with the others. A servant's life was good, an easier, simpler, one than that demanded of the noble class, full of obligations and choices . . . The servants were lucky. (66)

The reader figures out that the two new slaves are the characters with whom we are already acquainted, Aidan and Deidre. But the world as focalized through Kai's perspective does not see the history of these individuals. In fact, the reader's knowledge of this history only accentuates that which Kai's perspective does not have—the conditions of their arrival. He just sees them as servants in his kitchen, and his main context for understanding them is the kitchen, which is, in his mind, a fun place. The chronological gap is filled later on in the narrative. When the narrative shifts back to Aidan's focalization, and only after Aidan and Kai become friends, Aidan thinks back to his arrival at Dar Kush, thus giving the reader the missing information. The term for this technique is the completing analepsis: a return to fill in an earlier gap in the narrative. Here, it is used to reinterpret Kai's initial observations: "If he [Aidan] hadn't found a way to catch Kai's eye, he feared he might have been unhinged by the mind-numbing combination of boredom and fatigue" (87). We learn that the meeting with Kai and their friendship is partially a product of Aidan's own initiative and stratagems. Kai notices Aidan in the kitchen in the first place not just because he is asserting the power of his gaze over his slaves but also because *Aidan wanted to be noticed.* Through this technique, we follow the limitations of characters' knowledge, the blind spots, that make their narrative understandings rational and reasonable to themselves.

The reasonableness of narrative explanations relies on the predictive knowledge of race. This can be seen when Barnes further inhabits the logic of racial counterfactuals at the level of his characters' practical reasoning. Kai and Aidan engage in counterfactual scenarios as they repeatedly imagine what each one would do if they were in the position of the other. For example, Kai says to Aidan, "If you really knew [what my life is like], you'd be happy to be white. An' a slave. When the Aztecs come, you don't have to go off and fight an' die. Oh, no—you have strong black arms to protec' you" (150). In having Kai the slave owner use the counterfactual in order to justify slavery, Barnes highlights the blind spots of this imagination of reversal and the way in which it can be used to mask the inequalities and asymmetries of master and slave. As Barnes demonstrates in further uses of the counterfactual, these imaginings invariably do not place them in a relationship of symmetry but rather foreground the particularity of their positions, the fact that they do live in different worlds that ultimately cannot be traversed by the counterfactual.

One particular subplot hinges on these forms of counterfactual reasoning. Kai takes a mistress named Sophia, but Aidan and Sophia eventually fall in love. Both Kai and Aidan engage in counterfactual reasoning in order to think through their ethical obligations. Aidan imagines:

> And if he was, if Kai *was* his friend, and a man of honor, then what had Aidan done? He ground his fist against his temples as his heartbeat slowed, the adrenaline fading. No! He had done nothing wrong! This was madness! He was a man who had been torn from his home, his father killed, sister sold away and mother destroyed, that Kai's family might profit by his misery. And after long years he had found love. If Kai was worthy of friendship, then on some level he had to understand that. But if he was . . . If he wasn't . . . (233)

The counterfactual is used here to come up with a basic description of the world—a world in which Kai is his friend. But the very uncertainty of the counterfactual here—"if he was . . . If he wasn't"—calls attention to the shaping of the facts of the world and thereby the shaping of the grounds on which judgments of right or wrong are made. Similarly, Kai engages in his own kind of reasoning based in counterfactuals: "Kai remembered Sophia's touch, her lips, her whispers in the dark, thought of the peace he had experienced in her arms and knew that in another world, a different world, he could have found contentment there. . . . But he could never treat her as an equal, never really join with her in the eyes of men, let alone the sight of Allah. And if not, what was he thinking? Just how selfish was he?" (237). Kai had hitherto used the counterfactual—if Sophia were not a slave—in order to justify his sexual use of her as a benevolent, loving one. But far from using the counterfactual to demonstrate the same principles as they apply to different people (as it is used in legal cases and other alternate histories as we have seen), Barnes uses it to show the unbridgeable gap between peoples and the exploitative fantasies and illusions that it engenders. The institution of slavery as it is portrayed here is built on the illusion of the counterfactual—if Kai were his friend; if Sophia were a lover and not a slave—in order to reconcile differences in position and structure inequality. Barnes ultimately narrates the failure of the counterfactual to bridge that distance: "You have your world. I have mine" (237).

When Aidan and Kai take up arms together and imagine what might happen should they win a pivotal battle, Barnes uses the counterfactual again to demonstrate the unequal circumstances and consequences of the same event for them:

> "Yes. If we . . . if you live tomorrow, you are free."
> "And if you live, Kai—what do you win?"
> He thought for a time. "A chance to go home," he said finally. (382)

Instead of suggesting, as Tsouras does, that when white and black men take up arms they are fighting for the same thing (freedom), the uncertainty of Kai's answer pushes the counterfactual to consider how the question of freedom *for whom* becomes a real factor in measuring the desirability of an action. If Tsouras uses general descriptions of the absolute desirability of freedom in order to give "solidity" to his narrative probabilities, Barnes shows the way in which what counts as "probable" produces conditions that limit the general descriptions themselves. In this sense, he uses the counterfactual to embrace uncertainty in the service of reshaping the grounds of our narrative explanations.

So far the racial counterfactual has been understood as a crucial mode of antiblack worldmaking in both legal reasoning and alternate history. It is a narrative strategy that facilitates the logics of causality and abstract principles of symmetry and equality in ways that structure the pathways of racial *inequality*. Its effectiveness in reproducing antiblack racism is seen in its ability to convince readers of particular horizons of expectation when it comes to the history of emancipation. At the same time, Barnes and Bisson push the limits of counterfactual imagining by displacing the kernel that holds together the continuity of antiblack violence from the Civil War through civil rights—the predictive law of an inevitable emancipation. I now move from alternate histories of the U.S. Civil War to alternate histories of World War II, another scenario that has been crucial to racial jurisprudence, in particular via the testing of the constitutionality of Japanese internment in *Korematsu v. United States* (1944).

CHAPTER 8

Alternate Histories of World War II; or, How the Race Concept Organizes the World

The attractiveness of scenarios of war for alternate history writers is not surprising: war as a historical object raises all kinds of contingencies, necessities, possible explanations, and unusual circumstances. The scenarios of the U.S. Civil War and World War II, however, raise in particular the issue of racial organization at national and global levels. Both scenarios are deeply implicated in reimagining the place and significance of racial organization in the making of the modern world and of future worlds. As Eric Porter writes in the context of analyzing W. E. B. Du Bois's late writings, "World War II . . . presents a test case for the race concept as both a signifier of a racialized social order and a conceptual framework for understanding how the world operates, in part through the practice of war. . . . The new imperial order throws down the gauntlet to the racisms of fascism and old colonialisms, but it is also predicated on a continuation of a series of racial exclusions, precisely through its refusal to recognize the extent to which the race concept organizes the world."[1] This "refusal to recognize the extent to which the race concept organizes the world" is operative across legal writing and alternate histories. This language of refusal structures how and when race signifies and how we are made to participate in this world organization. From the ongoing refusals of Reconstruction through World War II, we see both continuities and discontinuities between the scenarios of antiblack and anti-Japanese racism. Together they display a set of narrative strategies that have shaped legal doctrine and the "common sense" built into a "racialized social order."

Alternate histories of World War II provide another dimension to the relationship between racial counterfactualism and the structure of racial organization explored in the previous chapter: the development of racial distinction as a sign such that it indexes the certainty, coherence, and continuity of the world. In this chapter, I return to equal protection jurisprudence, in particular *Korematsu v. United States*, in order to first locate the shifts in how racial distinction becomes a sign and how it is rendered meaningful. I then analyze alternate histories of World War II in order to show how racism gets embedded in ways that ensure the immediacy of a given experience in time and space. In short, how we have come to participate in worlds built through racial distinction.

Strict Scrutiny

I return to equal protection jurisprudence because of the powerful effect its mechanisms have had on creating race as a particular kind of perceptual object. In the aftermath of the Civil Rights Act of 1964 and the Equal Employment Opportunity Act of 1972, as well as the various court cases that put into motion institutional mechanisms around antidiscrimination law,[2] a legal vocabulary developed in order to categorize, measure, locate, and define race and racism. As we saw from Part III, Gary Becker and other economists helped develop the vocabulary and methodology in ways that both narrowed the measuring sticks for racism and embedded race into our mechanisms for calculating outcomes and value. A similar process, arguably influenced by Becker's methodology, occurred in legal vocabulary as well.[3] *De jure racism, de facto racism, disparate impact, disparate treatment, strict scrutiny.* These terms shaped how racism as it occurred in the social world was to be addressed legally. In doing so, they also shaped when and how race was noticed.

As Imani Perry writes, "In U.S. race talk, we generally define racism as comprising two components: intentionality and determinism. More specifically, racism requires both the intent to disadvantage someone on the basis of race and the belief that a person must necessarily be a particular way or have particular characteristics because he or she belongs to a specific racial group. Likewise, in constitutional law, with the exception of the employment discrimination context, in order to prevail, one must show intent to establish racial discrimination."[4] Additionally, "in constitutional law, courts fixate on a concept of equality that depends upon treating 'like' in 'like' fashion, that is, treating person A in the same fashion as person B, irrespective of differences in race or national origin . . .. Federal courts have not completely abandoned the idea that remediation of cultural and institutional practices of discrimination is lawful, but they are seen as barely legitimate departures from the principle of equality."[5] What Perry is referring to here is "strict scrutiny," the high standard with which any law that departs from this principle of treating "like" in "like" fashion must meet in order to be lawful. These two descriptions shape what counts as legally actionable racism, narrowly defining it in terms of intent and making it extremely hard for any action that does not conform to their notion of equality to be lawful.

The language and doctrinal significance of "strict scrutiny" for racial jurisprudence takes a decisive turn and development in *Korematsu v. United States* (1944). Han writes that *Korematsu* "affirms formally for the first time the strict judicial review of racially discriminatory policy."[6] Obasogie writes, "*Korematsu* established the now familiar constitutional structure whereby courts deploy strict scrutiny—where a law must be narrowly tailored to serve a compelling government interest—to laws implicating race, national origin, and alienage." He further notes, "Ironically, this first articulation of what is now known as strict scrutiny nonetheless led the Court to uphold the executive order allowing the internment of Japanese Americans."[7] Indeed, the court first decided that the law must be "narrowly tailored to serve a compelling government interest" when it considered the constitutionality of Executive Order No. 34 of the Commanding General of the Western Command, U.S. Army, which directed that after May 9, 1942, all persons of Japanese ancestry should be excluded from a specific area. The court determined that these executive orders were constitutional because they met the criteria of a compelling governmental interest—namely, wartime security. As I analyze below, the form of the explanation upholding the executive order depended on a constellation of ways of seeing put into place by strict scrutiny.

When strict scrutiny is imposed, it already manages the perception of race into an equation between the targeting of racial characteristics in the law and the statutory purpose of the law. In his defense that the purpose of the Executive Order has nothing to do with merely targeting racial characteristics for unequal treatment, Justice Black delivers the majority opinion, making clear demarcations between a purpose described as nonracial and a very narrow notion of racial antagonism: "It should be noted, to begin with, that all legal restrictions which curtail the civil rights of a single racial group are immediately suspect. That is not to say that all such restrictions are unconstitutional. It is to say that courts must subject them to the most rigid scrutiny. Pressing public necessity may sometimes justify the existence of such restrictions; racial antagonism never can."[8]

The method of looking for a narrowly tailored purpose produces this strict division between what is "racial" and what is "nonracial." I will quote a large portion of Black's opinion in order for us to see the syntactical movement of the ruling and the modes of racial attribution that it puts in place. Justice Black writes in his opinion:

> It is said that we are dealing here with the case of imprisonment of a citizen in a concentration camp solely because of his ancestry, without evidence or inquiry concerning his loyalty and good disposition towards the United States. Our task would be simple, our duty clear, were this a case involving the imprisonment of a loyal citizen in a concentration camp because of racial prejudice. Regardless of the true nature of the assembly and relocation centers—and we deem it unjustifiable to call them concentration camps with all the ugly connotations that term implies—we are dealing specifically with nothing but an exclusion order. To cast this case into outlines of racial prejudice, without reference to the real military dangers which were presented, merely confuses the issue. Korematsu was not excluded from the Military Area because of hostility to him or his race. He *was* excluded because we are at war with the Japanese Empire, because the properly constituted military authorities feared an invasion of our West Coast and felt constrained to take proper security measures, because they decided that the military urgency of the situation demanded that all citizens of Japanese ancestry be segregated from the West Coast temporarily, and finally, because Congress, reposing its confidence in this time of war in our military leaders—as inevitably it must—determined that they should have the power to do just this. There was evidence of disloyalty on the part of some, the military authorities considered that the need for action was great, and time was short. We cannot—by availing ourselves of the calm perspective of hindsight—now say that at that time these actions were unjustified.[9]

In Justice Black's written opinion, he is at pains to distinguish between a racial purpose and a nonracial purpose. Because "racial purpose" is narrowly defined as racial prejudice, it is carefully sectioned off from "nonracial" purposes, as if the *only* racial purpose is racial animus or prejudice, as if there could not possibly be a link or relation between racial restrictions (the targeting of racial minorities) and "nonracial" purposes (at least in the descriptive sense), namely, the protection of property and well-being for peoples living on the West Coast and in the United States. Since "West Coast" and "United States" are entities to which one does not ordinarily affix race as a qualifying descriptor, Justice Black can redescribe the purpose of the statute in nonracial terms even as the possessive pronoun "*our* West Coast" belies the interest in protecting peoples defined in opposition to citizens of Japanese ancestry. The narrowing of racial referentiality in the sense of describing a law that "targets" racial minorities simultaneously allows for and even constructs the grounds for the displacing of racial purpose into another set of narrative logics.

In replacing the "outlines of racial prejudice" with the "time of war," Black makes sure that the temporality of war becomes the main framework for understanding the sequence of events. Notice the verb tenses in Black's opinion: "the real military dangers which were presented" (past participle); "we are at war with the Japanese Empire" (present); "feared an invasion of our West Coast" (projected future); "we cannot now say that . . . at that time" (eliminating everything except the immediate present of the war). Justice Black continually leaves out what Peter Brooks calls the "occluded middle"—the "middle ground and middle condition"[10]—namely, the never resolved question of the relationship between the "Japanese Empire" and U.S. citizens of Japanese ancestry. Instead, Justice Black moves back and forth between the imaginatively far and the temporally near: we are at war with the Japanese empire and there was *imminent* danger on the West Coast. The occluded middle includes everything from the actual determination of loyalty or nonloyalty to the question of race to the actual determination of an imminent threat or danger.

This occlusion is all the more evident when we see the reliance on evidence of what happened after the internment in order to support the internment itself, even though the strict scrutiny process is all about statutory purpose. In this regard, Black's use of what Freud calls "kettle logic" is striking. Freud describes "kettle logic" as part of the defensive logics of dream-work in which "there is accordingly no such thing as an 'either-or,' only a simultaneous juxtaposition" of terms.[11] Justice Black states, "There was evidence of disloyalty on the part of some, the military authorities considered that the need for action was great, and time was short."[12] Each of these statements concatenated together are not so much contradictory as they are in Freud's kettle-logic joke as they place side-by-side reasons from distinct moments in time as if they were all known and well established at the moment of the implementation of the executive order. There is a temporal obfuscation here: the consideration of the need for action is clearly not based on the evidence of disloyalty, since that was only collected after the executive orders were issued. "There was evidence of disloyalty on the part of some" takes the point of view of the future after the internment. "The military authorities considered that the need for action was great" takes the point of view of a time leading up to the exclusion order. "Time was short" takes the point of view of the time of war, a kind of ever-present condition. The "both-and" logic of adding up these statements produces a time in which all these conditions are present at the same time, embedding race into the meaning of the sequence.

In this sense, strict scrutiny is formative of the decision in that it frames a targeting-equals-purpose temporality that excludes the middle ground from consideration, a middle ground occupied by the projected relationship between race and war. Each of the dissenting opinions points to this "excluded middle" in different ways. The dissent from Justice Roberts puts the events in chronological order, suggesting that there was no way that Korematsu could possibly abide by the mutually exclusive terms of the executive orders: "A chronological recitation of events will make it plain that the petitioner's supposed offense did not, in truth, consist in his refusal voluntarily to leave the area which included his home in obedience to the order excluding him therefrom. Critical attention must be given to the dates and sequence of events."[13] Justice Murphy dissents, saying, "Yet no reasonable relation to an 'immediate, imminent, and impending' public danger is evident to support this racial restriction which is one of the most sweeping and complete deprivations of constitutional rights in the history of this nation in the absence of martial law."[14] Both of these dissenting opinions question the understanding of sequence and what-comes-after that frames the causal force of the affirming opinion.

In her discussion of *Korematsu*, Sora Han writes that "strict scrutiny, as a matter of its logical structure, is more worried about nation than race."[15] She identifies in the opinions the establishment of a conditional relationship between nation and race: "if one, then not the other," if there is national interest, then it cannot be an interest implicated with racial animus. I would add that within this conditional logic, the linguistic field of racial meaning is being shifted. The meaning of race is narrowed to solely racial animus or prejudice at the same time that its capacity to index a situation is expanded. As we saw in the opinion, even as the racial language is deemed illegitimate, the use of the implied counterfactual—if Japan invades America—expands the meanings of race so that it exceeds the parameters set out by strict scrutiny. As soon as the question of race is embedded within a spatio-temporal continuity—if Japan invades America, then we need to incarcerate all persons of Japanese ancestry—the projection of race across the past and future has replaced any analysis of racial determination in the "present." One can also say here that race has become ever present across these multiple temporalities: "There was evidence of disloyalty on the part of some, the military authorities considered that the need for action was great, and time was short."

"Strict scrutiny" as it is applied in *Korematsu*, then, might be said to facilitate a shift from one register of perception to another. This register is best understood in terms of what Charles Peirce calls the "index" or "indications." In "What Is a Sign," Peirce writes of this category of sign: "secondly, there are *indications*, or indices; which show something about things, on account of their being physically connected with them."[16] Indices are connected to the objects that they signify through some correspondence in fact, some physical, actual, or imagined causal connection. As Peirce goes on to clarify,

> To identify an object, we generally state its place at a stated time; and in every case must show how an experience of it can be connected with the previous experience of the hearer. To state a time, we must reckon from a known epoch. . . . When we say the epoch must be known, we mean it must be connected with the hearer's experience. . . . So no place can be described, except relatively to some known place; and the unit of distance used must be defined by reference to some bar or other object which people can actually use directly or indirectly in measurement.[17]

The index, according to Peirce, produces a correlation in a specific space and time in order to produce meaningfulness. It is distinguished from two other categories of sign—the icon and the symbol. Examples of icons are portraits—representations that are supposed to be connected to their objects via some qualitative sense of likeness or similarity. Symbols are "general signs, which have become associated with their meanings by usage."[18] Signs can partake of the character of more than one register—that is, it can be both an icon and an index, or an index and a symbol. The added character of the index is its production of meaningfulness through its connection with some other event, occurrence, or experience in time and space.

Models for thinking about the function of the sign in relation to race have drawn primarily on interpretations of Ferdinand Saussure and the gap between sign and referent.[19] Because of this emphasis, analyses of the "social construction" of race have tended to emphasize that notion of the sign that Peirce describes as "symbolic": an order of signification based on conventional usage and the association of an idea—most often a denigrating one—with a sign. It is the enforcing of these conventional usages in political projects and everyday language that constitutes the social signification of race for theorists such as Omi and Winant.[20] But Peirce's distinctions between icon, index, and symbol, and especially his elaboration of indexicality, offer a new angle on how we think about the relationship between racial signs and racial organization. The iconic register gets at how racial signs produce its modes of classification and the cognitive habits that produce likeness and denigrating images. The symbolic register gets at the conventional usages of race that form more general rules and regularities. The indexical register gets at something else: the function of the racial sign in the way that it makes immediate specific connections in the here and now. Indices, according to Peirce, "direct the attention to their objects by blind compulsion," "startle us," and "mark the junction between two portions of experience."[21] Peirce describes the index's crucial role in locating, constituting, and putting together the "here and now": "some indices," he says, "are more or less detailed directions for what the hearer is to do in order to place himself in direct experiential or other connection with the thing meant."[22]

To return to the development of "strict scrutiny" in *Korematsu v. United States*, we see the indexicality of race heightened in this case and its iconicity rendered less salient. The correlation of Japaneseness with a time and space is expanded via Justice Black's articulation of "Japanese" with the multiple temporalities of war. The majority opinion does nothing less than produce a new sense of time and space that is able to select out and render meaningful a particular way in which race is made to indicate and point to reality. This is not just a form of "acontextual ahistoricism" because it is not just removing contexts and history. It is putting together and directing attention to "two portions of experience"—war with Japan and the day-to-day presence of Japanese Americans—that forcefully comprise a new time and space. To think about racial sign as index is to analyze these connections between racial signs and the construction of what Umberto Eco calls "a world of reference."[23]

In the next section, I track this shift toward using race as "index" in alternate histories of World War II. Like *Korematsu*, these alternate histories are responses to the fantasy and anxieties of a racialized social order made powerfully visible through World War II. They develop this indexicality of race and take it to even further imaginative ends. Analyzing their narrative strategies, I reveal the ongoing imaginative struggle captured by Porter above: the "refusal to recognize the extent to which the race concept organizes the world." I survey a set of alternate histories, from Peter Tsouras to Harry Turtledove, which often console the reader with ways to organize time and space such that its coherence need not be questioned too deeply. I then turn to Philip K. Dick's *The Man in the High Castle*, a work whose critical potential lies not so much in imagining an alternate world as it does in forcing readers to confront the dependence of the world's coherence on racism.

Counterfactual Worlds and Asiatic Racialization

In alternate histories of World War II, the presence of Japan in relation to the question of racial organization is both present and absent. As several commentators on alternate histories of World War II have observed, the scenario of Hitler's victory and the centrality of Germany's role is explored far more often than Japan's in this subgenre.[24] While this quantitative difference is suggestive, it is ultimately outside the scope of this chapter to survey all the alternate histories of World War II in order to measure the relative over-representation of German scenarios and speculate on what that might mean. Rather, I focus on two narrative logics and scenarios that do appear in the relatively fewer instances where Japanese "victory" is imagined: (1) the scenario in which Japanese forces are able to win battles but ultimately can never win the war or hold on to its gains; (2) the scenario in which Germany and Japan divide up the United States between them. These two narrative patterns take us to the limits of imagining a world whose racial organization would be radically different. Those limits speak to the extent to which race is used to index the time and space of our ongoing present.

The first narrative logic replicates conventional historical thinking that Japan would not have enough resources to ultimately hold on to its short-lived gains. Peter Tsouras's edited volume, *Rising Sun Victorious* (2001), is one of the few volumes that develops counterfactual scenarios of World War II that center on Japan. But it is notable that, despite its title, almost all of the stories actually culminate in the eventual defeat of the Japanese. The common narrative trajectory of these stories obeys the following general rule: something changes that allows the Japanese to win a few more battles and pose a greater threat, but Japan is ultimately defeated by the superior strength of the West. In the "Japanese Raj," although Japan is able to wrest India from Britain, they are ultimately driven back out: "the same forces that doomed the British Raj turned out also to make sure that the Japanese Indian Empire, and its impact on India and the subcontinent, would be even briefer than its predecessor."[25] The added line that "its impact on India" would be "even briefer" describes how the historical consequences of Japanese rule are foreclosed from narrative consideration. In "Nagumo's Luck," the Japanese are able to win the Battle of Midway, but "the balance of forces began to swing in America's favor."[26] The Japanese win battles in these counterfactual scenarios but are not imagined as being able to win the war. *Rising Sun Victorious* oddly promises to represent something—a Japanese victory—that it ultimately does not represent.

Even a work like Harry Turtledove's *Days of Infamy* forecloses the imagination of Japan on the world-historical stage. This novel does, from beginning to end, concentrate on Japanese forces as they take over, subjugate, and control Hawaii. But even here, the historical consequences of a Japanese victory is foreclosed because the narrative repeatedly suggests both that the United States will continue to fight and that the United States loses their battles because of their own arrogance and refusal to take Japan seriously—not because of any structural or "durable" factor that is more difficult to change. In a conversation between two American officers after the Japanese victory, the counterfactual scenario of Japanese victory is likened to the U.S. Civil War. This scenario creates a transhistorical logic that places the "victory" within a larger picture of the inevitability of U.S. dominance: "'We'll do what we need to do,' Sharp said. 'If it takes a little longer than we figured at first—then it does, that's all. When the Federals marched down to Bull Run, they thought they'd win in a hurry, too. It didn't work like that, but they didn't lose, either, not in the end.'"[27] In the ceremony that recognizes Japanese authority at the end of the novel, various hints are dropped that Japan's status as a colonial power is short-lived and that forces in Hawaii are biding their time until the next overthrow. The final lines of the novel both use the mood of the conditional and narrow the scope in order to describe Japanese power: Japan "had sunk two U.S. carriers and smashed up a third. As long as they could keep that up, Hawaii would remain untroubled—by the Americans, anyhow. . . . Now they had to make sure the newly revived kingdom stayed as independent as Japan wanted it to be—and not a bit more."[28] Of course, in the second novel of this series, *The End of the Beginning*, the retaking of Hawaii from the Japanese does eventually happen.

Both Turtledove and the multiple authors of the stories in *Rising Sun Victorious* subscribe to a narrative logic that sees Japan's power as realized in the short-term temporal units of "days" and "battles" but not on larger historical scales. Moreover, they rely on articulating an indexical relationship between racial markers and history in which two portions of experience are mashed together, creating a dynamic connection between sign and an imagined cause. In *Days of Infamy*, for example, one of the storylines follows a Japanese American named Kenzo Takahashi living in Hawaii when Japan and the United States begin their conflict: "Since the attack on Pearl Harbor, though. . . . All of a sudden, his *haole* friends didn't want to know him any more. . . . And he knew those *haoles* and their folks were lining up to buy the fish he and his father and brother brought in. They didn't mind doing that at all. . . . And now . . . now he was nothing but a lousy Jap."[29] It is easy to think about this moment of racialization as one where Kenzo becomes "nothing but a lousy Jap" through the construction of derogatory stereotypes built on conventional usages of "racial foreignness." But that is not what happens. Kenzo becomes a "lousy Jap" because two divergent portions of experience—the attack on Pearl Harbor and daily, interpersonal interactions—have been imagined as an "organic pair," dynamically connected to each other. The repeated "now" in the quotation above gets at how racism goes beyond discrimination of individuals to indexing and organizing the space and time of the present.

While this example certainly lends sympathy to Kenzo's character as the object of racial discrimination, thus calling attention to the moral failures of racism, the indexical function of race is left untouched. One does not begin with the description that Kenzo is a "lousy Jap" and then form an explanation about Pearl Harbor. The event happens and the explanation—the linking of one experience to another—produces the description. Thus, the form that racism takes in *Days of Infamy* is one where the incontrovertibility of the explanation is used to organize the world racially. And that organization has to do with putting two experiences into a real relationship as actuality, making the coherence of the world dependent on racial distinction. The words "Jap" or "Japs" populates virtually every page of *Days of Infamy*—435 instances, to be exact. But the magnitude of racism here is not because it is calling specific characters or even groups through a derogatory usage. It is powerful because it operates as an index that links up racial distinction to larger orders of experience and therefore creates the conditions by which the present and future are formed. When one character contemplates going to the grocery store in Wahiawa after the attack on Pearl Harbor, she thinks to herself, "And Japs ran most of them. She'd learned not to give that a second thought. Now she was going to have to unlearn it again. Things had changed. Exactly how they'd changed . . . well, she'd just have to wait and see."[30] "Japs" here becomes a sign of change effected through a world-historical event, one that reframes both the past and the future. Like the narrative logic of *Korematsu*, what is occluded from consideration is the actual relationship between Japanese people and the attack.

The use of race to index the immediate connection between the event of Pearl Harbor and all Japanese people produces a framework that assures its reader that the "Jap" is always organized as the object of containment, threat, and scrutiny. Thus, while *Days of Infamy* imagines an alternate history, it never imagines an alternate world. Its narrative strategies are strikingly close to those of *Korematsu*. The other predominant strain of alternate histories seems to go further in imagining both an alternate history and an alternate world. William Shirer's "If Hitler Had Won World War II" (1961), Cyril Kornbluth's "Two Dooms" (1958), and most famously in literary tradition, Philip K. Dick's *The Man in the High Castle* (1962) all depict the joint German-Japanese occupation of the United States. In Shirer's work, the Japanese occupation of the United States is described as comparatively benign to the German occupation. Shirer writes, "Although the Japanese occupation has been far from gentle, especially in the first months, when the Nipponese soldiers ran riot, in the end it has been mild compared to that of the Nazi Germans. The Japanese have been primarily interested in exploiting the Western third of the country. . . . Since getting the Americans to produce and deliver these products, the Japanese have left them pretty much to themselves in other respects. . . . There is a semblance of municipal and state self-government under the Japanese governors and the Governor-General at San Francisco. Life for Americans has become at least bearable."[31] Kornbluth's and Dick's scenarios are similar, but they make one modification: they concentrate most of their narrative energy in their alternate histories in depicting the Japanified world even as the horrors of the alternate history are reserved for the imagination of German atrocities. Further, they make this envisioning of a thoroughly Japanified world seem easy. In investigating the ease with which the racial counterfactual is effected, we must inquire in what ways the reader is asked to confront or disavow the relationship between coherence and racism.

For both Kornbluth and Dick, the initial signs for the reader that we are in an alternate world are conventional associations between objects and images of Japaneseness. In "Two Dooms," where a man wakes up from a drug-induced trance into a world in which the United States did *not* develop and use atomic weapons, the first sign of how the world is organized is a Samurai sword: "Savage nicks left by bayonets—and swords? . . . It was a piece of swordblade six inches long, hand-honed to a perfect edge, with a couple of nicks in it . . . It had a perceptible curve that would fit into only one shape: the Samurai sword of Japan."[32] In Dick's *The Man in the High Castle*, the reader is immediately immersed into an alternate historical world—the Rocky Mountain States—that is quickly filled out with images that draw out a time and space of Japaneseness. Instead of instant coffee there is "instant tea"; on the streets there are "women in their long colorful silk dresses."[33] Within the first page of the novel, a dialogue is represented in which both Mr. R. Childan and Mr. Tagomi speak in a stilted, formal English that invokes stereotyped representations of Japanese people speaking English: "Extensive inquiries . . . which I've had made at my own expense, Mr. Tagomi, sir, regarding the promised parcel. . . . Could I bring various desirable items out to your business location?" (4). These signs that allow the reader to build the world of the novel are both images and indices in Peirce's sense: they correspond to and create a likeness with images of Japaneseness at the same time that they create a correlation in a specific time, space, and situation. What makes this world Japanese is not just that it is populated with Japanese people or even objects. It is that these objects, images, and signs produce an organic connection between the experiences of walking, doing business, and getting something to drink with Japaneseness.

In both Kornbluth and Dick, the narrative diegesis relies on the easy visibility of Japanese cultural and social norms: a sword, a flag, stereotyped speech, concerns about "face" and "place," social order, rigidity, overpoliteness, fashion and style. Gavriel Rosenfeld describes all three works in this intertextual chain as "present[ing] highly dystopian portraits of the Nazi occupation of the United States."[34] But this description does not give an accurate sense of either the Kornbluth or the Dick novel, both of which concentrate a great deal more of their narrative diegesis on the Japanese occupation of the United States rather than the Nazi occupation of the United States. Rosenfeld's inaccuracy of description is telling in that it erases the importance of the easy legibility of Japanese images in creating a coherent, rational world of explanations, causes, and outcomes. Indeed, in *The Man in the High Castle*, whereas the Japanese occupation can be fully imagined, the Nazi occupation cannot. In the novel, there are two main plot lines. One is set in San Francisco in the Japan-occupied Rocky Mountain States focusing on a Japanese ambassador, Mr. Tagomi, and efforts to circumvent a potentially devastating new war with Germany. The other follows the movements of Juliana Frink from Canon City, Colorado, to Cheyenne, Wyoming. Juliana Frink and Joe Cinnadella (a suspected assassin) travel to meet Hawthorne Abendsen, author of an alternate history novel called *The Grasshopper Lies Heavy* in which the Allied forces win the war. With these plot and setting bifurcations, the Japanese-occupied San Francisco is fully imagined with "jinrikisha" runners, "pinocs," "chinks," clean streets, high skyscrapers, and clear hierarchies. The Nazi presence in this world is never realized at the level of setting, space, and time. It is formed and vehicularized through Joe Cinnadella—an irrational, crazy, lean, good-looking guy who is the embodiment of the assassin and pure evil.

Because of this bifurcated plot structure, Japanese and Nazi occupation operate at very different registers in the narrative discourse. In *The Man in the High Castle*, Dick does not spend a lot of time telling us how the world came to be like this. This novel gives us a fully realized world and how we got here is only minimally explained. The effect of the bifurcation is that Japanese occupation is realized through the mode of description while the German occupation is given through the mode of explanation. The world of the novel is initially presented to the reader as focalized through Childan, and he produces the terms of these different modes of representation. Contrast, for example, the following initial ways in which Japan and Germany are figured in the making of the world:

> The radio of the pedecab blared out popular tunes, competing with the radios of other cabs, cars and buses. Childan did not hear; he was used to it. Nor did he take notice of the enormous neon signs with their permanent ads obliterating the front of virtually every large building. After all, he had his own sign; at night it blazed on and off in company with all the others of the city. What other way did one advertise? One had to be realistic. . . . And it was pleasurable to be peddled along by another human being, to feel the straining muscles of the *chink* transmitted in the form of regular vibrations; a sort of relaxing machine, Childan reflected. To be pulled instead of having to pull. And—to have, if even for a moment, higher place. . . .
>
> One had to blame the Germans for the situation. Tendency to bite off more than they could chew. After all, they had barely managed to win the war, and at once they had gone off to conquer the solar system, while at home they had passed edicts which . . . well, at least the idea was good. And after all, they had been successful with the Jews and Gypsies and Bible Students. And the Slavs had been rolled back two thousand years' worth. . . . And those great glossy magazines printed in Munich and circulated around to all the libraries and newsstands . . . one could see the full-page color pictures for oneself: the blue-eyed, blond-haired Aryan settlers who now industriously tilled, culled, plowed, and so forth in the vast grain bowl of the world, the Ukraine.

> . . . You didn't see pictures of drunken dull-witted Poles any more, slouched on sagging porches or hawking a few sickly turnips at the village market. All a thing of the past, like rutted dirt roads that once turned to slop in the rainy season, bogging down the carts. (22–23, 24)

The Japanese occupation is envisioned as a change that is barely noticed. It has already been a part of the descriptive iconography of the city and it has changed our mindsets and behaviors in subtle ways, such as the sustained attention to hierarchies of social position, prestige, and rank. The descriptions of Childan and his behavior invoke the Japanese occupation at the level of atmosphere, and its lived reality is fully realized in Childan's anxieties about his behavior and the small pleasures he can take in his position—being pulled along by a pedecab "*chink*." The racism here is embedded into the landscape and what that landscape makes possible for Childan.

The distinction that "One had to blame the Germans for the situation" marks a split in narrative presentation. The German relationship to the existing world is constructed at the level of sequence, explanation, and causality. The explanation projects from a certain German mindset—a "tendency" that is at base an irrational megalomania—in order to demonstrate Germany's ordering of the world as a set of large-scale historical projects. Germany appears in the novel less as a fully realized description of what the world might look like and more as an abstract principle to either shy away from or embrace. As Childan muses, "So it all came back to what he had told his fellow store owners; what the Nazis have which we lack is—nobility. Admire them for their love of work or their efficiency . . . but it's the dream that stirs one. . . . Now, the Japanese on the other hand. I know them pretty well; I do business with them, after all, day in and day out. They are—let's face it—Orientals. Yellow people. We whites have to bow to them because they hold the power. But we watch Germany; we see what can be done where whites have conquered, and it's quite different" (25).

This "difference" could be described along the lines of Shirer above as a contrast between Japan imagined as a more "benign" conqueror and Germany as the more malevolent one. The parameters of this contrast follow and extrapolate from popular representations in the wake of World War II that described Nazism in the terms of the most extreme irrational evils and U.S. representations of Japan in terms of familiarity and Orientalism—respect and denigration, benevolent *and* unassimilable. The "evil" of Nazism is imagined in individual-racial terms and a collective fantasy of Aryan superiority. The "evil" of Japanese occupation is the evil of reverse assimilation, of being culturally and stylistically made into Japanese. However, this popular contrast encoded by both Dick and Kornbluth obscures the reasons the Japan-occupied world is so much more legible than the German-occupied world. The reason is the crucial role that the familiarity of racial signs as indices plays in establishing the coherence of the imagined world. If the Nazi swastika operates primarily in the "iconic" register to convey the idea of race hatred, the rising sun operates in a more indexical register to link two portions of experience. Remember that in our initial introduction to the alternate world, Dick uses the reader's recourse to the familiar—the immediate readability of Japanese culture and style in order to render coherent a time and space. In order to make a world in which Japan now owns the United States most visible and legible, the narrative diegesis relies on representations of speech, culture, and manners drawn from racist representations of Japanese people and society. The projectibility of the counterfactual depends on the relationship between noticing race and racial organization. In a novel in which reality is continually being questioned, racial organization emerges as its guarantee.

One of the main critical problems that scholars have addressed in *The Man in the High Castle* is the epistemological status of reality. All alternate histories force us to question how we know history, but Dick doubles down on the genre by including within it a book called *The Grasshopper Lies Heavy*, which virtually everyone in the novel is reading. This novel-within-the-novel depicts a world in which the Allied forces do win the war, and the ending of the novel famously raises the question of whether the characters are living in the world of *The Grasshopper Lies Heavy* or the world of *The Man in the High Castle* and further, how they would know.[35] Despite all the attention paid to the question of metaphysical reality in *The Man in the High Castle*, though, little attention has been paid to the role that race plays in indexing the present for both the characters and the reader. What does it mean that the novel's "sense of the real" is predicated on the indexical function of race, its capacity to produce a meaningful correlation in a specific time and space?[36] Far from showing the pathologies of racism in a topsy-turvy world, Dick's work shows the embeddedness of racism in our descriptions of the world and how the *only* legible world is a racist one.

The most crucial example of race being used to create certainty in the world is when Tagomi slips into an alternate reality late in the novel. After killing a couple of SS officers, Tagomi questions everything around him and feels a deep void. He goes to Childan's store in order to find some tangible thing that will allow him to "return to the world." He contemplates: "Still without what I need if I am to return to the world" (226). When Tagomi sits on a park bench and closes his eyes, he opens them to an alternate world. The point of entry to this alternate world, even before the reader knows that Tagomi has entered into an alternate reality, is the possibility of racism. A policeman talks to Mr. Tagomi and he thinks, "My chance at nirvana. Gone. Interrupted by that white barbarian. Neanderthal *yank*. That subhuman supposing I worked a child's puerile toy. Rising from the bench he took a few steps unsteadily. Must calm down. Dreadful low-class jingoistic racist invectives, unworthy of me" (230–31). Even as he denounces his own racism, it is the thing that assures him of his location in the world. But the main marker that registers the fact of a different world is that there are no pedecabs: "Mr. Tagomi halted at the curb. No pedecabs. He walked along the sidewalk instead. . . . Mad dream, Mr. Tagomi thought. Must wake up. Where are the pedecabs today?" (231). The pedecab is an excellent example of Peirce's index, for it "show[s] something about things, on account of their being physically connected with them" and it "forces his attention." Tagomi's whole sense of reality and his ability to orient himself rely on the presence of pedecabs—an index of how one inhabits the class and racial stratification of the Pacific States of America. Indeed, the marker of his return to the Pacific States of America is the presence of two Chinese boys and their assurance that there are pedecabs in San Francisco: "You're sure they were pedecabs? You distinctly saw the drivers peddling?" (234). Reality is rendered certain through referring the Chinese boys to the index of pedecabs.

At the heart of this scene from an alternate world is a moment when Tagomi goes to a "lunch counter" where all the seats are occupied. After demanding a seat, Tagomi is met with anti-Japanese racism:

> Ahead, a dingy lunch counter. Only whites within, all supping. Mr. Tagomi pushed open the wooden swinging doors. Smell of coffee. Grotesque jukebox in corner blaring out; he winced and made his way to the counter. All stools taken by whites. Mr. Tagomi exclaimed. Several whites looked up. *But none departed their places. None yielded their stools to him. They merely resumed supping.*
>
> "I insist!" Mr. Tagomi said loudly to the first white; he shouted in the man's ear.
>
> The man put down his coffee mug and said, "Watch it, Tojo."
>
> Mr. Tagomi looked to the other whites; all watched with hostile expressions. And none stirred. (231–32)

Two iconic scenes are enfolded into this one: first, the lunch counter sit-in whereby African Americans protest segregation, the first of which happened on February 1, 1960, in Greensboro, South Carolina, just a couple years before *The Man in the High Castle* was published; second, the scene of discrimination where African Americans are refused service and not given seats at the table, a scene that provides the backdrop through which the lunch counter sit-in as an act of protest gains notice. Tagomi knows that he is no longer in his reality when his mere presence does not have a demonstrable racial consequence that would reorganize the lunch counter according to his reality. Dick's use of the scene shows a function of racism that goes beyond legal segregation or discriminatory practices of employment and hiring: it is a perceptual apparatus for situating persons and actions into the certainty of the here and now. Tagomi's cognition of space and time depends on the capacity to refer the presumptive coherence of people's races to a sequence of racism and thereby give certainty to otherwise disparate, unconnected, or meaningless phenomenon. Its mirroring of a scene that would have been all over the newspapers at the time of Dick's writing helps the reader identify Tagomi's alternate reality as *our* reality and the expected racist outcomes. *Both* the legibility of our world and the legibility of Tagomi's alternate reality rely on race. But they rely on race not just because of the visibility of racial categorization and norms of behavior, but because race organizes the very coherence on which the experience of reality depends. The "dingy lunch counter" provides the index that signals how racism is the "proper" sequence for the invocation of race.

This moment could be read as a protest against racism by showing the "arbitrarily disposed roles of social reality"[37] and a critique of the elevation of racial differences over a more common humanity. That reading relies on the opposition between race as particularity versus a more human universalism. I read the moment instead as a penetrating description of how the race concept organizes the world. The critical potential of Dick's alternate history is not that it imagines an alternate world or gives us a mode of antiracist worldmaking. Rather, it forces the reader to confront the degree to which the race concept organizes a sense of reality, indeed, our entry *into* a coherent time and space.

Racial Coherence

As is well known, Dick was preoccupied with the constitution of reality. His narratives repeatedly turn to questions of paranoia, schizophrenia, delusion, and multiple worlds.[38] But his alternate history produces not a confrontation with the continually changing formations of subjective psychic reality but with the limits of imagination. In his and other alternate histories of World War II considered here, that limit is the use of race as index, a use that these narratives return to again and again to put two portions of experience together in a meaningful relation. This tracing of an imaginative limit resonates with the work of Adrian Piper, a philosopher and artist who has produced some of the most innovative work attempting to disrupt this relationship between racism and what she calls the "indexical present."

Piper theorizes racism through a cognitive framework built around Kant: "If we were finally to fail to identify the thing or state of affairs in question as having a consistent set of properties . . . we would have no experiences of it at all. . . . For a Kantian rationalist, then, the cognitive organization of experience according to consistent and coherent concepts is a necessary condition of being a rationally unified subject."[39] Using this framework, Piper details all of the defensive, pseudorationalizations that allow a (white) self to maintain consistency through the denial of the other—that is, through xenophobic and racist responses. Racism is constitutive to the rational unity of certain subjects and Piper builds her installation art in order to intervene in that circuit between racism and rational unity. She calls attention to the ritualized racism at the level of the everyday that forms exactly what we mean by civility, politeness, and decorum. Racism in this way is embedded into our social interactions such that we do not have a rational subject *without* racism. Piper's artwork in turn works off of this theory by forcing the viewer to encounter the racial other in immediate experience, the introduction of an alternative here-and-now that disrupts the work of the easy cognitive classification and organization of experience. She writes, "My purpose is to transform the viewer psychologically, by presenting him or her with an unavoidable concrete reality that cuts through the defensive rationalizations by which we insulate ourselves against the facts of our political responsibility."[40]

Piper's desire here is to puncture, to break this circuit between rational unity and racism by introducing an "unavoidable concrete reality" that reshapes the indexical present. But Tagomi's alternations between realities suggest something a bit more disturbing, for the "unavoidable concrete reality" that he turns to is precisely the racial sign as constituting the continuity of space and time: the pedecab, the jingoistic invective, the dingy lunch counter. As we have seen throughout, race establishes experience in space and time. The counterfactual switching of positions that Tagomi undergoes—the world in which whites dominate and Asiatics are subordinated—is not, then, an instance whereby the arbitrariness of racial positions is critiqued. Indeed, Tagomi does not return to "his world" with some greater understanding of the circumstances of white people in the Pacific States of America. The mirroring of alternatives shows the utter collapse of distinctions between rationality and irrationality when it comes to situating subjects in the world.

In *The Psychoses*, Jacques Lacan makes a crucial distinction in suggesting that psychoses are so important to study because they get at the more general constitution of reality. Not, as Freud suggests, because psychotics represent an extreme version of a hermeneutic process that all subjects perform—logically linking various connections to extreme ends. But because psychotic phenomenon mimic the constitution of reality whereby something coherent is referred to something else. Lacan writes,

> What characterizes a normal subject is precisely that he never takes seriously certain realities that he recognizes exist. You are surrounded by all sorts of realities about which you are in no doubt, some of which are particularly threatening, but you don't take them fully seriously . . . and maintain yourselves in an average, basic . . . state of blissful uncertainty. . . . But, contrary to the normal subject for whom reality is always in the right place, he [the psychotic] is certain of something, which is that what is at issue—ranging from hallucination to interpretation—regards him.[41]

In the alternate histories and in *Korematsu*, this "certainty" is constituted through the uses of race that I have been tracing. The "unsatisfying" ending of Dick's novel opens the world of the novel to potentially be reinterpreted as a delusional world only made real through the psychic commitments of the characters. But Dick also extends this to the narrative diegesis itself where race structures our "worlds of reference"—delusional or not. This makes it extremely difficult *not* to participate in the racist structures of the world.

The imaginative task, then, is dislocating those "worlds of reference" and the narrative strategies that undergird them. In this sense, the lunch counter sit-in is one example of such an imaginative act. As it was practiced in the 1960s and invoked by Dick in *The Man in the High Castle*, it must have created a situation that would have seemed something like an alternate world to the white customers and restaurant owners. By being in the "wrong" place and extending their presence over time, the protesters restructured space and time. By occupying a place and time in the white paranoid imagination and by indexing a different kind of meaningful experience—the serving of black people by white people—they insert themselves into the projection of reality. The convergence of an iconic scene of black-white conflict that signals the continuing struggle to articulate black freedom with the counterfactual imagination of Japan's victory in World

War II nicely links the two sections of my consideration of alternate history. Their reversal and mirroring in Dick's novel, however, trace less a disjunctive reordering of space and time and more the way in which alternate histories run up against the limits of imagining what could happen.

Those limits begin with the narrative strategies for locating and relocating race. Race is a figure *for* thought, and as we have seen above, to produce alternate histories that actually imagine alternate worlds requires us to relocate race within our worlds of reference. Barnes strategically locates racist representations in order to produce alternate lines of thought, ones that avoid the formal symmetry of the racial counterfactual. Dick forces the reader to confront the organizing force of the race as index. I turn in the conclusion to one last intervention in the use of race in the making of the modern world, one that draws a line between the major historical moments imagined and reimagined by the popular fictions that I have considered: the U.S. Civil War, the Russo-Japanese War, and World War II.

CONCLUSION

On the Possibilities of an Antiracist Racial Worldmaking

Racial Worldmaking has brought genre and race together in curious, sometimes unlikely combinations. I do so not in order to explore how genre can be a vehicle for either racist representation or the critique of racist ideologies as a mix of attitudes and ideas. I do not subordinate one to the logics and categories of the other. Rather, I read their deep interrelations as affordances that build in knowledges and form the pathways by which we inhabit and participate in the world. Yellow peril future war fictions, plantation romances of Reconstruction, sword and sorcery and racial capitalism, alternate histories of the Civil War and World War II. Each of these configurations embeds race in our anticipations and expectations of the world. As we have seen, sometimes they get us to notice race at levels beyond biological differences such that racism is "built into" the context, the atmosphere, or the structures of decision making and causality. Sometimes, though, authors reflect back on these narrative and interpretive strategies and they relocate race in ways that both make visible this embedding of race and produce alternate, oppositional forms of antiracist worldmaking. Frank Yerby, Samuel Delany, Steven Barnes, Terry Bisson, and Philip K. Dick all do versions of this alternate worldmaking.

In identifying these narrative and interpretive strategies, I have been able to track processes of race-making and world-building that challenge prominent historical explanations of the transformation of racial meanings in the twentieth century: on the one hand, the trajectory from biological racism to cultural racism; on the other hand, the transition from overt to covert racism. First, we see the supplementation of biological science and physical anthropology with other temporal modes for generating meaning through race, namely historiography, economics, cultural anthropology, and legal reasoning. Second, we see the convergence of these disciplines with the role of popular genres throughout the twentieth and early twenty-first century in directing the modal imagination of race and in creating the conditions by which race gets embedded in the making of present and future world(s).

In our current moment, we have seen the coexistence of two seemingly opposed phenomena. As Imani Perry observes, "Since the mid-1960s, Americans have lived within a nation that announces racial equality, democracy, and fairness as fundamental to its creed. During the same period, Americans have witnessed little movement in the most egregious signs of racial inequality."[1] The historical and methodological reframing accomplished in the previous chapters helps us understand these phenomena not as contradictions but as mutually constitutive. It offers a different protocol of racial reading that hinges not on the stability of racial representations that can be traced back to sociohistorical referents but on the ongoing production of racial salience—how and when we notice race. Fictional and nonfictional genres alike instruct readers in the process of noticing race. They do so at the level of language, but their organizing force resides in units of meaning between language and structure such as sequence, narrative retrospection, anticipation, the formation of expectations, the organization of foreground/background. Through these analyses we gain insight into the multiple relationships among race, racism, and race critique. As we have seen, mechanisms used to *identify* discrimination in the economy and the law become ways of *embedding* discrimination within our everyday comprehension of social structures. Likewise, the use of race is not only racist when it targets individuals or groups with invidious intent or effect. Uses of race produce conditions for making racism a built-in knowledge for our participation in the world.

My critique, then, is located not so much in the recognition of racial ideologies as they are in changing the modes through which we grasp the world. I conclude with one final example of a critique along these lines in order to develop strategies of antiracist racial worldmaking.[2] It is not easily recognizable since it was not done through critiquing the deployment of "world" as a category of racial meaning but through *inhabiting* it in a different way. This alternative line of thought about how race builds worlds is articulated through W. E. B. Du Bois's interventions at the edges of genre, race, and world. Du Bois's fiction displaying his clear participation in genres such as romance, fantasy, and science fiction has garnered increasing attention.[3] And his canonical *Souls of Black Folk* has long been recognized for its mixed genre. But in works that draw out the relationships between historiography and romance, historical speculation and the politics of race, and science fiction and race relations, we see how his theorizations of genre, race, and world come together. Moreover, the line of thought he develops both connects the historical moments that form important cruxes in *Racial Worldmaking* and frames them as powerful dramas of racial organization at the global level. These are, of course, the Russo-Japanese War, the U.S. Civil War and Reconstruction, and the World Wars.

When Lothrop Stoddard develops his notion of a world besieged by the "rising tide of color" and encapsulates a particular way of apprehending the world through race as an organizing principle, he curiously quotes Du Bois in support of his claims.[4] His citation of Du Bois is both inappropriate and appropriate. It is appropriate because Du Bois is similarly marshaling forth an emergent understanding that articulates race and "world" together as a complex entity and that forces on the reader new and distinct perceptual organizations. Indeed, Du Bois's phrases "worlds of color," "the color of Asia," "the color of Europe," "the colored world" *look* and *sound* a lot like Stoddard's own phrases.[5] Like Stoddard, Du Bois observed the Russo-Japanese War with great interest, seeing in it an epochal shift. In his 1906 essay, "The Color Line Belts the World," Du Bois writes, "For the first time in a thousand years a great white nation has measured arms with a colored nation and has been found wanting. The Russo-Japanese war has marked an epoch. The magic of the word 'white' is already broken, and the Color Line in civilization has been crossed in modern times as it was in the great past. The awakening of the yellow races is certain. That the awakening of the brown and black races will follow in time, no unprejudiced student of history can doubt."[6] Stoddard looks on this "awakening" with fear and dread and the felt need to construct a racial mode of cognition that renders the world graspable in terms of that fear. Du Bois sees hope and the potential beginning of a revolution of labor at the scale of the "world."

In this sense, Stoddard's citation of Du Bois is wholly inappropriate because it places Du Bois's language of "white world," "colored world," and "worlds of color" into an itinerary of thought that is precisely opposed to Du Bois's aims. Visible through this instance of quotation and appropriation is a struggle over how to perceive race in/as worlds. Unlike the yellow peril genre that imagines Japanese civilizational "prowess" as a completely unprecedented first in history, Du Bois qualifies this sentiment by saying "the Color Line in civilization has been crossed in modern times *as it was in the great past*." Unlike the yellow peril genre that holds the conflict between the white and yellow races as the main historical fact, Du Bois does not designate others to the dustbin of history: "That the awakening of the brown and black races will follow in time, no unprejudiced student of history can doubt." The figuration of "worlds" that articulate race in different ways is present throughout Du Bois's oeuvre. His early and recently excavated essay, "The Afro-American" articulates a sense of being "born into a universe which in addition to all horizontal boundaries is separated by a straight perpendicular fissure into a white and black hemisphere."[7] This sense of peering through the veil into another world is one of the crucial figures on which *The Souls of Black Folk* dwells. With its chapters on "The Color of Asia," "The Colored World," and "The Color of Europe," *Darkwater: Voices from Within the Veil* articulates Du Bois's understanding of World War I as a struggle of racial organization. Finally, his 1925 essay, "Worlds of Color" is his way of linking up the "problem of the color-line" with global formations of colonialism, and he extends this topoi in his "White World" chapter in *Dusk of Dawn: Autobiography of a Race Concept* and the third book of his Mansart trilogy, titled *Worlds of Color*.

This insistent figuration of "worlds" did not go unnoticed. It is precisely this tendency to speak of "white worlds" and "colored worlds" that George Schuyler rails against in "The Negro-Art Hokum": "the Africamerican is subject to the same economic and social forces that mold the actions and thoughts of the white Americans. He is not living in a different world as some whites and a few Negroes would have us believe."[8] In ridiculing the overemphasis on racial differences manifested in this language of "different worlds," Schuyler makes no distinction at the level of the historical terms through which "Africamerican" and "white American" subjectivities are organized. For Du Bois, though, this is a crucial distinction. At the beginning of his chapter, "The White World," Du Bois writes:

> A man lives today not only in his physical environment and in the social environment of ideas and customs, laws and ideals; but that total environment is subjected to a new socio-physical environment of other groups, whose social environment he shares but in part . . . and this greater group environment was not a matter of mere ideas and thought; it was embodied in muscles and armed men, in scowling faces, in the majesty of judges and police and in human law which became divine. . . . I lived in an environment which I came to call the white world. . . . All this made me limited in physical movement and provincial in thought and dream. I could not stir, I could not act, I could not live, without taking into careful daily account the reaction of my white environing world.[9]

This matter of "world" cannot be conceived as Schuyler would have it as the same social forces (i.e., capitalism) being imposed on different subjects. It is distinct forms of organization that surround and shape the emergence of the African American as a historical possibility or impossibility. The difficulty in describing this co-constitution of social field and subject leads Du Bois in this chapter to return to the capacities of figuration. He writes, "Thus in my life the chief fact has been race—*not so much scientific race*, as that deep conviction of myriads of men that congenital differences among the main masses of human beings absolutely condition the individual destiny of every member of a group. . . . Yet, how shall I explain and clarify its meaning for a soul? Description fails—I have tried that . . . let me attempt its exposition by personifying my white and colored environment."[10] Race, for Du Bois, is a figure of and for thought. Here, he reflects on the different ways in which race is figured, and how these different strategies shape the possibilities of thinking and grasping the world. Du Bois understands the way in which race is used to fragment and specify social forces such that worlds are organized along differential lines.

No scholar has better elucidated the function of the figural senses of "worlds" as it operates in Du Bois's thought than Nahum Chandler. In his commentary on Du Bois's early essay, "The Afro-American," Chandler centers on Du Bois's "peculiar sense of world."[11] As Chandler puts it, "Du Bois . . . is on the track of outlining a complicated sense of world. The world in question is always one of worlds. It is a world that is itself, as such, an infrastructural organization of discontinuities . . . world here, while experienced in a certain way as if a whole, is yet also always already re-marked within that form of experience, that is to say, explicitly marked, as a categorically or oppositionally divided whole."[12] Worlds, as moments of historical and phenomenal possibility, are marked by this fissure—what Du Bois elsewhere calls the "veil"—that already exists in a world that is experienced "as if a whole." Crucial for my thinking on the subject, Chandler carefully excavates this understanding of the world: it organizes itself around the emergence of the African American; it is also shaped through the constitutive force of the African American on its infrastructures. As Chandler elsewhere explains, one cannot presuppose the constitution of the system or structure in which either the Euro-American or African American subject is constructed.[13] Instead, we must continually be alive to the question of historical possibility.[14]

For Du Bois, that historical possibility begins with the end of the world. In "The Comet," Du Bois's science fiction story included at the end of *Darkwater: Voices from within the Veil*, a black man named Jim Davis and a white woman named Julia are seemingly the only survivors in the world after a comet hits the Earth. The word "world" is insistently repeated throughout the story to show two movements. First, it highlights how even though Jim and Julia existed in the same "world," they were acted on by different social forces such that they did not actually share the same world: "Not that he [Jim] was not human, but he dwelt in a world so far from hers, so infinitely far, that he seldom even entered her thought."[15] Second, it shows an emerging sense of historical possibility as Jim and Julia recognize the construction of a future world that is not grasped as if whole but grasped through new intersubjective conditions of meeting: "He lifted up his mighty arms, and they cried to each other, almost with one voice, 'The world is dead.' 'Long live the——'"[16] This second iteration of "world" is never spoken as the potential of their intimate embrace is interrupted by Julia's family. This interruption ushers back into the world all of its racist structures and patterns. Julia's boyfriend gives Jim some money. A crowd threatens to lynch Jim Davis. The "world," in fact, is not gone. Only a part of it is. And what remains limits the historical and social possibilities of the African American subject.

Du Bois's figuration of worlds—especially in contradistinction to Stoddard's stagings of "world"—shows the struggles going on in the early twentieth century over making worlds thinkable and actionable; indeed, the process of making future worlds. This figuration applies not only to the imagination of future worlds but also to the speculations on past ones that shape the present. Like Yerby's critique of the historiography of Reconstruction analyzed in Part II, Du Bois critiques this historiography in *Black Reconstruction in America, 1860–1880*, not just for its misrepresentations but for the way in which they shaped the historical possibilities of black subjects through particular textual strategies of relocating racial meaning. He had his finger on the dangers of how history, romance, and propaganda intermingle over the contested formation of "worlds." In the last chapter, "The Propaganda of History," he summarizes the textbooks and histories of Reconstruction thus:

> In order to paint the South as a martyr to inescapable fate, to make the North the magnanimous emancipator, and to ridicule the Negro as the impossible joke in the whole development, we have in fifty years, by libel, innuendo, and silence, so completely misstated and obliterated the history of the Negro in America and his relation to its work and government that today it is almost unknown. This may be fine romance, but it is not science. It may be inspiring, but it is certainly not the truth. And beyond this it is dangerous. It is not only part foundation of our present lawlessness and loss of democratic ideals; it has, more than that, led the world to embrace and worship the color bar as social salvation and it is helping to range mankind in ranks of mutual hatred and contempt, at the summons of a cheap and false myth.[17]

Here Du Bois draws links between the histories that we have internalized through the multiple books and textbooks that tell the history of Reconstruction and the present and future worlds that they make possible. As Rebekka Fisher states in defining Du Bois's own historiographical method, "the past is reconstructed not only in a political effort to reframe the present but also to point in useful ways toward a viable future for black life."[18]

For Du Bois, the erasure of black Americans from the story of Reconstruction helps buttress and condition the historical possibilities of the present world. To counter this history, it is not enough to insert black voices and actions into existing historical events. In addition, Du Bois endeavors to show the way in which the organizing of racial distinction structures what can and cannot be done, what can and cannot be thought. As Du Bois puts it, "And then some unjust God leaned, laughing, over the ramparts of heaven and dropped a black man in the midst. It transformed the world. It turned democracy back to Roman Imperialism and Fascism; it restored caste and oligarchy."[19] This is not hyperbolic figuration here: what Du Bois attests to are the systems and structures that emerge in relation to black Americans in the constitution of what he calls the "sociophysical environment" of the "white world."

For example, in his chapter "The General Strike," Du Bois notes how the presence of black Americans themselves became a structure that governed the decisions and course of the Civil War and the possibility of the event of emancipation: "the Negro himself was not seriously considered by the majority of men, North or South. And yet from the very beginning, the Negro occupied the center of the stage because of very simple physical reasons: the war was in the South and in the South were 3,953,740 black slaves and 261,918 free Negroes. What was to be the relation of this mass of workers to the war?"[20] Dispelling the theories that the "Negro" either served faithfully their masters until "emancipation was thrust upon him" or that the "Negroes" were simply freed by advancing Northern armies—both theories of which rely on a base notion of black passivity—Du Bois reframes their presence in terms of the central function they played in terms of strategy in and around the war: labor. As *workers*, they were the key to the war, and as workers they exercised their agency in the world-organizing forces that had, up until then, ignored or erased the presence of black Americans:

> The North started out with the idea of fighting the war without touching slavery. They faced the fact, after severe fighting, that Negroes seemed a valuable asset as laborers, and they therefore declared them "contraband of war." It was but a step from that to attract and induce Negro labor to help the Northern armies. Slaves were urged and invited into the Northern armies; they became military laborers and

> spies; not simply military laborers, but laborers on the plantations, where the crops went to help the Federal army or were sold North. Thus wherever Northern armies appeared, Negro laborers came, and the North found itself actually freeing slaves before it had the slightest intention of doing so, indeed when it had every intention not to.[21]

In telling the story of the experience of the army with the refugees, Du Bois uncovers how the thought and actions of black laborers forced the issue of emancipation and slavery and shifted the world-organizing intentions and ideas of a North and South that essentially "ignored the Negro."[22] Du Bois pierces through the structures of explanation put into place by "ignoring the Negro" and installs new structures of explanation that get at the organizing forces put into place in and through the "Negro." This method is at the heart of his analysis of Reconstruction. This is why he starts his study with a chapter on "the black worker." The figuration present throughout the book—poetic descriptions of the "black worker," the "white worker," "the planter," the "poor white"—are all ways of personifying the forces of power that make these subjects possible or, in the case of the "black worker," impossible.

The historicism that Du Bois performs thus partakes of the figurations of romance and its ability to generalize about mood, temper, and desire. In characterizing the surge of black workers toward freedom, Du Bois writes, "There was joy in the South. It rose like perfume—like a prayer. Men stood quivering. Slim dark girls, wild and beautiful with wrinkled hair, wept silently; young women, black, tawny, white and golden, lifted shivering hands, and old and broken mothers, black and gray, raised great voices and shouted to God across the fields, and up to the rocks and the mountains."[23] He waxes romantic here. But he does so not to distort fact but to render certain facts—such as the fact of black labor during the war itself—visible. For Du Bois, conventional histories of Reconstruction obfuscate the thoughts and desires of black workers and thereby make possible a world order that marches forward into the future of Du Bois's present moment of 1935, the date of *Black Reconstruction's* publication.

Indeed, with chapters titled "Looking Backward" and "Looking Forward," Du Bois pinpoints this relationship between speculative modes of thought and race as a figure for thought. He connects Reconstruction and the struggle for black freedom with world war as moments of racial reorganization that otherwise would not be framed in this way. This is not a continuity based on the world wars as struggles for democracy but rather as formations of racial oligarchy. He writes at the end of the chapter "The White Worker":

> Then came this battle called Civil War, beginning in Kansas in 1854, and ending in the presidential election of 1876—twenty awful years. The slave went free; stood a brief moment in the sun; then moved back again toward slavery. The whole weight of America was thrown to color caste. . . . The upward moving of white labor was betrayed into wars for profit based on color caste. . . . The resulting color caste founded and retained by capitalism was adopted, forwarded and approved by white labor, and resulted in subordination of colored labor to white profits the world over. Thus the majority of the world's laborers, by the insistence of white labor, became the basis of a system of industry which ruined democracy and showed it perfect fruit in World War and Depression. And this book seeks to tell that story.[24]

What Du Bois limns are the powerful historiographical poetics that install a world-version that becomes the foundation for the "subordination of colored labor to white profits the world over" and the "basis of a system of industry which ruined democracy and showed its perfect fruit in World War and Depression." In tracing the continuities between world phenomena that are largely thought to be discontinuous—the U.S. Civil War and the developments of world war in Europe—Du Bois practices his own transformation of our worlds of reference.

This image of the continuity of the long history of black freedom struggle with world war relies on Du Bois's insistent use of race as personification for a set of forces. This use of personification can now be seen as a particular figure for countering the strategies of narrative explanation that we have seen in previous parts. While scholars have generally seen personification as a simplistic form of representation, such as Mr. Faithful or Ms. Happy, Du Bois's continued use of this strategy must be understood differently. If the indexical use of race discussed in Part IV stages the coherence of space and time such that racist explanations are already embedded in the (prior) understanding of a situation, we might see the use of personification as a strategy to make racism readable in terms of organizing forces. Such a narrative strategy recognizes the real historical effects that persons as representatives of sets of interests have. It counteracts the *resistance to being read* on the part of those who wish to be identified simply as the objective voice of the law or some other social institution.[25] In representing persons *as* the force of particular interests, Du Bois is constructing the terms for a different kind of historical explanation on a large scale.

For example, in his late work, *Worlds of Color*, Du Bois imagines a meeting in which representatives of nations involved on the world-historical stage of World War II get together in order to ensure the ends of industrialism and a capitalism based on racial exclusions. The meeting consists of "British industrialists and bankers, French business men of the type which originated the cartel idea, German army officers and representatives of Krupp and Thyssen; the Japanese ambassador was there and, of course, the chief heads of American corporations in steel, oil, food, fibers, and power production."[26] Together this group ensures war in the service of keeping back socialism and ensuring the division of production, trade, and finance in the world between Britain, France, Germany, and the United States. The men involved in this meeting do not simply represent national interests. They represent the combination of national and economic interests in the service of a broad set of racial exclusions. They could be personified simply as "Steel" or "Oil" or "Banks," and this personification is not a simplification so much as it is a figurative act that renders the relation between actions and interests transparent.

Du Bois narrates a proposal put forth in the meeting: if Roosevelt is re-elected president of the United States, then Japan will attack the United States, thereby precipitating and ensuring war. The rationale for this proposal is voiced in the collective voice of a small core committee: "War alone will insure our present profits and bring greater profits and power in the future. If, of course, there could be progress without war, we could consider peace. History has proven that impossible. By war alone can socialism finally be conquered."[27] This episode in *Worlds of Color* is not "alternate history" per se, but here Du Bois speculates on the conditions through which the historical event of Pearl Harbor is actualized. Pearl Harbor is not attacked simply because of Japanese imperialism. It is attacked in order to ensure the continuity of particular interests. The personification of these forces alerts us to another world, one that was built on circumscribing and foreclosing alternative possibilities. It is in this sense that the use of personification helps transform our worlds of reference.

The relationship between racial salience and the organization of the world remains a crucial point of discursive and imaginative struggle in the making of future worlds. In pursuing this relationship further, we might well remind ourselves of Du Bois's formulation concerning the difficulty in *locating* race and racism. In *Darkwater*, Du Bois narrates a conversation between himself and a pale friend who charges him with being too sensitive. The pale friend charges him with proving that racism is something that occurs everywhere and everyday. Du Bois's persona responds: "They [racism] do happen. Not all each day, surely not. But now and then—now seldom, now, sudden; now after a week, now in a chain of awful minutes; not everywhere, but anywhere—in Boston, in Atlanta."[28] *"Not everywhere, but anywhere."* Du Bois's formulation captures the spatio-temporal component of racism as a built-in knowledge for making the world. In doing so, he clarifies the task of an antiracist racial worldmaking. To render our racist worlds incoherent. To reimagine "anywhere."

ACKNOWLEDGMENTS

This book began with a class discussion that I had while teaching a course in multiethnic literature at University of California, Davis. We were reading Chang-rae Lee's *Aloft* and it became clear to me that we had no shared ground for determining when a particular scene, sentence, or sequence was *about* race. In fact, we did not agree on whether it was there to be read at all. From that moment on, I thought a great deal about how and in what ways we have been taught to notice race as meaningful in some contexts and not others. I wondered about our protocols for reading race. That sense of wonder slowly became this book.

This project thus owes a great deal of its development to teaching. I am grateful to the many undergraduate and graduate students at Davis who have thought through these protocols with me in discussing race, science fiction, and fantasy. My colleagues at Davis have been with me every step of the way in producing a lively and supportive environment. I wrote this book from its earliest drafts in dialogue with writing group partners Seeta Chaganti and Jon Rossini. Those dinner conversations, critiques, and feedback have shaped every aspect of this book. Early conversations with Colin Milburn on all things science fictional and on Samuel Delany's work in particular helped set the terms of my engagement. Feedback and insight from Margie Ferguson, Hsuan Hsu, John Marx, David Simpson, Matthew Vernon, and Claire Waters at a faculty presentation occurred at a critical point when I was putting all the disparate parts together. Gina Bloom, Joshua Clover, Fran Dolan, Beth Freeman, Danielle Heard, Desirée Martín, Elizabeth Miller, Parama Roy, Scott Simmon, Matthew Stratton, and Michael Ziser have been wonderful interlocutors over the years. Nathan Brown and David Lloyd offered theoretical queries that shaped my critical engagements.

I am grateful to audiences at Södertörn University, Harvard University, UC-Irvine, University of Warwick, Pennsylvania State University, and University of Tampere. Tobias Hubinette, Johanna Gondouin, Veronica

Hollinger, Gerry Canavan, Sianne Ngai, Lauren Berlant, Laura Scales, Geoff Ward, Lawrence Buell, and Osagie Obasogie all provided encouragement, suggestions, and crucial queries along the way. Panel presentations at conference meetings of the American Studies Association, Asian American Studies Association, International Association for the Fantastic in the Arts, and Modern Language Association helped me test out various ideas. I am especially grateful to Adrienne Brown and Britt Rusert for organizing a "Race and Genre Fiction" roundtable that occurred at a pivotal point in framing my project, as well as questions and conversation with Bill Gleason, Yogita Goyal, and Rachel Watson. Conversations with Jordana Rosenberg regarding Samuel Delany's work were crucial. Dialogues with Michael Levy, Isiah Lavender III, Helen Young, and John Rieder deepened my engagements with science fiction and fantasy. Suggestions at the level of argument from Mark Bould and Michael Omi on article versions helped clarify my stakes.

A University of California Center for New Racial Studies grant funded important archival research at the Eaton Collection of Science Fiction and Fantasy at UC Riverside and the Howard Gottlieb Archival Research Center at Boston University. I am grateful to the librarians there. UC Davis has provided research support for materials and travel. Michael Mlekoday helped with finalizing the bibliography and proofreading. Richard Morrison framed and found the right fit for this project as only the best editors can do. The two anonymous readers for Fordham University Press provided the best kind of critique: deep understanding of what I was after coupled with forceful critique on how to make it better.

I am fortunate to share each and every day with Liane, Seneca, and Chloe.

NOTES

INTRODUCTION: RACIAL WORLDMAKING

1. Coates, *Between the World and Me*, 78.

2. Haughwout, Mayer, and Tracy conclude that there was "no evidence of adverse pricing by race, ethnicity or sex of the borrower in either the initial rate or the reset margin" ("Subprime Mortgage Pricing," 21). Ghent, Hernández-Murillo, and Owyang *do* find evidence of adverse pricing, but conclude, "The adverse pricing we describe may not necessarily reflect explicit discrimination or bias on the part of lenders, and in our analysis we offer some alternative explanations" ("Differences in Subprime Loan Pricing," 3).

3. See Wyly, Atia, Lee, and Mendez, "Race, Gender and Statistical Representation"; Rugh and Massey, "Racial Segregation."

4. Dymski, Hernandez, and Mohanty, "Race, Power," 26.

5. See Anita Singh, "Avatar Hit by Accusations of Racism," *Telegraph*, January 11, 2010, and the comment written by iwannabeNa'Vi, http://www.telegraph.co.uk/culture/film/film-news/6968020/Avatar-hit-by-claims-of-racism.html (accessed December 10, 2016).

6. Koshy, "Why the Humanities Matter," 1542.

7. Perry argues that this standard does not capture the character of racism today, which is antideterminist and correlational (*More Beautiful and More Terrible*, loc. 395).

8. Omi and Winant, *Racial Formation* (2015), 125.

9. Omi and Winant, *Racial Formation* (1994), 55.

10. Omi and Winant, *Racial Formation* (2015), 111. The full restatement of the thesis in the later editions actually reinforces the primacy of the "nonreducible *visual dimension*": "Race is a concept, a representation or signification of identity that refers to different types of human bodies, to the perceived corporeal and phenotypic markers of difference and the meanings and social practices that are ascribed to these differences" (111).

11. Obasogie, *Blinded by Sight*, loc. 377.

12. Ibid., loc. 764.

13. Ibid., loc. 183. Obasogie's research shows this empirically through qualitative analysis of blind persons' experiences and descriptions of race. Counterintuitively, Obasogie learns, blind people describe race in visual terms, showing "how social relations and forces produce visual experiences" (loc. 718).

14. Omi and Winant, *Racial Formation* (2015), 124.

15. Ibid., 125.

16. Ibid., 128. This statement is a change from the 1994 edition, which relies more on the function of racial essentialism: "A racial project can be defined as *racist* if and only if it *creates or reproduces structures of domination based on essentialist categories of race*" (71).

17. Omi and Winant, *Racial Formation* (2015), 129.

18. Alcoff, "Philosophy and Racial Identity," 31.

19. "Notice," v. *OED Online*, Oxford University Press, December 2016 (accessed January 12, 2017).

20. I think of "noticing" in terms of Wittgenstein's philosophies of perception where he defines the experience of "noticing an aspect": "I contemplate a face, and then suddenly notice its likeness to another. I *see* that it has not changed; and yet I see it differently. I call this experience 'noticing an aspect.'" This experience of "noticing an aspect" or "seeing something as something" redefines perception in two ways, and Wittgenstein famously uses the duck-rabbit image as an illustration. First, we can see a rabbit as a duck because we can use other concepts to organize our perceptions of that object. Second, we see something *as* something because it has an internal relation to other objects based on the applicability of a set of concepts to both of them. Wittgenstein writes, "What I perceive in the dawning of an aspect is not a property of the object, but an internal relation between it and other objects" (Wittgenstein, *Philosophical*, 212). As Mulhall explains, this internal relation has been established via "conceptual or grammatical structures": "for Wittgenstein . . . grammar is that which tells us what kind of an object anything is" (*On Being in the World*, 130–31).

21. Massumi, *Parables for the Virtual*, 231.

22. See Goldberg, *Racist Culture*; Smedley, *Race in North America*; and Hill, *Everyday Language of White Racism*.

23. Quoted in Swaine, Lewis, and Roberts, "Grand Jury Decline."

24. McCracken, *Pulp*, 20. See chapter 1 for a fuller discussion of the history of popular genre fiction and its difference from earlier forms of popular culture.

25. Classic analyses of genre include Fowler, *Kinds of Literature*, and Frye, *Anatomy of Criticism*.

26. Derrida, "Law of Genre," 230.

27. Here, the classificatory function of genre as pure, fixed categories gives way to understanding genre in terms of expectation, potentiality, and emergence (Dimock, "Migration across Genres," 98).

28. Frow thinks Derrida goes too far in the other direction, positing the absolute singularity of the text against genre as constraint (*Genre*, 26–28).

29. Ibid., 30, 1, 7.

30. Hayot, *On Literary Worlds*, 72.

31. For an analysis of literature's construction of space-time relations, see Bakhtin's notion of the "chronotope" in *The Dialogic Imagination.* For Herman's delineation of mechanisms for producing space and time in the "storyworld," a term that encompasses links between "worlds evoked by narratives" and narratives "as blueprints for world-creation," see his "Scope and Aims of *Storyworlds*," vii.

32. Wolf, *Building Imaginary Worlds*, 17.

33. Herman, "Narrative Worldmaking." Pavel recognizes the ontological dimensions of fictional worlds: "Texts, media, are not just referential paths leading to worlds: to read a text or to look at a painting means already to inhabit their worlds" (*Fictional Worlds*, 74). For Goodman, the relationship between actual and possible worlds is not merely one of intervening: "no such thing as the real world, no unique, ready-made absolute reality apart from and independent of all versions and visions. Rather, there are many right world-versions, some of them irreconcilable with others; and thus there are many worlds if any. A version is not so much made right by a world as a world is made by a right version" (*Of Mind and Other Matters*, 127).

34. Wolf, *Building Imaginary Worlds*, 17.

35. See Radway, *Reading the Romance*; Bacon-Smith, *Science Fiction Culture*; Jenkins, *Textual Poachers*.

36. See Suvin, *Metamorphoses of Science Fiction*, 98. See also Freedman for his revision of Suvin's definition to consider this cognitive component as a "cognition effect" (*Critical Theory and Science Fiction*, 13–23).

37. Gerrig, *Experiencing Narrative Worlds*, 46, 41, 130, 132.

38. In *Dreaming by the Book*, Scarry conceives of literature as instructing readers in very precise ways to imagine things and to give "vivacity, solidity, persistence, and givenness" to the "perceptible world" (loc. 549).

39. Piper, "Impartiality, Compassion, and Modal Imagination," 726.

40. Ibid., 730.

41. Currie, *About Time*, loc. 177.

42. Hollinger, "Humanity 2.0," 267.

43. Bourdieu, *Distinction*, 33. Recent critical attention to these popular forms through literary and cultural studies has attempted to work against these dominant attitudes in various ways. See Radway, *Reading the Romance*;

Lynn Pearce, *Romance Writing*; Bacon-Smith, *Enterprising Women*; and Jenkins, *Textual Poachers*.

44. Delany, *Starboard Wine*, 188.

45. T. Roberts, *Aesthetics of Junk Fiction*, 133.

46. Radway, *Reading the Romance*, 201, 202.

47. Gibson, *Ecological Approach*, esp. chapter 8.

48. Kilgore's essay counteracts this tendency by turning critical attention toward African American science fiction writers ("Beyond the History We Know," 119). Jarrett's *Deans and Truants*, for example, historicizes racial realism as a particular normative constraint on expression by black authors.

49. See Sohn, *Racial Asymmetries*. Tsou, *Unquiet Tropes*, uses trope to rethink the assumptions behind referential reading practices that remain anchored in the givenness of the body and in the self-evident presentation of Asian American subjects in order to speak to sociohistorical reality. See also Pak and Tsou, "Introduction," 172–73. For work centered on aesthetics against the politics of racial referentiality, see Jeon, *Racial Things, Racial Forms*; Shockley, *Renegade Poetics*; C. Lee, *The Semblance of Identity*; Wang, *Thinking Its Presence*.

50. See Aldama, *Your Brain on Latino Comics*; see also Saldívar's "Second Elevation of the Novel" and "Historical Fantasy," which use a narratological approach to conceptualize a "postrace aesthetic" in readings of Colson Whitehead, Salvador Plascencia, and Junot Diaz.

51. Rieder, *Colonialism*.

52. See Lavender, *Race in American Science Fiction*. There are many good essays and books on race and science fiction, including work on authors such as Octavia Butler, Samuel Delany, Nalo Hopkinson, and Ted Chiang, among others. For a few notable examples, see Vint, "Only by Experience"; Tucker, *Sense of Wonder*; Dubey, *Signs and Cities*; Foster, *Souls of Cyberfolk*; Carrington, *Speculative Blackness*.

53. See B. Huang, *Contesting Genres*. Thoma, *Asian American Women's Popular Literature*, considers genre fiction by Asian American women in the context of neoliberal cultures of consumption in order to analyze the shaping of models of citizenship for Asian American women.

54. Lye, "Racial Form," 99.

55. Here I borrow and extend Chuh's influential formulation of Asian American studies as a "subjectless discourse." This critical orientation focuses on the "regulatory matrices" and situations through which the term "Asian American" "comes to have meaning" (*Imagine Otherwise*, 9, 11).

56. Sylvia Wynter's invocation of "genre of the human" is one theorization of this interaction. "Genre of the human" is her phrase for the link between "storytelling and biological being" that has historically instituted a

coloniality of being, one that excises the non-Western from models of humanness (McKittrick, *Sylvia Wynter*, loc. 819). Wynter traces this idea most clearly in "Unsettling the Coloniality." Her formulations are influential in constructing what other theorists call an "anti-black world." See Gordon for his discussion of the "facts" of blackness as "materially constituted realms" (*Her Majesty's Other Children*, 76). See also Weheliye, *Habeas Viscus*.

57. Several scholars have observed the close relationship between popular fictions and contemporaneous social changes and contradictions. S. Hall observes the "elements of recognition and identification, something approaching a recreation of recognisable experiences and attitudes, to which people are responding" in popular culture in "Notes on Deconstructing 'the Popular,'" 233. See also Glover and McCracken, "Introduction."

58. See Dillon, "Imagining Indigenous Futurisms," and Ramirez's articles on Chicanafuturism, including "Afrofuturism/Chicanafuturism," and "El fantasma en la máquina."

59. At the time of this writing, lawsuits in federal district courts are ongoing in relation to claims that admissions at various universities—Harvard University and University of North Carolina, Chapel Hill, in particular—discriminate against Asian applicants.

60. See Mullen, *Afro-Orientalism*; and Vijay Prashad, *Everybody Was Kung Fu Fighting*.

61. See Koshy, "Morphing Race into Ethnicity," 28; C. J. Kim, "Racial Triangulation of Asian Americans." See also Okihiro's pivotal article, "Is Yellow Black or White?," in *Margins and Mainstreams*.

62. See Saxton, *Indispensable Enemy*. For a model in which Asiatic racialization is not seen as a middle term but as a prior term that reroutes the triangulated model in interesting ways, see Jung, *Coolies and Cane*.

63. Lye, "Afro-Asian Analogy."

64. See Hsu's warnings about analogy in comparativism in "Sitting in Darkness." See also Lye, "Afro-Asian Analogy."

65. Frow, *Genre*, 104.

66. Omi and Winant, *Racial Formation* (2015), 114.

67. See Wiegman, *American Anatomies*, for her synthesis of the trajectory of the race concept from natural history to biological racism. Much of the writing on race that contested its biological and physical anthropological foundations worked off of a historical trajectory of this sort. For an exemplary instance, see Ruth Benedict, *Race*. See also Gossett, *Race*; Gould, *Mismeasure of Man*; Stanton, *Leopard's Spots*; Harding, *"Racial" Economy of Science*.

68. See Gilroy, *Against Race*; Duster, *Backdoor to Eugenics*; Haraway, "Universal Donors."

69. Stoler, "Racial Histories," 185.

70. Fredrickson, *Racism*, 100.

71. J. L. Jackson, *Racial Paranoia*, 87.

72. Bonilla-Silva, *Racism without Racists*, loc. 204.

73. In defining race as a "master category," Omi and Winant focus on the "act of categorizing people and assigning different attributes to such categories" (*Racial Formation* [2015], 105).

74. Chun, "Race and/as Technology, 11.

75. Stoler, "Racial Histories," 185.

76. Kendi, *Stamped from the Beginning*, 8.

77. Gilroy, *Against Race*, 58, 57, 42, 68.

78. Eshun, "Further Considerations on Afrofuturism," 289. This phrase occurs in the context of an argument where Eshun analyzes how the use and commodification of future projections and information in generating capital structures the present and destines Africa to decades of immiseration through debt and divestment. Eshun goes on to define the project of Afrofuturism not merely as imagining futures with black people or in correcting that history of the future but rather as "concerned with the possibilities for intervention within the dimension of the predictive, the projected, the proleptic, the envisioned, the virtual, the anticipatory and the future conditional" (293).

79. Loury, *Anatomy of Racial Inequality*, loc. 556; my italics.

80. Loury writes that his social-cognitive approach "may be usefully contrasted with an approach derived from the science/art of *biological taxonomy*. There, one endeavors to classify human beings on the basis of natural variation in genetic endowments across geographically isolated subpopulations" ("Anatomy of Racial Inequality," 241).

81. Ibid., 238–39, 241.

1. WORLDS OF COLOR

1. See "Rosy Snow" (1884); Kersting, *White World*.

2. See Pitt, "White World," 128; Hood, *Christmas Evans*, 13.

3. The denotation of the "white city" in the 1893 Chicago World's Fair is related to this geopolitical usage of "white world." For a critique of the racial formation of the "white city," see Reed, *"All the World Is Here!"*

4. See Jung, *Coolies and Cane*; Lowe, *Intimacies of Four Continents*; Wong, *Racial Reconstruction*; Glenn, *Unequal Freedom*.

5. Goodman, *Of Mind and Other Matters*, 132; Goodman, *Languages of Art*, 88.

6. Lye, *America's Asia*, complicates this conventional understanding, making the argument that "yellow peril" and "model-minority discourses" are not distinct stages of Asiatic racialization but, rather, two parts of the same racial form (see esp. 47–96).

7. See Berlant's discussion of genre in relation to the emerging event in *Cruel Optimism*, 6–7.

8. See Heidegger, "Age of the World Picture," 129. I am drawing on Heidegger's argument that what characterizes modern knowledge production is the grasping of the world as picture: "'To get the picture' throbs with being acquainted with something, with being equipped and prepared for it. Where the world becomes picture, what is, in its entirety, is juxtaposed as that for which man is prepared and which, correspondingly, he therefore intends to bring before himself and have before himself" (129). Heidegger here is concerned with those procedures that bind the world to the procedures of knowing. See also Krishnan, "Reading Globalization from the Margin," who defines the global as a "peculiar way of making the world visible and legible" (41).

9. London, "Give Battle to Retard Enemy," 105.

10. We already hear the strains in assumptions based in physical anthropology in the orientalist writings of the 1880s. For example, Percival Lowell qualifies any simple designation of the Japanese as "primitive," while still measuring the Japanese on a scale of civilization: "To say that the Japanese are not a savage tribe is of course unnecessary. . . . At present we go halfway in recognition of these people by bestowing upon them a demi-diploma of mental development called semi-civilization, neglecting, however, to specify in what the fractional qualification consists." Lowell locates his grounds for primitivism not in bodies but in the language, famously calling it "backward" in a civilizational sense in response to the fact that you read Japanese from right to left. See Lowell, *Soul of the Far East*, quoted in Yunte Huang, *Transpacific Displacements*, 28.

11. Lye, *America's Asia*, 47–96, highlights Jack London's role in relation to the problem of "Asiatic modernity" posed by the Japanese military victory over Russia. She shows one way in which this perceptual problem was resolved: through a yoking of the "sophisticated" Japanese with the "primitivist" Chinese in creating a dual-pronged yellow peril that was never simply a stereotype but more a representational system. Her interest in showing the developments of racial representation in nonanthropomorphic directions is similar to my own.

12. London, "Yellow Peril," 349.

13. See Tsou, *Unquiet Tropes*, chap. 4, for a survey and tropological reading of Asian deceit.

14. London, "If Japan Wakens China," 358.

15. Hough further argues that this imagination of invasion, pervasive across popular culture and fiction alike, is used to rationalize and justify the actions of the United States during World War II, including the use of atomic bombs. See Hough, "Demon Courage and Dread Engines," 23–39. I similarly

engage London, H. G. Wells, and others in order to delineate the specific epistemologies put in place through these speculative forms of knowledge.

16. Ibid., 361.

17. Weale, *Conflict of Colour*, 113; italics mine.

18. Weale, "Conflict of Color," 12122.

19. Ibid., 12023.

20. The genre of "future history" within the field of science fiction as defined through John Campbell and Robert Heinlein denotes the continuity across a set of serialized or scattered publications. More broadly, it refers to stories that are set in the future that then go on to tell the history of how it came to be. See Csicsery-Ronay, *Seven Beauties of Science Fiction*, esp. "Future History," for a broad analysis of SF's multiple forms of engaging "future history."

21. Weale, "Conflict of Color," 12023–24.

22. Goodman, *Ways of Worldmaking*, enumerates specific processes through which different world-versions are formed. The two that I draw on to describe Weale's linguistic and descriptive strategies here are "weighting" and "ordering." "Weighting" is sorting the same classes of entities that make up the world "differently into relevant and irrelevant kinds" (10). "Ordering" is making different worlds by changing the order of derivation. As Goodman states, "perceived patterns change under different orderings; the patterns perceived under a twelve-tone scale are quite different from those perceived under the traditional eight-tone scale" (13).

23. Weale, *Conflict of Colour*, 111–12.

24. Stoddard, *Rising Tide of Color*, 3–5.

25. Ibid., 5–6.

26. Ibid., 12.

27. Weale, *Conflict of Colour*, 87.

28. I do not include works such as Arthur Vinton's *Looking Further Backward* (1890), which tells the history of a future world in which China has become a global empire from the point of view of that future. What all of my works have in common is the narrative construction of *anticipating* the yellow peril. See Hayot, *Hypothetical Mandarin*, 148–71, for a reading of *Looking Further Backward* that centers on precisely its tangential relation to popular invasion novels.

29. Weale, *Conflict of Colour*, 116.

30. Ibid.

31. Stoddard, *Rising Tide of Color*, 29.

32. Ibid., 124.

33. See Thompson, *Yellow Peril, 1890–1924*, and Takaki, *Strangers from a Different Shore*.

34. Okihiro, *Margins and Mainstreams*, 119.

35. See "The 'Yellow Peril' Mystique: Origins and Vicissitudes of a Racist Discourse," in Lyman, *Roads to Dystopia*, 65–111.

36. Sohn, "Alien/Asian," summarizes: "the yellow peril traditionally operates with an overtly racist representation predicated on the danger it represents to the West's economic and military primacy" (7).

37. Daniels, *Concentration Camps, U.S.A.*, documents this escalation through newspaper accounts at the time. He states, "In addition to the usual economic and racial arguments, arguments that stressed a lowering of the standard of living and the impossibility of assimilation, the *Chronicle* injected two new and ugly elements into the agitation: sex and war" (10–11).

38. Both Lye, *America's Asia*, and Ferreira Da Silva, *Toward a Global Idea of Race*, point to ways in which yellow peril discourse operates within global formations of race. Lye writes, "Despite the increasing thematization of East-West conflict in world politics, disparate geopolitical interests undermined the certainty of any line that could be drawn between 'East' and 'West.' . . . The Western imperialist struggle *for* Asia was therefore itself depicted as a struggle *between* East and West" (22–23). Ferreira da Silva argues, "In the period between 1875 and the 1930s, the racial would reorganize the global space" (194). The intertwining of this globality and a teleological historicism renders European and U.S. subjects in terms of transparency and what Ferreira da Silva calls the "others of Europe" in terms of "affectability."

39. Respectively, Wells, *War in the Air*, 235; "Predicts War with Japanese," *Los Angeles Herald*, August 18, 1908; "Presents a New Yellow Peril," *San Francisco Call*, February, 1, 1908, 9.

40. For "yellow flood," see Weale, *Coming Struggle in Eastern Asia*, 101. For "yellow wave," see Shiel, *Yellow Wave*. For "yellow peril in action," see Manson, *Yellow Peril in Action*, analyzed in more detail below.

41. Wu, *Yellow Peril*, 39.

42. Pearson, *National Life and Character*, 16.

43. Stepan, *Idea of Race in Science*, notes the shift in "race science" to a "sense of man as primarily a biological being, embedded in nature and governed by biological laws" (4). Wiegman, *American Anatomies*, draws some further conclusions from Stepan's analysis, stating, "In the ascendancy of biology . . . the concept of 'race' will undergo significant transformation, losing the kind of fluidity it achieved in natural history as a product of climate and civilization, as a variation within the human species, to become a rather stable and primary characteristic for defining the nature of the body, both its organic and ontological consistency" (30). For accounts of the historical genealogy of concepts of race as they move from the domain of natural history to a biological concept, see Bernasconi and Lott, *Idea of Race*, and Stanton, *Leopard's Spots*.

44. Thompson, *Yellow Peril*, 18.
45. Pearson, *National Character*, 68.
46. Ibid., 50; my italics.
47. Koselleck, *Practice of Conceptual History*, 135–36.
48. Ibid., 107.
49. Ibid.
50. Ibid., 112.
51. Thompson's *Yellow Peril* details the importance of Adams's treatise for the history of yellow perilism.
52. Adams, *Law of Civilization and Decay*, 1–2.
53. Koselleck, *Practice of Conceptual History*, 112.
54. Pearson, *National Life and Character*, 14.
55. "The Perils," *San Francisco Call*, October 29, 1910, 4.
56. "Sounds a Warning to the United States," *San Francisco Call*, August 12, 1907, 4.
57. "Conger Is Not Going to China," *San Francisco Call*, August 25, 1905, 2.
58. "Predicts War with Japanese," *Los Angeles Herald*, August 18, 1908, 9.
59. "Orientalism Is Spreading Danger," *Los Angeles Herald*, June 27, 1905, 1; "Yellow Peril War Declared," *Los Angeles Herald*, March 4, 1910, 11; "Presents a New Yellow Peril," *San Francisco Call*, February 1, 1908, 9.
60. "Germany Fears Japanese Victory Would Mean the Exclusion of the White Race from Asia," *San Francisco Call*, February 14, 1904, 23.

2. FUTURES PAST OF ASIATIC RACIALIZATION

1. See Franklin, "How America's Fictions" and *War Stars*; Clarke, *Voices Prophesying War*.
2. Clarke, "Future-War Fiction," 13.
3. Chesney, *Battle of Dorking*, 21.
4. Ibid., 22.
5. Ibid.
6. Ibid., 1.
7. Clarke, "Future-War Fiction," 15.
8. Ibid. Clarke identifies these histories with writers like "Guizot, Thierry, Michelet, Francis Parker, Macaulay, Carlyle, Buckle, von Ranke, Treitschke" (15).
9. Guynn and Stahuljak, "Introduction," 1–2.
10. Clarke, "Future-War Fiction," 15.
11. Manson, *Yellow Peril in Action*, 5.
12. Ibid., 3.
13. Ibid., 12.
14. Ibid., 16.

15. Burton, "Prophet of Pearl Harbor," 8.
16. Boothe, introduction, 5.
17. Ibid., 2.
18. Ibid., 24.
19. Lea, *Valor of Ignorance*, 8.
20. Ibid., 10.
21. Ibid.
22. Ibid., 13.
23. Burton, "Prophet of Pearl Harbor," 8.
24. See Yamamura's argument about the use of the term "alien" in *Valor of Ignorance* in chapter 2 of his "Science Fiction Futures."
25. Lea, *Valor of Ignorance*, 23.
26. Ibid., 158.
27. William Delisle Hay, "The Fate of the Inferior Races," quoted in Clarke, "Future-War Fiction," 11.
28. For an excellent reading of future war novels and yellow peril with particular emphasis on Chinese invasion, see Hayot, *Hypothetical Mandarin*. For a reading of the relationship between political discourse and Palmer's future war novel, see Rieder, "Palmer's *The Invasion of New York*," 85–103.
29. Henry Norman writes, "Japan's eyes would turn first to China . . . she would mould China to her will," quoted in *Review of Reviews* 29, ed. W. T. Stead (January–June 1904): 252. George Lynch states, "I believe that the ideal of Japan . . . is to put herself at the head of an awakened and modernized China, and form a great Asiatic confederacy." Lynch quoted in "Japanization of China," *American Monthly Review of Reviews* 29 (1904): 468. Alexander Ular writes of the "formation of a formidable Yellow Block, the existence of which would entail a racial struggle alike merciless and fatal for Europe." Ular, "Europe's Failure, Japan's Opportunity," *Review of Reviews* 29 (1904): 251.
30. For the context of Shiel's publication of *The Empress of the Earth* in terms of what may have drawn Shiel to the subject matter, see Squires, "Some Contemporary Themes," 249–329. For the idea that Louis Tracy may have suggested the future war format to Shiel, see Stableford, "Politics of Evolution," 372.
31. Shiel, *Yellow Danger*, 335.
32. Hayot, *Hypothetical Mandarin*, 150.
33. Ibid., 149.
34. See Wu, *Yellow Peril.*
35. The *Saturday Review* describes the novel thus: "It is horrible, exciting, impossible, alluring, fascinating, but above all, it is audacious." Review of "The Yellow Danger: A Romance." *Saturday Review* (1898), 448. This review is included in Morse, *Shiel in Diverse Hands*, 113.

36. Shiel, *Yellow Danger*, 44.
37. Ibid., 4, 10–11.
38. Ibid., 15–16.
39. Ibid., 28, 30–31.
40. Ibid., 12–13.
41. Worth, "Reversible Empire," has an excellent related argument that links the logic of race to an "ahistorical timelessness" (105) and a "racial recoding of the world," in his discussion of two contemporaneous future war novels, George Griffith's *The Angel of the Revolution* (1893) and Louis Tracy's *The Final War* (1896). Worth links this logic of race to an evolutionary time based in social Darwinism and a "narrative of technological superiority" (111).
42. Shiel, *Yellow Danger*, 45.
43. Ibid., 29.
44. Quoted in a review of *The Yellow Danger* in the *Academy Supplement*, July 30, 1898, 105–6.
45. The reviewer prefaces his quote from the novel with these statements: "The best portions of the book are those which describe Hardy's naval actions . . . he makes the encounters perfectly conceivable. The book is punctuated with them, and they are of enthralling interest. People tired of the exiguous newspaper accounts of the engagement in the American-Spanish War will find positive refreshment in Mr. Shiel's full and convincing methods." Review in ibid., 105–6.
46. Quoted in Squires, "Some Contemporary Themes," 297. This essay includes various excerpts from Stead's writings that show his own interest and anxieties concerning Japan's victory against Russia.
47. Squires, afterword to *China in Arms.*
48. H. G. Wells, preface to *The Sleeper Awakes*, 238.
49. See the *Saturday Review* reviews of "Prince Zaleski" and "The Rajah's Sapphire," which "were presumably written by H. G. Wells," in Morse, *Shiel in Diverse Hands*, 112–13. See also an article on Wells's impact on Shiel and Shiel's impact on Wells: George Hay, "Shiel versus the Renegade Romantic," in *Shiel in Diverse Hands*, 109–12.
50. Parrinder, *Shadows of the Future*, 78. Haynes, *H. G. Wells*, reads *The War in the Air* within the context of scientific industrialism and war, as well as Wells's narrative techniques for showing the impact of war on individuals with no mention of the yellow peril. Hammond, in his entry on *The War in the Air*, does not mention the yellow peril at all. This tradition of reading is maintained in an examination of detachment, war, and technology in Mollmann, "Air-Ships and the Technological Revolution."
51. H. G. Wells, "Preface to the 1921 Edition," in *War in the Air* (2005), 278.

52. H. G. Wells, "Preface to the 1941 Edition," in *War in the Air* (2005), 279.

53. Wynter, introduction to *The War in the Air*, xxi–xxii.

54. For an excellent reading of race and colonialism in H. G. Wells's *The Island of Dr. Moreau*, see John Rieder, *Colonialism and the Emergence of Science Fiction*, esp. chap. 4. See also Hough's contextualization of *The War in the Air* in relation to popular formations of Japanese invasion as "techno-orientalist" ("Demon Courage," 36).

55. Squires, "Some Contemporary Themes," 299.

56. H. G. Wells, *War in the Air* (1908), 97–98.

57. Ibid., 98.

58. Ibid., 235–36.

59. Ibid., 107.

60. Ibid., 251. This language echoes that found in Griffith's *The Angel of the Revolution*: "The fierce flood of war had swept away all smaller distinctions. It was necessary to rise to the altitude of the problem of the Government, not of nations, but of the world" (307).

61. This is a rephrasing of Stephen Greenblatt's understanding of the anecdote or fragment as giving us a "touch of the real." See Gallagher and Greenblatt, *Practicing New Historicism*.

62. H. G. Wells, *War in the Air* (1908), 297.

63. Ibid., 149.

64. Ibid., 178–79.

65. Ibid., 184.

66. Ibid., 186.

67. Wu writes in *The Yellow Peril*: "The water imagery appears in all four of these novels, where the solid entity of Chinese stream out of China, pour into the United States, and wash away all opposition in a cresting flood tide" (39).

68. H. G. Wells, *War in the Air* (1908), 277, 273.

69. Wong's renewed attention in "In a Future Tense" to the alternate history/counterfactual form of some of these fictions helpfully reinvigorates our analysis of these works. She argues that the speculative fiction around Chinese invasion lent a particular political utility for exclusion legislation and the legally actionable scenarios that they created in order to facilitate the retroactive *and* projective taking away of rights from U.S. citizens of Chinese descent.

70. See Roh, Huang, and Niu, *Techno-Orientalism*, 12.

3. ROMANCE AND RACISM AFTER THE CIVIL WAR

1. Listing several popular works in the late 1880s and into the 1890s, Jeremy Wells, *Romances*, writes, "It is remarkable . . . that the resonance [of

plantation fiction] seemed actually to increase as the nineteenth century came to an end, with such works as Francis Hopkinson Smith's *Colonel Carter of Cartersville* (1891) and Thomas Nelson Page's *Red Rock* (1898) numbering among the more popular American novels of the 1890s. It is more remarkable still that it continued well into the twentieth century, long after most of those who might actually have known life on an old plantation had gone the way of Foster's 'old massa . . . in de cold, cold ground'" (3).

2. For a survey of plantation fiction that locates its heart in the nineteenth century and then gradually fades from view by the twentieth century, see Grammer, "Plantation Fiction."

3. Luck, *Body of Property*, 142–43.

4. For arguments that post–Civil War plantation fiction takes on both nationalist and imperialist projects, see J. Wells, *Romances*; on the impact of Reconstruction on U.S. imperialism well into the twentieth century, see Stecopoulos, *Reconstructing the World*; on the role of romance in imagining national reconciliation after the U.S. Civil War, see Silber, *Romance of Reunion*; on plantation fiction and the afterlife of property relations, see Luck, *Body of Property*.

5. See Grammer, "Plantation Fiction," for this story's place in the literary history of plantation fiction.

6. Hale, *Making Whiteness*, loc. 950, 989.

7. Ibid., loc. 1017.

8. Greeson, *Our South*, usefully contextualizes and analyzes familiar notions of the plantation romance as "idyll" within an understanding of the ideological work it does toward national consciousness; see esp. Part I.

9. See Grammer, "Plantation Fiction."

10. Other analyses distinguish between the ideological work being done by the early twentieth-century plantation romances and the romance of history. For Woodward, *Origins of the New South*, these reinterpretations of the past link up with the economic development of a new white rising middle class built around industry. For Hale, *Making Whiteness*, the reinterpretation of history grounds a modern whiteness within the logics of segregation. See also J. Wells, *Romances*, and Gray, *Writing the South*.

11. Cowley, "Going with the Wind," 161–62.

12. Cripps, "Winds of Change," 139. As Cripps suggests, both writers who followed Cowley in lambasting the novel for its refurbishing of the "plantation legend" and critics on the right, "doctrinaire Southerners expecting a reflowering of the old myths" and not getting it critiqued Mitchell's novel. The inability to satisfy either of these groups exemplifies the in-between position of Mitchell's novel in terms of its representational politics of race (140).

13. D. Roberts, *Myth of Aunt Jemima*, 171.

14. For an analysis of Thomas Dixon's works in relationship to scientific racism and the racialization of character, see Boeckmann, *Question of Character*, 11–98.

15. O'Brien, "Race, Romance," 162–63. For analyses of racial imagery, see Williamson, "How Black Was Rhett Butler?"

16. McPherson, *Reconstructing Dixie*, 63–64. In foregrounding Mitchell's construction of a new woman and a new man in her romance, Jones, "*GWTW* and Others," 372–73, does not mention race at all in her analysis.

17. I draw on work in the philosophy of aesthetics for this conception of how different strategies of verbal discourse construct different organizations of meaning. Goodman, *Of Mind and Other Matters*, 55, describes "routes of reference" as the "various relationships that may obtain between a term or other sign or symbol and what it refers to." These relationships include verbal denotation (naming, predication, description), notation (like a music score), exemplification (reference by a sample to a feature of the sample), and expression (exemplification of a label or feature that metaphorically rather than literally denotes).

18. Dixon, *Leopard's Spots*, loc. 145.

19. Ibid., loc. 153.

20. J. Wells, *Romances*, 115.

21. Dixon, *Leopard's Spots*, loc. 154

22. Ibid., loc. 1681.

23. Williamson, "How Black Was Rhett Butler?," writes, "Margaret Mitchell grew up in a white Georgia world very much pervaded by a fear of the black beast rapist. And yet in *Gone with the Wind* there is no potential black rapist worthy of mention in more than a few lines, and none at all important enough to be given a name" (87). O'Brien, "Race, Romance," writes that Mitchell shifts the racial politics of the sexual attack because the attackers include two men, one black, one white: "With the identification of the area as 'the refuge of negro and white criminals,' race is subordinated to economic and social factors" (161).

24. Richardson, "Mammy's 'Mules,'" highlights these rules as they pertain to marriage and courtship, and she points specifically to Mammy's role articulating these "time-honored scripts and protocols of southern social life." But even as "Mammy is the *rule* model to whom we need to look for a thorough epistemology of the character Scarlett," her exclusion from femininity "emphasized her own subordination" (54, 75).

25. I draw on M.-L. Ryan's framework for thinking about the relations among the many possible worlds within a narrative system: "From the viewpoint of its participants, the goal of the narrative game—which is for them

the game of life—is to make TAW [textual actual world] coincide with as many as possible of their private worlds. . . . The moves of the game are the actions through which characters attempt to alter relations between worlds" (*Possible Worlds*, 119–20).

26. Mitchell, *Gone with the Wind*, 8. Subsequent references are noted parenthetically in the text.

27. The servants of Tara are introduced only in relation to the objects they bring: "the little black girl who carried her [Ellen's] basket of keys"; "there was the click of china and the rattle of silver as Pork, the valet-butler of Tara, laid the table for supper" (*GWTW*, 8).

28. In the context of analyzing the Mammy figure and the relationship between black and white femininity, McPherson, "Seeing in Black and White," focuses on this manipulation of foreground and background: "the figure of Mammy provides the (dark) background against which the (white) image of Scarlett can take shape" (521).

29. McPherson gives other examples of this animalistic imagery (ibid.).

30. For example, Mitchell writes, "Will, like Mammy, seemed to know things without being told" (*GWTW*, 550), and Careen "treated Will as gently as a brother and took him as much for granted as she did Pork" (513).

31. I derive this notion of landscape from Samuel Delany's many uses of the word. For example, Delany, *Longer Views*, 308, writes of the science fiction writer's "delight over inserting new facts into unfamiliar landscapes," implying by "landscape" something more like the linguistic and social field of the fiction.

32. Will's status as "white" is raised several times, most often in connection with how marriageable he is. See the discussions on 513 and 715.

33. Radway, *Reading the Romance*, 201, 202.

34. T. Roberts, *Aesthetics of Junk Fiction*, 133.

35. This fact is cited as Mitchell's transformation of the plantation romance convention and her departure from the myth of the iconic black rapist. See Williamson, "How Black Was Rhett Butler?" and O'Brien, "Race, Romance."

36. The movie version directed by Victor Fleming famously and controversially eliminates even this reference, using "social club" instead of the Klan. Haskell, *Frankly, My Dear*, 203.

37. O'Brien, "Race, Romance," analyzes this almost-rape scene, stating, "the scene is more clearly drawn in terms of a criminal or social violation rather than merely a racial act. . . . By this means, Mitchell isolates the affair from the main flow of the narrative or plot line. It is simply one more dramatic event rather than an integral part of the plot. . . . By presenting the scene this way, Mitchell shifts the motivation from racial differences to criminal behavior in general" (161). As I demonstrate, this scene is actually crucial

in the romance plot (the move from Frank to Rhett) and in the development of Scarlett's character in relation to the role of the Ku Klux Klan and its place in the South. By focusing on the detail that a black *and* a white man participate in the assault, O'Brien misses the function of racial attribution in the novel's narrative organization. In dismissing race as merely figurative and therefore "background material," O'Brien concludes, "Mitchell's novel would still hold together and still make sense if all the comments on black character were eliminated or even if black characters disappeared" (162–63). But it is my contention that the novel relies precisely on the reader's participation in racial attribution for both its coherence and much of its narrative pleasures.

38. These two scenes have often been read either singularly or together as depictions of sexual assault and how race and gender are mobilized through them. For a useful synthesis of critical readings of these scenes of sexual assault and a linking of the two scenes along the lines of Scarlett's relationship to the Reconstruction economy, see Barker, "Reconstructing Scarlett."

39. In "How Black Was Rhett Butler?," Williamson argues that the imagery of blackness in the racialized figuration of Rhett is used to reconstruct fears of the "black rapist" that are missing at the "literal" level of the text. O'Brien, "Race, Romance," comments on it in order to dismiss it. Young analyzes what it suggests not so much about Rhett but about Scarlett. For Young, the "brownness" of Rhett neutralizes his masculinity as social threat, and instead is the vehicle by which Scarlett gains sexual pleasure, fulfilling audience expectations and allowing them to "become dark" surreptitiously. E. Young, *Disarming the Nation*, writes, "In *Gone with the Wind*'s climactic moment, the white woman's implicit racial 'darkness,' coupled with her explicit subjugation, is the foundation of her sexual ecstasy" (271–72).

40. T. Ryan, *Calls and Responses*, argues that the novel "obfuscates the nature of slavery and consequent divisions in American society by constructing them as issues of social class rather than race" (22). By focusing on class "rather than race," Ryan sees this rhetoric as in the service of an aristocratic vision of the U.S. South. My argument departs from Ryan's in reading the reconfigurations of class and race as they serve to reconstruct whiteness beyond its "aristocratic" frameworks of superiority.

4. RECONSTRUCTING RACIAL PERCEPTION

1. C. L. R. James, *American Civilization*, 129–30.
2. B. Jackson, "Silver Foxes," 651
3. Ibid., 652.
4. A common way of disavowing racial aspects in these romances is to locate them in the "background." Wendt, "Amber Hued Romances," writes, "Against a background of pre-Civil War New Orleans, probably the most

exotic and glamorous place and period an historical novelist could select from the American scene, the youthful Frank Yerby has written a lurid, swift paced tale of a red haired Irish gambler named Stephen Fox, who won and lost a sugar cane empire while winning and losing the woman he thought he loved" (G3). Locke, "Reason and Race," situates *Foxes* similarly, with the effect of downplaying any "social significance": "On grander, more colorful but less socially significant canvas, Frank Yerby has written The Foxes of Harrow (Dial)—a romantic historical best-seller. Superior to most novels of this genre in his carefully drawn historical background of early 19th century New Orleans, Yerby's smooth romancing accomplishes an interesting tour de force, giving him the right to a vast audience and a deeper influence when and if he should later choose to write more seriously realistic fiction, whether of Negro life or American life in general" (20).

5. Yerby, *Foxes of Harrow*, 25. Subsequent citations are noted parenthetically in the text.

6. At the copyediting phase, "nigger" is often changed to "Negro" or "nigra." In this passage, "café noir" is replaced by "black coffee," thus obscuring the parallelism of "café noir" and "café au lait" and the juxtaposition of how one likes their coffee with how one likes the racial composition of their women. See "*Foxes of Harrow*, typescript."

7. At the copyediting stage, Yerby's phrase "like a nigger" was replaced with "like a Negro." The original is closer to Mitchell's phrase. See "*Foxes of Harrow*, typescript."

8. The name Odalie resonates with the orientalist painterly tradition of the odalisque, which represents a slave or concubine figure, thus further showing how the white woman's "other"—be it slave or blackness—is internal to the constitution of the white woman heroine in plantation romance. Thanks to Seeta Chaganti for this reference.

9. Jarrett, *Deans and Truants*, writes of the resolution of Stephen Fox's ideological relationship to the race problem: "If *The Foxes of Harrow* begins by defining Stephen's Americanness in terms of his consent to southern values, the novel ends by redefining it as a product of his ideological dissent on the race problem" (161).

10. Haskell, *Frankly, My Dear*, writes, "when the book was finally finished and published in 1936, with the movie following in 1939, it was the Depression that weighed on everyone's minds. According to the cards of the preview audiences, almost all saw the movie as a reflection of their own experience. To these viewers *Gone with the Wind* was both escape and parallel: a story of struggle and survival during a national catastrophe, but at a romantic remove. Scarlett's evolution from seductress to woman of action exerted an enormous pull as a fable for working women" (11). Hale, *Making Whiteness*, focuses, too, on a white order in a "desperate struggle for survival with their

very own values" in arguing that *Gone with the Wind* elaborates a new southern formation of middle-class whiteness that responds to conditions in the 1930s (loc. 5347).

11. Notions of an individuality that acts within a race-neutral landscape have long stymied efforts to address racial inequality. Du Bois, *Black Reconstruction in America*, called the belief that "wealth is mainly the result of its owner's effort and that any average worker can by thrift become a capitalist" the "great American assumption." He argues that this belief, revived and rearticulated at different historical moments, was a powerful justification for postslavery industrial development in the South and connected the needs of capital with the economic disfranchisement of the freed population (182–83). As Turner, *Awakening to Race*, writes, this assumption has had an "enduring reign in U.S. political culture" and that "popular disregard for how structure constrains agency . . . impedes clear thinking about the causes of racial inequality" (5).

12. For a synthesis of some of these critical responses that call out Yerby for the absence of race, as well as a counter-reading that analyzes various racial themes in Yerby's novels, see Moore, "Guilt of the Victim." For a contextualization of Yerby's move toward a career as a popular writer as a critique of the dictates of "race-problem" literature and a counter-reading of *Foxes of Harrow* that studies Stephen's complex ideological conflicts with regard to slavery, see Jarrett, *Deans and Truants*, 143–67. For an analysis of Yerby as a debunker of various historical myths, see D. T. Turner, "Frank Yerby as Debunker."

13. Yerby, "Notes of Background Material."

14. Ibid.

15. To say that it was "finished" is a bit of a simplification. What I am signaling is a broad sense of questioning the scientific "facts" of race that the UNESCO declarations ushered forth. For a contextualization and analysis of the institutional history of these UNESCO statements in relation to the formation of racism and antiracism, see Balibar, "Racism Revisited." Among other things, Balibar notes that UNESCO "had to issue not one but two declarations on race and racism, the second after the first was challenged by some scientific authorities (notably the British Royal Academy)" (1634). This suggests not a model of the "end" of one mode of thought and the beginning of another but rather one of "continuous tension and reformulation that even today make the critique of racism a work in progress" (1634).

5. THE "FACTS" OF BLACKNESS AND ANTHROPOLOGICAL WORLDS

1. Lieber, "Letter," 21.

2. Farah Mendlesohn's *Rhetorics of Fantasy* mentions S&S as an influence on quest fantasy and for its emphasis on action. Sword and sorcery is mentioned for its popularity as a series and for its interest in the deep past

in Paul Kincaid's, Kari Maund's, and Edward James's contributions to the *Cambridge Companion to Fantasy Literature*. For field-defining criticism from psychoanalytic, structuralist, and formal perspectives, respectively, see R. Jackson, *Fantasy*; Todorov, *Fantastic*; and Atteberry, *Strategies of Fantasy*.

3. Delany, *Silent Interviews*, 226, refers to S&S as a "largely infantile genre." Paul Kincaid calls Howard a writer of "swashbuckling adventure" combined with "weird fiction" in "American Fantasy 1820–1950," in E. James, *Cambridge Companion to Fantasy Literature*, 45.

4. For J. R. R. Tolkien's place in the development of epic fantasy, see Edward James, "Tolkien, Lewis and the Explosion of Genre Fantasy," in E. James, *Cambridge Companion to Fantasy Literature*; Shippey, *Road to Middle-Earth*; Haber, *Meditations on Middle-Earth;* and chapter 2 of Atteberry, *Strategies of Fantasy*.

5. Bould, "Dreadful Credibility of Absurd Things," 81.

6. Fabian, *Time and the Other*, 55.

7. For a detailed account of the use of maps in building worlds, see Wolf, *Building Imaginary Worlds*, 155–64.

8. See Rearick, "Why Is the Only Orc," 861–62. Fimi, *Tolkien, Race and Cultural History*, traces the construction of the worlds as a vestige of specific ideologies of race based either in now-discounted biological or anthropological explanations. H. Young, "Diversity and Difference," re-evaluates the function of diversity in Tolkien as "essential to cultural renewal" (352).

9. See Ahmed, "Is 'Game of Thrones' Too White?"; Rastogi, "Is 'Game of Thrones' Racist?"; and Marvin, "Game of Thrones, Racism."

10. Martin comments, "Most of these people have obviously not read the books. If they had, they would know there is no racial component to slavery as practiced on Essos. It is based on slavery as it existed in the ancient world. The Romans and Greeks were just as willing to enslave other Greeks and Romans as they were Celts, Goths, Germans, and Africans. It's on the page." See "Not a Blog," http://grrm.livejournal.com/325946.html?page=2#comments.

11. I derive this description of a classical account of allegory from Fletcher, *Allegory*, and Teskey, *Allegory and Violence*. My own understanding of allegory also takes into consideration De Man's description in *Blindness and Insight* of the mode in relation to the temporality of meaning in which one of the main features of allegory is the noncoincidence of language with itself.

12. S. J. Kim, "Beyond Black and White," critiques the dead-end nature of these debates, arguing for the paucity of semiotic approaches to race because they either conveniently notice or overlook race, depending on the political argument they are making. My argument differs in that, for me, the discursive

readings do not go far *enough* in analyzing discourse as a structure of perception.

13. Suvin, *Metamorphoses of Science Fiction*, 88, 86. This viewpoint shapes Suvin's critique of fantasy. See "Considering the Sense of 'Fantasy' or 'Fantastic Fiction': An Effusion," reprinted in *Metamorphoses*, 381–443. See also Mieville, "Marxism and Fantasy," for arguments in support of fantasy's cognitive potential.

14. Lovecraft, letter to Donald Wollheim.

15. See Mendlesohn, *Rhetorics of Fantasy*, xiv. Mendlesohn's four categories of fantasy—the portal-quest, the immersive, the intrusive, and the liminal—are built from her interest in synthesizing the reader-relationship to the fantastic. I am not so much interested in these categories as I am in attending to the processes and cognitive effects of the relationship among the reader, primary world, and fantasy world.

16. Shanks, "Hyborian Age Archaeology," 13, traces the influence of contemporaneous work in anthropology, geology, archaeology, and history on Howard's creation of the Hyborian Age. My emphasis is on the way readers engaged in and imagined this world-building process.

17. De Camp, "Exegeses of Hyborian Age," 13.

18. Kidd, Letter to *AMRA* 2, no. 5.

19. See Clark, Miller, and de Camp, "Informal Biography of Conan"; Boardman, "Ocean Trade"; de Camp, "Hyborian Technology." For these and other similar essays, see de Camp, *Blade of Conan*.

20. Boardman, "Ocean Trade," 49–50.

21. De Camp, "Hyborian Technology," 57.

22. Carter, "Real Hyborian Age"; my italics.

23. Miller, "Lord of the Black Throne," 78.

24. Ibid., 79.

25. The examples used by Saler are Lovecraft's Cthulhu mythos, Tolkien's Middle-earth, and Sherlock Holmes's Baker Street.

26. Saler, *As If*, loc. 127.

27. Burns, "Letter," 5.

28. Bradley, "Some Strange Sounding Names," 13.

29. Anderson, "Who Were the Aesir," 11.

30. Scithers, "Balthus of the Tauran," 20.

31. De Camp, "Pseudohistory," 15.

32. Ibid., 15–18.

33. De Camp, "Range," 227, 228.

34. Anderson, "Response to 'Range,'" 9.

35. Brackett, "And as for the Admixture," 235, 241.

36. Howard, "Hyborian Age," 367.

37. Teskey, *Allegory and Violence*, 4.
38. Howard, "Hyborian Age," 370.
39. Ibid., 372; italics mine.
40. Ibid., 370, 372.
41. Ibid., 372.
42. Teskey, *Allegory and Violence*, 62.
43. Debates over Howard's racist attitudes take up his correspondence with H. P. Lovecraft. For a reading of their letters along these lines, see Joshi, "Barbarism vs. Civilization."
44. Lieber, "Howard's Style," 26–27.
45. Goodman, *Of Mind and Other Matters*, 55.
46. Others include pictorial denotation, quotation, but I am only focusing on those varieties above. See his chapter "Routes of Reference," in ibid, 55–71.
47. Ibid., 62.
48. Ibid., 67–68.
49. Howard, *Bloody Crown of Conan*, 83.
50. Barthes, "Introduction to the Structural," 249.
51. Ibid., 249.
52. Howard, "Iron Shadows of the Moon," 197.
53. Ibid., 197.
54. Ibid., 191.
55. Howard, "Queen of the Black Coast," 145.
56. Howard, *Conquering Sword of Conan*, 54.
57. Ibid., 51.
58. Gossett, *Race*, loc. 5126. See his chapter on "The Scientific Revolt against Racism" for a contextualization of Franz Boas's antiracism. For further analysis of Boas's role in relation to scientific racism, see Stocking, *Race, Culture, and Evolution*. For an analysis of the continuity between biological and cultural understandings of race, see Balibar, "Civic Universalism," 215–16.
59. Shanks, "Hyborian Age Archaeology," 17. Similarly, M. Hall, "Crash Go the Civilizations," contextualizes Howard's uses of race in relation to an "essentialist view of race, religion, and nation" and the "racialist thinking of eugenics" (88–89).
60. Reardon, *Race to the Finish*, 31.
61. "Statement on Race, Paris, July 1950," in *Four Statements on Race Question*, 30.
62. Ibid., 33.
63. "Statement on the Nature of Race and Race Differences, Paris, June 1951," in *Four Statements on Race Question*, 37.

64. "Proposals on the Biological Aspects of Race," in *Four Statements on Race Question*, 47.

65. Visweswaran, "Race and Culture of Anthropology," 73.

66. Balibar, "Racism Revisited," 1633.

67. Benedict, *Race and Racism*, 63.

68. Ibid., 28, 33.

6. FANTASIES OF BLACKNESS AND RACIAL CAPITALISM

1. Saunders's construction of an African-centered cosmology that reroutes the masculine and colonialist codes of sword and sorcery has influenced contemporary "sword-and-soul" writers. For an account of this genealogy, see Charles Saunders, "The Soul in the Sword," and Milton Davis, "A Gathering at the Meeting Tree," in Davis and Saunders, *Griots*.

2. De Camp, "Editing Conan," in *Spell of Conan*, 118–19.

3. De Camp, "The Trail of Tranicos," in *Spell of Conan*, 48–49. In the table that de Camp produces to track the changes among various stories, this demon has one incarnation as an "Anonymous Negro Wizard" (50).

4. Fleury, "Redefining the Social." See also Porter, *Problem of the Future World*, which is an account of Myrdal's approach and influence on disciplinary approaches to racism in the United States.

5. Friedman, *Capitalism and Freedom*, 108.

6. Ibid., 109.

7. Hayek, *Law, Legislation and Liberty*, loc. 105.

8. Ibid., loc. 2137.

9. Ibid., loc. 2300.

10. Ibid., loc. 2593.

11. Becker, *Economics of Discrimination*, 1.

12. Becker, *Accounting for Tastes*, 139.

13. Becker, *Economic Approach to Human Behavior*, 8.

14. Becker, *Accounting for Tastes*, 140–41.

15. Becker, *Economics of Discrimination*, 15.

16. Ibid., 14.

17. Arrow, "Theory of Discrimination," 3–4.

18. Dymski, Hernandez, and Mohanty, "Race, Power," 2.

19. Ibid., 2. They explain further: "The reasons for economists' failure to identify racial inequality or exploitation as one of the causes of the subprime crisis are now clear. They largely rule out predatory racial behavior; and view the recurrence of systematic vulnerability in multiple markets for any subgroups of loan applicants as outside the boundaries of 'economic' analysis. And since other social scientists permit economists' definition to govern discussions about discrimination, there is little left to say. Once variables correlated

both with race and creditworthiness are ruled out of bounds, little if any empirical evidence can meet the double discrimination threshold of intent to harm and unfair treatment" (15).

20. Ibid., 2.

21. Ibid., 26.

22. P. Williams, *Seeing a Color-Blind Future*, 38–39.

23. Ibid., 39.

24. For a survey of these models, see Shelley Lundberg and Richard Startz, "Inequality and Race: Models and Policy," and Glenn Loury, "Conceptual Problems in the Enforcement of Anti-Discrimination Laws," in Arrow, Bowles, and Durlauf, *Meritocracy and Economic Inequality*, 269–317. See also Arrow, "What Has Economics to Say," 91–100.

25. Loury, "Relations before Transactions."

26. Arrow, "What Has Economics to Say," 98.

27. Ibid., 91.

28. Barrett, *Blackness and Value*, loc. 57–65. See chapter 1 for Barrett's development of the multiple relationships between the formation and formative violence of value and racial blackness.

29. Delany, *Silent Interviews*, 131–32.

30. Simmel, *Philosophy of Money*, 84.

31. Howard, *Conquering Sword of Conan*, 178.

32. Ibid., 184.

33. Ibid., 189.

34. Howard, "Vale of Lost Women," 294–95.

35. Ibid., 295

36. Ibid., 295.

37. Delany, "Generic Protocols," 176.

38. Delany, *Silent Interviews*, 226.

39. See Freedman, *Critical Theory and Science Fiction*, and Dubey, *Signs and Cities*, for discussions on Delany's *Stars in My Pocket Like Grains of Sand.*

40. For a synthesis of approaches to Delany's work in terms of race and an analysis of how Delany challenges these reading protocols, see my "World of Difference." The latest generation of Delany scholarship has largely focused on theorizations of genre, race, and sexuality. See Lavender, *Race in American Science Fiction*, and special issues on Delany in *American Literary History* 24, no. 4, and in *African American Review* 48, no. 3.

41. Delany, *Starboard Wine*, 31, famously speaks about this technique in commenting on Robert Heinlein's *Starship Troopers* and how one does not learn the protagonist's racial identity until two hundred pages into the novel.

42. Delany, *Silent Interviews*, 225–26.

43. For a discussion of Delany's engagements with poststructuralist thought, see Spencer, "Deconstructing Tales of Nevèrÿon," 14; Kelso, "'Across Never,'"; Johnston, "Discourses of Autobiographical Desires"; Delany, *Silent Interviews*, 127–64.

44. Delany, *Return to Nevèrÿon*, 21.

45. For analyses of intersections between race and capitalist processes, see J. K. Lee, *Urban Triage*; Hong, *Ruptures of American Capital*; and Chakravarty and Ferreira da Silva, "Race, Empire."

46. Roediger, *Wages of Whiteness*, identifies racial capitalism at the level of exploiting labor divides and depressing wages (for blacks) and creating intangible wages (for whites). E. Williams, *Slavery and Capitalism*, identifies the ways in which slavery accumulated capital and technological structures without which capitalism could not have emerged. Robinson, *Black Marxism*, analyzes the long history of racial capitalism and its importance at the center of the black radical tradition. Ferreira da Silva analyzes race as elements of representation (of economic incapacity and of moral attributes incongruous with economic being) that are used to extract profit from certain subjects and render them expropriable (see Chakravarty and Ferreira da Silva, "Accumulation, Dispossession, and Debt").

47. Precisely because of the understated, often incidental way in which racial markings and signs appear in the series, the early reception, marketing, and production of the Nevèrÿon series is marked by its lack of attention to race and the invisibility of race in its discourse.

48. Tucker, *Sense of Wonder*, 100–101.

49. Tucker writes, "The *Return to Nevèrÿon* series is paraliterary sword-and-sorcery fiction; these books are *not* historical novels about slavery in America. As important as such disclaimers are to keep in mind, however, it is impossible to ignore the centrality of the subject of slavery to the overall narrative" (ibid., 101).

50. One line of debate centers on the meaning of the "slave collar" and its potential resignification at the intersection of slavery, semiotics, and sexuality. See ibid., 135–45; Rosenberg and Rusert, "Framing Finance"; and Keizer, "'Obsidian Mine.'"

51. Delany, *Tales of Nevèrÿon* 238.

52. Ibid.

53. Delany, *Return to Nevèrÿon*, 222.

54. Delany, *Conversations with Samuel R. Delany*, 182.

55. Teskey, *Allegory and Violence*, 62.

56. Delany, *Silent Interviews*, 130.

57. For an analysis of Gorgik, Pryn, and Pheron within the context of the movements of capital, see Battis, "Delany's Queer Markets."

58. Delany, *Return to Nevèrÿon*, 23.

59. Marx, *Capital*, 797.

60. For analysis of the intersections among race, market processes, and sex work, see Scott, *Extravagant Abjection*, 204–54; and Delany, *Times Square Red*.

61. Delany, *Return to Nevèrÿon*, 132.

62. Ibid., 139.

63. Ibid., 141, 142.

64. Ibid., 170–71.

65. As Balibar, "Difference, Otherness, Exclusion," writes, "colour . . . is one of the most telling metonymies of race . . . but it is also the instrument of a new objectification of differences, which is not finite but infinite, not closed, but 'open,' on the model of the market. . . . Nobody knows what a 'colour' is, where it begins and where it ends" (28).

66. Delany, *Return to Nevèrÿon*, 182.

67. For critiques of contract and wage labor as vehicles or symbols of freedom, see Stanley, *From Bondage to Contract*; Hartman, *Scenes of Subjection*; and P. Williams, *Alchemy of Race and Rights*.

68. Lukin, "Wiggle Room of Theory," 171.

69. See P. Williams, *Open House*, 176, and *Rooster's Egg*, 232–43.

70. Melamed, *Represent and Destroy*, loc. 1899–1903.

7. RACIAL COUNTERFACTUALS AND THE UNCERTAIN EVENT OF EMANCIPATION

1. See Han's excellent critique of these academic tendencies in *Letters of the Law*, 3.

2. Ibid., 1, 3, 7.

3. See Rosenfeld's introduction to *The World Hitler Never Made* for a brief overview of the genre.

4. *A Time to Kill*, dir. Joel Schumacher (Warner Bros, 1996).

5. Ibid.

6. Ibid.

7. Goodman, *Fact, Fiction, and Forecast*, writes, "the assertion that a connection holds is made on the presumption that certain circumstances not stated in the antecedent obtain. . . . We do not assert that the counterfactual is true *if* the circumstances obtain; rather, in asserting the counterfactual we commit ourselves to the actual truth of the statements describing the requisite relevant conditions" (8).

8. Ibid., 20–21.

9. For useful explications of the emergence of race as a modern concept in epistemological terms, see Bernasconi, "Who Invented the Concept";

Wiegman, *American Anatomies*; I. Tucker, *Moment of Racial Sight*; and Chun, "Race and/as Technology."

10. Hawthorn, *Plausible Worlds*, points out that "what we first choose to explain, and the shape and direction of the explanations we suggest, are themselves informed by pictures of the possible" (158).

11. Strassfeld, "If . . ."

12. See Kray et al., "From What *Might* Have Been."

13. Best, *Fugitive's Properties*, loc. 3215–19.

14. Ibid., loc. 3018.

15. Ibid., loc. 3223, 3215.

16. Ibid., loc. 3189.

17. *Regents of the University of California v. Bakke.*

18. Fish, "Reverse Racism."

19. Williams, *Rooster's Egg*, 103–4.

20. *Ricci v. Destefano*, 3.

21. Ibid., 3.

22. Ibid.

23. Ginsburg states, "Can you be specific about what facts you think should be tried on remand?" and "You say there are or may be genuine issues of fact. So what are they?" and "What—what has New Haven done in fact?" (ibid., 31, 44).

24. Ibid., 23–24.

25. Strassfeld, "If . . . ," 3–4.

26. Han, *Letters of the Law*, 10.

27. See Ferguson, "Virtual History."

28. Prince, *Narrative as Theme*, 51.

29. Ibid., 51–52.

30. The list of alternate history works on Uchronia.net shows two main themes that dominate the genre: the U.S. Civil War and "what if Nazi Germany won World War II." For a good introduction to alternate history as a genre in terms of its relationship to time, see Hellekson, *Alternate History*. For a good analysis of the uses to which alternate histories are put in the case of imagining if Nazi Germany won World War II (refiguring historical memory, staging cultural commentary on history via its dystopian or utopian visions), see Rosenfeld, "Why Do We Ask 'What If?,'" in *History and Theory*, and *World Hitler Never Made*.

31. Gallagher, "When Did the Confederate States," 54.

32. Gallagher writes, "Numerous subsequent counterfactualists adopted Churchill's hypothesis that Confederate victory would soon have led to peaceful emancipation . . . and the South's voluntary manumission would have been followed by racial harmony. . . . Indeed, the sentiment is

so frequently repeated in these scenarios that the intertwining of two deep Truths becomes apparent: because manumission was inevitable in the natural course of things, Reconstruction was a counterproductive policy, which only bred impossible expectations and murderous resentments" (ibid., 55).

33. Dixon is discussed in Chapter 2.

34. Gallagher, "When Did the Confederate States," 61.

35. Ibid., 61.

36. Hawthorn, *Plausible Worlds*, 34–35.

37. Kantor, *If the South Had Won*, loc. 595.

38. Tsouras, "Confederate Black and Grey," 207.

39. Turtledove, *Guns of the South*, 257–58.

40. Ibid., 259; my emphasis.

41. Uncertain commons, *Speculate This!*, loc. 128, 158.

42. Thanks to Gerry Canavan for alerting me to this work.

43. See Hawthorn, *Plausible Worlds*, 158–59; Gallagher, "When Did the Confederate States," 59; and Ferguson, "Virtual History," 83–85.

44. Bisson, *Fire on the Mountain*, 49.

45. See Reynolds, *John Brown, Abolitionist*; Trodd and Stauffer, *Meteor of War*; and Du Bois, *John Brown*.

46. Bisson, *Fire on the Mountain*, 50.

47. Ibid., 50.

48. Ibid., 143.

49. Barnes, *Lion's Blood*, 365. All subsequent citations are from this edition and noted parenthetically in the text.

50. As Barthes, "Introduction," and Herman, *Basic Elements of Narrative*, make clear in different ways, sentences at the level of description can often serve explanatory functions in narrative.

51. By "horizon of expectation," I follow Hans Robert Jauss's coining of the phrase, which is used to describe the historically situated social norms and conventions through which readers structure and apprehend aesthetic works. See Jauss, *Toward an Aesthetic of Reception*, 22–23.

52. Genette, *Narrative Discourse*, 194–98.

8. ALTERNATE HISTORIES OF WORLD WAR II; OR, HOW THE RACE CONCEPT ORGANIZES THE WORLD

1. Porter, *Problem of the Future World*, 89.

2. See *Brown v. Board of Education*; *Shelley v. Kraemer*; *Metro Broadcasting, Inc., v. FCC*; and *Adarand Constructors v. Pena*, among others.

3. Ashenfelter and Oaxaca, "Economics of Discrimination," trace the impact of Becker's thinking on legal approaches to discrimination.

4. Perry, *More Beautiful and More Terrible*, loc. 388. As we saw from the previous chapters, *even in the context of employment discrimination*, intentional discrimination is rendered perceptible (because it is framed as antiwhite) *over* the claims of disparate treatment.

5. Ibid., loc. 403.

6. Han, *Letters of the Law*, 55.

7. Obasogie, *Blinded by Sight*, loc. 2834.

8. *Korematsu v. United States*, 216.

9. Ibid., 224.

10. Brooks, *Melodramatic Imagination*, 36.

11. Freud, *Jokes*, 254.

12. *Korematsu v. United States*, 224.

13. Justice Roberts dissent, *Korematsu v. United States.*

14. Justice Murphy dissent, *Korematsu v. United States.*

15. Han, *Letters of the Law*, 60. Han sees this logic as a species of colorblind judgment as opposed to common interpretations of the opinion as advancing xenophobia. See her fuller analysis in *Letters of the Law*, 55–65. My own reading expands on the particular ways of perceiving race codified in the opinion, ways that are related to using race as a predictive law.

16. Peirce, "What Is a Sign," 5.

17. Ibid., 7–8.

18. Ibid., 5.

19. Henry Louis Gates Jr., *Signifying Monkey*, draws on Saussurean notions of signification in order to modify and theorize the notion of "signifyin(g)." Gates writes, "Since Saussure, at least, the three terms *signification, signifier, signified* have been fundamental to our thinking about general linguistics and, of late, about criticism specifically. These neologisms in the academic-critical community are homonyms of terms in the black vernacular tradition perhaps two centuries old" (46).

20. See my critique of the process of signification as modeled by Omi and Winant in the introduction.

21. Peirce, *Philosophical Writings*, loc. 2119–29.

22. Ibid., loc. 2172.

23. Eco, *Role of the Reader*, 221.

24. See Elhefnawy, "'Two Dooms,'"; and G. W. Young, "Third Reich in Alternate History," 878.

25. Isby, "Japanese Raj," loc. 3430.

26. Forrest R. Lindsey, "Nagumo's Luck," in Tsouras, *Rising Sun Victorious*, loc. 2795.

27. Turtledove, *Days of Infamy*, loc. 8397.

28. Ibid., loc. 8596.

29. Ibid., loc. 2592.

30. Ibid., loc. 1631.

31. Shirer, "If Hitler Had Won," 34. For an interesting analysis of the reception of Shirer's piece, see Rosenfeld, *World Hitler Never Made*, 116.

32. Kornbluth, "Two Dooms," 12.

33. Dick, *Man in the High Castle*, 3. All subsequent citations are noted parenthetically in the text.

34. Rosenfeld, "Why Do We Ask," 96.

35. The ending of the novel is often cited as problematic in this regard. Rose, *Alien Encounters*, writes, "What Dick has done is to violate the ground rule that the text should regard its own world as real" (122). Robinson, "Novels of Philip K. Dick," calls the ending a "misplayed note" (98). Rieder, "Metafictive World," 214, 216, highlights the way in which ethical distinctions between good and bad are used to stabilize truth even as questions about truth might destabilize those ethical distinctions by undermining the grasp of reality.

36. Rieder, "Metafictive World," 222, writes that the novel's "sense of the real" is caught between ethical determinations and cognitive interpretations.

37. Ibid.

38. See Freedman, "Towards a Theory of Paranoia"; and Burt, "Kick Over the Scenery."

39. Piper, *Out of Order*, 2:219.

40. Ibid., 1:234.

41. Lacan, *Seminar*, 74–75.

CONCLUSION: ON THE POSSIBILITIES OF AN ANTIRACIST RACIAL WORLDMAKING

1. Perry, *More Beautiful and More Terrible*, loc. 340. For other formulations of this coexistence stressing coloniality on the one hand and the prison-industrial complex on the other, see Omi and Winant, "Race and Racism," 988; and Alexander, *New Jim Crow*, 1.

2. Scott, "Not-Yet Justice League," offers the useful formulation of trying to think an "anti-anti-black world."

3. See chapter 2 of Goyal, *Romance, Diaspora*; chapter 3 of Cooppan, *Worlds Within*; Edwards, "Late Romance"; Rusert and Brown, "Princess Steel"; and Gillman and Weinbaum, *Next to the Color Line*.

4. In describing the hate and indignation felt by the "colored world" against white peoples, Stoddard, *Rising Tide of Color*, cites Du Bois: "The Afro-American author, W. E. Burghardt Du Bois wrote of the colored world: 'These nations and races composing as they do a vast majority of humanity

are going to endure this treatment just as long as they must and not a moment longer. Then they are going to fight, and the War of the Color Line will outdo in savage inhumanity any war this world has yet seen. For colored folk have much to remember and they will not forget'" (14).

5. These phrases proliferate across Du Bois's work, especially in *Dusk of Dawn*; his article "Worlds of Color," published in *Foreign Affairs* (April 1925); and in volume 3 of the Mansart trilogy, *Worlds of Color*.

6. Dubois, "Color Line Belts the World," 34.

7. Du Bois, "Afro-American," 2.

8. Schuyler, "Negro-Art Hokum," 25.

9. Du Bois, *Dusk of Dawn*, 135–36.

10. Ibid., 139–40.

11. Chandler, "Of Horizon," 4.

12. Ibid., 14–15.

13. In his critique of Genovese's *Roll, Jordan Roll*, Chandler, *X*, writes, "we know that historical systems are irreducibly open, unfinished, and irresolvable in their movement" (loc. 2909).

14. See Chandler, *X*, esp. chapters 2 and 3.

15. Du Bois, "The Comet," in *Darkwater*, 259.

16. Ibid., 270.

17. Du Bois, *Black Reconstruction in America*, 723.

18. Fisher, "Democracy's Remains," 512.

19. Du Bois, *Black Reconstruction in America*, 30.

20. Ibid., 57.

21. Ibid., 66.

22. Ibid., 56.

23. Ibid., 124.

24. Ibid., 30.

25. These formulations are indebted to Barbara Johnson's reading of allegory in relation to identity politics. See Johnson, "Women and Allegory," in *Wake of Deconstruction*, esp. 70–73.

26. Du Bois, *Worlds of Color*, 112. For a link between this scene and a similar depiction of a scene of powerful world-historical actors in his romance, *Dark Princess*, see Edwards, "Late Romance." Edwards in that essay provides an excellent reading of the anachronisms that interrupt the flow of the narrative of *Worlds of Color*.

27. Du Bois, *Worlds of Color*, 113.

28. Du Bois, *Darkwater*, 223.

BIBLIOGRAPHY

Adams, Brooks. *The Law of Civilization and Decay: An Essay on History*. New York: Macmillan, 1896.

Adarand Constructors v. Pena. 515 U.S. 200 (1995).

Ahmed, Saladin. "Is 'Game of Thrones' Too White?" *Salon*, April 1, 2012. http://www.salon.com/2012/04/01/is_game_of_thrones_too_white. Accessed June 11, 2014.

Alcoff, Linda Martín. "Philosophy and Racial Identity." In *Ethnic and Racial Studies Today*, edited by Martin Bulmer and John Solomos, 29–45. London: Routledge, 1999.

Aldama, Frederick Luis. *Your Brain on Latino Comics*. Austin: University of Texas Press, 2009.

Alexander, Michelle. *The New Jim Crow: Mass Incarceration in the Age of Color Blindness*. New York: New Press, 2010.

American Literary History 24, no. 4 (2012), a symposium on Samuel Delany, 680–774.

Anderson, Poul. "Response to 'Range.'" *AMRA* 2, no. 33 (1965): 9. Transcribed from holdings of *AMRA* at Eaton Fanzine Collection, University of California, Riverside.

———. "Who Were the Aesir." *AMRA* 2, no. 3 (1959): 11.

Appadurai, Arjun. *The Future as Cultural Fact: Essays on the Global Condition*. London: Verso, 2013.

Arrow, Kenneth. "The Theory of Discrimination." In *Discrimination in Labor Markets*, edited by Orley Ashenfelter and Albert Rees, 3–33. Princeton, N.J.: Princeton University Press, 1973.

———. "What Has Economics to Say about Racial Discrimination?" *Journal of Economic Perspectives* 12, no. 2 (Spring 1998): 91–100.

Arrow, Kenneth, Samuel Bowles, and Steven Durlauf, eds. *Meritocracy and Economic Inequality*. Princeton, N.J.: Princeton University Press, 2000.

Ashenfelter, Orley, and Ronald Oaxaca. "The Economics of Discrimination: Economists Enter the Courtroom." *American Economic Review* 77, no. 2 (1987): 321–25.

Atteberry, Brian. *Strategies of Fantasy*. Bloomington: Indiana University Press, 1992.

Bacon-Smith, Camille. *Enterprising Women: Television Fandom and the Creation of Popular Myth*. Philadelphia: University of Pennsylvania Press, 1991.

———. *Science Fiction Culture*. Philadelphia: University of Pennsylvania Press, 1999.

Bakhtin, Mikhail. *The Dialogic Imagination: Four Essays*. Translated by Michael Holquist and Caryl Emerson. Austin: University of Texas Press, 1982.

Balibar, Étienne. "Civic Universalism and Its Internal Exclusions: The Issue of Anthropological Difference." *boundary 2* 39, no. 1 (2012): 207–29.

———. "Difference, Otherness, Exclusion." *Parallax* 11, no. 1 (2005): 19–34.

———. "Racism Revisited: Sources, Relevance, and Aporia of a Modern Concept." *PMLA* 123, no. 5 (2008): 1630–39.

Barker, Deborah. "Reconstructing Scarlett and the Economy of Rape in *Gone with the Wind*." In *New Approaches to "Gone with the Wind*," edited by James Crank, 110–35. Baton Rouge: Louisiana State University Press, 2015.

Barnes, Steven. *Lion's Blood: A Novel of Slavery and Freedom in an Alternate America*. New York: Warner Books, 2002.

Barrett, Lindon. *Blackness and Value: Seeing Double*. Cambridge, U.K.: Cambridge University Press, 1999. Kindle edition.

Barthes, Roland. "Introduction to the Structural Analysis of Narrative." In *Image, Music, Text*, by Roland Barthes, translated by Stephen Heath, 79–125. New York: Farrar, Straus and Giroux, 1977.

Battis, Jes. "Delany's Queer Markets: Nevèrÿon and the Texture of Capital." *Science Fiction Studies* 36, no. 3 (2009): 478–89.

Becker, Gary. *Accounting for Tastes*. Cambridge, Mass.: Harvard University Press, 1996.

———. *The Economic Approach to Human Behavior*. Chicago: University of Chicago Press, 1978.

———. *The Economics of Discrimination*. Chicago: University of Chicago Press, 1971.

Benedict, Ruth. *Race: Science and Politics*. New York: Viking Press, 1943.

———. *Race and Racism*. London: Routledge and Kegan Paul, 1942.

Berlant, Lauren. *Cruel Optimism*. Durham, N.C.: Duke University Press, 2013.

Bernasconi, Robert. "Who Invented the Concept of Race? Kant's Role in the Enlightenment Construction of Race." In *Race*, edited by Robert Bernasconi, 11–37. Malden, U.K.: Blackwell, 2001.

Bernasconi, Robert, and Tommy Lott, eds. *The Idea of Race*. New York: Hackett, 2000.

Best, Stephen. *Fugitive's Properties: Law and the Poetics of Possession*. Chicago: University of Chicago Press, 2004.

Bisson, Terry. *Fire on the Mountain.* Oakland, Calif.: PM Press, 1988.
Boardman, John. "Ocean Trade in the Hyborian Age." In *The Blade of Conan*, edited by L. Sprague de Camp, 45–51. New York: Ace Books, 1979.
Boeckmann, Cathy. *A Question of Character: Scientific Racism and the Genres of American Fiction, 1892–1912.* Tuscaloosa: University of Alabama Press, 2000.
Bonilla-Silva, Eduardo. *Racism without Racists: Color-Blind Racism and the Persistence of Racial Inequality in America.* 4th ed. Lanham: Rowman and Littlefield, 2014. E-book edition.
Boothe, Clare. Introduction to *The Valor of Ignorance*, by Homer Lea, 1–31. New York: Harper and Brothers, 1942.
Bould, Mark. "The Dreadful Credibility of Absurd Things: A Tendency in Fantasy Theory." *Historical Materialism* 10, no. 4 (2002): 51–88.
Bourdieu, Pierre. *Distinction.* Translated by Richard Nice. Cambridge, Mass.: Harvard University Press, 1987.
Brackett, Leigh. ". . . And as for the Admixture of Cultures on Imaginary Worlds." In *The Blade of Conan*, edited by L. Sprague de Camp, 235–43. New York: Ace Books, 1979.
Bradley, Marion Zimmer. "Some Strange Sounding Names." *AMRA* 2, no. 12 (1960): 13. Transcribed from holdings of *AMRA* at Eaton Fanzine Collection, University of California, Riverside.
Brooks, Peter. *The Melodramatic Imagination.* New Haven, Conn.: Yale University Press, 1976.
Brown v. Board of Education of Topeka. 347 U.S. 483 (1954).
Bruner, Jerome. *Actual Minds, Possible Worlds.* Cambridge, Mass.: Harvard University Press, 1986.
Burns, T. A. "Letter." *AMRA* 2, no. 13 (1960): 5. Transcribed from holdings of *AMRA* at Eaton Fanzine Collection, University of California, Riverside.
Burt, Stephen. "Kick Over the Scenery." *London Review of Books* 30, no. 13 (2008): 23–25.
Burton, Wilbur. "The Prophet of Pearl Harbor." *Saturday Review of Literature* 25, no. 14 (1942): 8.
Callon, Michel. "The Embeddedness of Economic Markets in Economics." In *Laws of the Markets*, edited by Michel Callon, 1–58. Oxford: Blackwell, 1998.
Cantor, Mackinlay. *If the South Had Won the Civil War.* New York: Forge Books, 1960. Kindle edition.
Carrington, André. *Speculative Blackness: The Future of Race in Science Fiction.* Minneapolis: University of Minnesota Press, 2016.
Carter, Lin. "The Real Hyborian Age." In *The Blade of Conan*, edited by L. Sprague de Camp, 70–71. New York: Ace Books, 1979.

Chakravarty, Paula, and Denise Ferreira da Silva. "Accumulation, Dispossession, and Debt: The Racial Logic of Global Capitalism." *American Quarterly* 64, no. 3 (2012): 361–85.

Chakravarty, Paula, and Denise Ferreira da Silva, eds. "Special Issue: Race, Empire, and the Crisis of the Subprime." *American Quarterly* 64, no. 3 (2012).

Chandler, Nahum D. "Of Horizon—An Introduction to 'The Afro-American' by W. E. B. DuBois—circa 1894." *Journal of Transnational American Studies* 2, no. 1 (2010). http://escholarship.org/uc/item/8q64g6kw. Accessed February 27, 2017.

———. *X: The Problem of the Negro as a Problem for Thought.* New York: Fordham University Press, 2014. Kindle edition.

Chesney, George Tomkyns. *The Battle of Dorking.* North Charleston, S.C.: CreateSpace, 2012. Originally published in 1871.

Chuh, Kandice. *Imagine Otherwise.* Durham, N.C.: Duke University Press, 2003.

Chun, Wendy. "Race and/as Technology; or, How to Do Things to Race." *Camera Obscura* 24, no. 1 70 (2009): 7–35.

Churchill, Winston. "If Lee Had Not Won the Battle of Gettysburg." *Wisconsin Magazine of History* 44, no. 4 (1961): 243–51.

Clark, John D., P. Schuyler Miller, and L. Sprague de Camp. "An Informal Biography of Conan the Cimmerian." In *The Blade of Conan,* edited by L. Sprague de Camp, 9–45. New York: Ace Books, 1979.

Clarke, I. F. "Future-War Fiction: The First Main Phase, 1871–1900." In *Future Wars,* edited by David Seed, 9–32. Liverpool: Liverpool University Press, 2012.

———. *Voices Prophesying War: Future Wars, 1763–3749.* Oxford: Oxford University Press, 1992.

Coates, Ta-Nehisi. *Between the World and Me.* New York: Spiegel and Grau, 2015.

Cone, Helen Gray. "Rosy Snow." *St. Nicholas Magazine* 11 (May 1884): 529.

Cooppan, Vilashini. *Worlds Within: National Narratives and Global Connections in Postcolonial Writing.* Stanford, Calif.: Stanford University Press, 2009.

Cowley, Malcolm. "Going with the Wind." *New Republic,* September 16, 1936, 161–62.

Cripps, Thomas. "Winds of Change: *Gone with the Wind* and Racism as a National Issue." In *Recasting: "Gone with the Wind" in American Culture,* edited by Darden Asbury Pyron, 137–52. Miami: University Presses of Florida, 1983.

Csicsery-Ronay, Istvan, Jr. *Seven Beauties of Science Fiction.* Middletown, Conn.: Wesleyan University Press, 2008.

Currie, Mark. *About Time: Narrative, Fiction and the Philosophy of Time*. Edinburgh: Edinburgh University Press, 2007. Kindle edition.

Daniels, Roger, *Concentration Camps, U.S.A.* New York: Holt, Rinehart and Winston, 1972.

Davis, Milton J., and Charles Saunders. *Griots: A Sword and Soul Anthology*. Atlanta: MVMedia, 2011.

de Camp, L. Sprague. "Exegeses of Hyborian Age." *AMRA* 2, no. 6 (1959): 13. Transcribed from holdings of *AMRA* at Eaton Fanzine Collection, University of California, Riverside.

———. "Hyborian Technology." In *The Blade of Conan*, edited by L. Sprague de Camp, 9–85. New York: Ace Books, 1979.

———. "Pseudohistory." In *AMRA* 2, no. 70 (1980): 15. Transcribed from holdings of *AMRA* at Eaton Fanzine Collection, University of California, Riverside.

de Camp, L. Sprague, ed. *The Blade of Conan*. New York: Ace Books, 1979.

———. *The Spell of Conan*. New York: Ace Books, 1980.

Delany, Samuel. *Conversations with Samuel R. Delany*. Jackson: University of Mississippi Press, 2009.

———. "Generic Protocols: Science Fiction and the Mundane." In *The Technological Imagination*, edited by Teresa de Lauretis et al., 175–93. Madison, Wis.: Coda Press, 1980.

———. *Longer Views*. Hanover, N.H.: University Press of New England, 1996.

———. *Return to Nevèrÿon*. Hanover, N.H.: University Press of New England, 1987.

———. *Shorter Views: Queer Thoughts and the Politics of the Paraliterary*. Hanover, N.H.: University Press of New England, 1999.

———. *Silent Interviews: On Language, Race, Sex, Science Fiction, and Some Comics*. Hanover, N.H.: University Press of New England, 1994.

———. *Starboard Wine*. New York: Dragon Press, 1984.

———. *Times Square Red, Times Square Blue*. New York: New York University Press, 1999.

De Man, Paul. *Blindness and Insight: Essays in the Rhetoric of Romanticism*. Minneapolis: University of Minnesota Press, 1983.

Derrida, Jacques. "The Law of Genre." In *Acts of Literature*, translated by Avital Ronell. New York: Routledge, 1992.

Dick, Philip K. *The Man in the High Castle*. New York: Vintage, 1992.

Dillon, Grace L. "Imagining Indigenous Futurisms: An Interview with Stephen Graham Jones." *Paradoxa* 26 (2014): 211–16.

Dimock, Wai Chee. "Migration across Genres." In *The Work of Genre*, edited by Robyn Warhol, 96–128. Cambridge, Mass.: English Institute in collaboration with the American Council of Learned Societies, 2011.

Dixon, Thomas, Jr. *The Leopard's Spots: A Romance of the White Man's Burden, 1865 to 1900*. Rochester, N.Y.: Starry Night Publishing, 2009. Originally published in 1902. Kindle edition.

Dubey, Madhu. *Signs and Cities: Black Literary Postmodernism*. Chicago: University of Chicago Press, 2003.

Dubois, W. E. B. "The Afro-American." *Journal of Transnational American Studies* 2, no. 1 (2010). http://escholarship.org/uc/item/2pm9g4q2. Accessed February 27, 2017.

———. *Black Reconstruction in America, 1860–1880*. New York: Free Press, 1935.

———. "The Color Line Belts the World." In *W. E. B. DuBois on Asia: Crossing the World Color Line*, edited by Bill Mullen and Cathryn Watson, 33–35. Jackson: University of Mississippi Press, 2005.

———. *Darkwater: Voices from within the Veil*. New York: AMS Press, 1969.

———. *Dusk of Dawn: Autobiography of a Race Concept*. New Brunswick, N.J.: Transaction, 1968.

———. *John Brown*. Oxford: Oxford University Press, 2007.

———. "The Negro Mind Reaches Out." In *The New Negro*, edited by Alain Locke, 385–415. New York: Atheneum, 1992. Originally published in 1925.

———. *The Souls of Black Folk*. New York: Penguin, 1996.

———. *Worlds of Color*. New York: Oxford University Press, 2007.

Duster, Troy. *Backdoor to Eugenics*. New York: Routledge, 1990.

Dymski, Gary A., Jesus Hernandez, and Lisa Mohanty. "Race, Power, and the Subprime/Foreclosure Crisis: A Mesoanalysis." *Levy Economics Institute Working Paper Collection* (2011): 26.

Eco, Umberto. *The Role of the Reader: Explorations in the Semiotics of Texts*. Bloomington: Indiana University Press, 1984.

Edwards, Brent. "Late Romance." In *Next to the Color Line: Gender, Sexuality, and W. E. B. DuBois*, edited by Susan Gillman and Alys Weinbaum, 124–50. Durham, N.C.: Duke University Press, 2007.

Elhefnawy, Nader. "'Two Dooms' and the Memory of World War II in Alternate History." *Internet Review of Science Fiction* 6 (August 2008). http://www.irosf.com/q/zine/article/10452. Accessed August 31, 2014.

Eshun, Kodwo. "Further Considerations on Afrofuturism." *CR: The New Centennial Review* 3, no. 2 (2003): 287–302.

Fabian, Johannes. *Time and the Other: How Anthropology Makes Its Object*. New York: Columbia University Press, 1983.

Ferguson, Niall. "Virtual History: Towards a 'Chaotic' Theory of the Past." In *Virtual History: Alternatives and Counterfactuals*, edited by Niall Ferguson, 1–91. New York: Basic Books, 1997.

Ferreira da Silva, Denise. *Toward a Global Idea of Race*. Minneapolis: University of Minnesota Press, 2007.

Fimi, Dimitra. *Tolkien, Race and Cultural History.* New York: Palgrave Macmillan, 2009.

Fineman, Joel. "The Structure of Allegorical Desire." In *Allegory and Representation*, edited by Stephen Greenblatt, 26–46. Baltimore: Johns Hopkins University Press, 1981.

Fish, Stanley. "Reverse Racism; or, How the Pot Got to Call the Kettle Black." *Atlantic Monthly*, November 1, 1993. https://www.theatlantic.com/magazine/archive/1993/11/reverse-racism-or-how-the-pot-got-to-call-the-kettle-black/304638. Accessed September 14, 2012.

Fisher, Rebekka Rutledge. "Democracy's Remains: The Hermeneutic Historiography of *Black Reconstruction*." *South Atlantic Quarterly* 112, no. 3 (2013): 507–27.

Fletcher, Angus. *Allegory: The Theory of a Symbolic Mode.* Ithaca, N.Y.: Cornell University Press, 1964.

Fleury, Jean-Baptiste. "Redefining the Social in a Changing Society: Origins and Reception of Gary Becker's *The Economics of Discrimination*." http://economix.fr/pdf/workshops/2009_altruism/Fleury_rev2.pdf. Accessed May 26, 2014.

Foster, Thomas. *Souls of Cyberfolk.* Minneapolis: University of Minnesota Press, 2005.

Foucault, Michel. *Society Must Be Defended.* Translated by David Macey. New York: Picador, 2003.

Four Statements on the Race Question. France: UNESCO, 1969.

Fowler, Alastair. *Kinds of Literature.* Oxford: Oxford University Press, 1982.

"*Foxes of Harrow*, typescript, setting copy with printers' notation." Frank Yerby Collection, Howard Gottlieb Archival Research Center, Boston University.

Franklin, H. Bruce. "How America's Fictions of Future War Have Changed the World." In *Future Wars*, edited by David Seed, 32–49. Liverpool: Liverpool University Press, 2012.

———. *War Stars: The Superweapon and the American Imaginary.* Oxford: Oxford University Press, 1988.

Fredrickson, George. *Racism: A Short History.* Princeton, N.J.: Princeton University Press, 2002.

Freedman, Carl. *Critical Theory and Science Fiction.* Middletown, Conn.: Wesleyan University Press, 2000.

———. "Towards a Theory of Paranoia: The Science Fiction of Philip K. Dick." *Science Fiction Studies* 11, no. 1 (1984): 15–24.

Freud, Sigmund. *Jokes and Their Relation to the Unconscious: Standard Edition.* Translated by James Strachey. New York: W. W. Norton, 1960.

Friedman, Milton. *Capitalism and Freedom.* Chicago: University of Chicago Press, 1962.

Frow, John. *Genre: The New Critical Idiom.* London: Routledge, 2015.

Frye, Northrop. *Anatomy of Criticism*. Princeton, N.J.: Princeton University Press, 1957.

Gallagher, Catherine. "When Did the Confederate States of America Free the Slaves?" *Representations* 98 (2007): 53–61.

Gallagher, Catherine, and Stephen Greenblatt. *Practicing New Historicism*. Chicago: University of Chicago Press, 2001.

Gates, Henry Louis, Jr. *Figures in Black*. Oxford: Oxford University Press, 1987.

———. *Loose Canons*. Oxford: Oxford University Press, 1993.

———. *The Signifying Monkey: A Theory of Afro-American Literary Criticism*. New York: Oxford University Press, 1988.

Genette, Gerard. *Narrative Discourse: An Essay in Method*. Translated by Jane Lewin. Ithaca, N.Y.: Cornell University Press, 1980.

Gerrig, Richard J. *Experiencing Narrative Worlds*. New Haven, Conn.: Yale University Press, 1993.

Ghent, Andra C., Rubén Hernández-Murillo, and Michael T. Owyang. "Differences in Subprime Loan Pricing across Races and Neighborhoods." *Federal Reserve Bank of St. Louis Working Papers*, March 2014. https://research.stlouisfed.org/wp/2011/2011-033.pdf. Accessed February 28, 2017.

Gibson, James Jerome. *An Ecological Approach to Visual Perception*. Boston: Houghton Mifflin, 1979.

Gillman, Susan, and Alys Weinbaum, eds. *Next to the Color Line: Gender, Sexuality, and W. E. B. DuBois*. Durham, N.C.: Duke University Press, 2007.

Gilroy, Paul. *Against Race*. Cambridge, Mass.: Harvard University Press, 2000.

Glenn, Evelyn Nakano. *Unequal Freedom*. Cambridge, Mass.: Harvard University Press, 2002.

Glover, David, and Scott McCracken. Introduction to *The Cambridge Companion to Popular Fiction*, edited by David Glover and Scott McCracken, 1–14. Cambridge: Cambridge University Press, 2012.

Goffman, Erving. *Frame Analysis: An Essay on the Organization of Experience*. Boston: Northeastern University Press, 1974.

Goldberg, David Theo. *Racist Culture: Philosophy and the Politics of Meaning*. Cambridge, Mass.: Blackwell, 1993.

Goodman, Nelson. *Fact, Fiction, and Forecast*. Cambridge, Mass.: Harvard University Press, 1979.

———. *Languages of Art*. Indianapolis: Bobs-Merrill, 1968.

———. *Of Mind and Other Matters*. Cambridge, Mass.: Harvard University Press, 1984.

———. *Ways of Worldmaking*. Indianapolis: Hackett, 1978.

Gordon, Lewis. *Her Majesty's Other Children*. Lanham, Md.: Rowman and Littlefield, 1997.

Gossett, Thomas F. *Race: The History of an Idea in America.* Edited with a foreword by Shelley Fisher Fishkin and Arnold Rampersad. Oxford: Oxford University Press, 1997.

Gould, Stephen Jay. *The Mismeasure of Man.* New York: Norton, 1996.

Goyal, Yogita. *Romance, Diaspora and Black Atlantic Literature.* Cambridge: Cambridge University Press, 2010.

Grammer, John. "Plantation Fiction." In *A Companion to the Literature and Culture of the American South*, edited by Richard Gray and Owen Robinson, 58–75. Malden, U.K.: Blackwell, 2004.

Gray, Richard. *Writing the South: Ideas of an American Region.* Baton Rouge: Louisiana State University Press, 1997.

Greeson, Jennifer. *Our South: Geographic Fantasy and the Rise of National Literature.* Cambridge, Mass.: Harvard University Press, 2010.

Griffith, George. *The Angel of the Revolution.* London: Tower Publishing, 1894.

Guynn, Noah, and Zrinka Stahuljak. "Introduction: Historicity, Violence, and the Medieval Francophone World: *Memoire Hysterisee.*" In *Violence and the Writing of History*, edited by Noah Guynn and Zrinka Stahuljak, 1–19. Woodridge, U.K.: D. S. Brewer, 2013.

Haber, Karen, ed. *Meditations on Middle-Earth.* New York: St. Martin's Press, 2001.

Hale, Grace Elizabeth. *Making Whiteness: The Culture of Segregation in the South, 1890–1940.* New York: Vintage Books, 2010.

Hall, Mark. "Crash Go the Civilizations: Some Notes on Robert E. Howard's Use of History and Anthropology." In *The Robert E. Howard Reader*, edited by Darrell Schweitzer, 82–94. San Bernardino, Calif.: Borgo Press, 2010.

Hall, Stuart. "Notes on Deconstructing 'the Popular.'" In *People's History and Socialist Theory*, edited by Raphael Samuel, 227–42. London: Routledge and Kegan Paul, 1981.

Hammond, J. R. Entry on *The War in the Air.* In *An H. G. Wells Companion*, by J. R. Hammond, 107–9. London: Macmillan, 1979.

Han, Sora. *Letters of the Law: Race and the Fantasy of Colorblindness in American Law.* Stanford, Calif.: Stanford University Press, 2015. Kindle edition.

Haraway, Donna. "Universal Donors in a Vampire Culture: It's All in the Family: Biological Kinship Categories in the Twentieth Century United States." In *Uncommon Ground: Toward Reinventing Nature*, edited by William Cronon, 321–78. New York: W. W. Norton, 1995.

Harding, Sandra. *The "Racial" Economy of Science: Toward a Democratic Future.* Bloomington: Indiana University Press, 1993.

Hartman, Saidiya. *Scenes of Subjection.* Oxford: Oxford University Press, 1997.

Haskell, Molly. *Frankly, My Dear.* New Haven, Conn.: Yale University Press, 2009.

Haughwout, Andrew, Christopher Mayer, and Joseph Tracy. "Subprime Mortgage Pricing: The Impact of Race, Ethnicity, and Gender on the Cost of Borrowing." *Federal Reserve Bank of New York Staff Reports* 368, April 2009.

Hawthorn, Geoffrey. *Plausible Worlds.* Cambridge, U.K.: Cambridge University Press, 1993.

Hayek, Friedrich. *Law, Legislation and Liberty.* Vol. 2, *The Mirage of Social Justice.* Chicago: University of Chicago Press, 1976.

Haynes, Rosslyn. *H. G. Wells: Discoverer of the Future.* New York: New York University Press, 1980.

Hay, George. "Shiel versus the Renegade Romantic." In *Shiel in Diverse Hands: A Collection of Essays on M. P. Shiel*, edited by A. Reynolds Morse, 109–12. Cleveland: Reynolds Morse Foundation, 1983.

Hayot, Eric. *The Hypothetical Mandarin.* Oxford: Oxford University Press, 2009.

———. *On Literary Worlds.* Oxford: Oxford University Press, 2012.

Heidegger, Martin. "Age of the World Picture." In *The Question concerning Technology and Other Essays*, by Martin Heidegger, translated by William Lovitt, 115–54. New York: Harper and Row, 1977.

Hellekson, Karen. *The Alternate History: Refiguring Historical Time.* Kent, Ohio: Kent State University Press, 2001.

Herman, David. *Basic Elements of Narrative.* Oxford: Blackwell, 2009.

———. "Narrative Ways of Worldmaking." In *Narratology in the Age of Cross-Disciplinary Narrative Research*, edited by Sandra Heinen and Roy Sommer, 71–87. Berlin: De Gruyter, 2009.

———. "Narrative Worldmaking across Media and Disciplines." American Council of Learned Societies, Focus on Research Series. https://www.acls.org/news/5-24-11. Accessed February 26, 2017.

———. "The Scope and Aims of *Storyworlds.*" *Storyworlds: A Journal of Narrative Studies* 1 (2009): vii–x.

Hill, Jane. *The Everyday Language of White Racism.* Malden, U.K.: Wiley-Blackwell, 2008.

Hollinger, Veronica. "Humanity 2.0: Retrospective, Abjection, and the Future-to-Come." *Paradoxa* 26 (2014): 268–83.

Hong, Grace. *The Ruptures of American Capital.* Minneapolis: University of Minnesota Press, 2006.

Hood, Edwin Paxton. *Christmas Evans, the Preacher of Wild Wales.* London: Hodder and Stoughton, 1883.

Hough, Kenneth. "Demon Courage and Dread Engines: America's Reaction to the Russo-Japanese War and the Genesis of the Japanese Invasion Sublime." In *Techno-Orientalism: Imagining Asia in Speculative Fiction, History, and Media*, edited by David S. Roh, Betsy Huang, and Greta A. Niu, 23–39. New Brunswick, N.J.: Rutgers University Press, 2015.

Howard, Robert. "Beyond the Black River." In *The Conquering Sword of Conan*, by Robert Howard, 45–100. New York: Del Rey, 2005

———. *The Bloody Crown of Conan*. New York: Del Rey Books, 2003.

———. *The Coming of Conan the Cimmerian*. New York: Random House, 2002.

———. *The Conquering Sword of Conan*. New York: Del Rey, 2005.

———. "The Hyborian Age." In *The Coming of Conan the Cimmerian*, by Robert Howard, 364–80. New York: Random House, 2002.

———. "Iron Shadows of the Moon." In *The Coming of Conan the Cimmerian*, by Robert Howard, 179–205. New York: Random House, 2002.

———. "The Man-Eaters of Zamboula." In *The Conquering Sword of Conan*, by Robert Howard, 177–207. New York: Del Rey, 2005.

———. "Queen of the Black Coast." In *The Coming of Conan the Cimmerian* by Robert Howard, 115–39. New York: Random House, 2002.

———. "The Vale of Lost Women." In *The Coming of Conan the Cimmerian*, by Robert Howard, 294–309. New York: Random House, 2002.

Hsu, Hsuan. "Sitting in Darkness: Mark Twain and America's Asia." *American Literary History* 25, no. 1 (2013): 69–84.

Huang, Betsy. *Contesting Genres in Contemporary Asian American Fiction*. New York: Palgrave, 2010.

Huang, Yunte. *Transpacific Displacements*. Berkeley: University of California Press, 2002.

Isby, David C. "The Japanese Raj." In *Rising Sun Victorious: An Alternate History of the Pacific War*, edited by Peter G. Tsouras, 166–86. Novato, Calif.: Presidio Press, 2007.

Jackson, Blyden. "Silver Foxes." *Journal of Negro Education* 15, no. 4 (1946): 649–52.

Jackson, John L. *Racial Paranoia: The Unintended Consequences of Political Correctness*. New York: Basic Books, 2008.

Jackson, Rosemary. *Fantasy: The Literature of Subversion*. London: Methuen, 1981.

James, C. L. R. *American Civilization*. London: Blackwell, 1993.

James, Edward, ed. *The Cambridge Companion to Fantasy Literature*. Cambridge: Cambridge University Press, 2012.

Jameson, Fredric. *Signatures of the Visible*. New York: Routledge, 2011.

"Japanization of China." *American Monthly Review of Reviews* 29 (1904).

Jarrett, Gene. *Deans and Truants: Race and Realism in African American Literature*. Philadelphia: University of Pennsylvania Press, 2007.

Jauss, Hans Robert. *Toward an Aesthetic of Reception*. Minneapolis: University of Minnesota Press, 1982.

Jenkins, Henry. *Textual Poachers*. London: Routledge, 1992.

Jeon, Joseph. *Racial Things, Racial Forms*. Iowa City: University of Iowa Press, 2012.

Jerng, Mark C. "A World of Difference: Samuel Delany's Dhalgren and the Protocols of Racial Reading." *American Literature* 83, no. 2 (2011): 251–78.

Johnson, Barbara. *The Wake of Deconstruction*. Oxford: Blackwell, 1994.

Johnston, Georgia. "Discourses of Autobiographical Desires: Samuel Delany's *Nevèrÿon* series." *Biography* 30, no. 1 (Winter 2007): 48–60.

Jones, Anne Goodwyn. "*Gone with the Wind* and Others: Popular Fiction, 1920–1950." In *The History of Southern Literature*, edited by Louis D. Rubin Jr. et al., 363–74. Baton Rouge: Louisiana State University Press, 1990.

Joshi, S. T. "Barbarism vs. Civilization: Robert E. Howard and H. P. Lovecraft in Their Correspondence." In *The Robert E. Howard Reader*, edited by Darrell Schweitzer, 51–82. San Bernardino, Calif.: Borgo Press, 2010.

Jung, Moon-Ho. *Coolies and Cane*. Baltimore: Johns Hopkins University Press, 2008.

Kantor, Mackinlay. *If the South Had Won the Civil War*. New York: Forge Books, 2001. Originally published in 1960.

Keizer, Arlene. "'Obsidian Mine': The Psychic Aftermath of Slavery." *American Literary History* 24, no. 4 (2012): 686–701.

Kelso, Sylvia. "'Across Never': Postmodern Theory and Narrative Praxis in Samuel R. Delany's Nevèrÿon Cycle." *Science Fiction Studies* 24, no. 2 (1997): 289–301.

Kendi, Ibram X. *Stamped from the Beginning: The Definitive History of Racist Ideas in America*. New York: Nation Books, 2016.

Kersting, Rudolf. *The White World: Life and Adventures within the Arctic Circle*. New York: Lewis Scribner, 1902.

Kidd, Justin. Letter to *AMRA* 2, no. 5. Transcribed from holdings of *AMRA* at Eaton Fanzine Collection, University of California, Riverside.

Kilgore, De Witt Douglas. "Beyond the History We Know." In *Afro-Future Females*, edited by Marleen S. Barr, 119–29. Columbus: Ohio University Press, 2008.

Kim, Claire Jean. "Racial Triangulation of Asian Americans." In *Asian Americans and Politics: Perspectives, Experiences, Prospects*, edited by Gordon H. Chang, 39–78. Stanford, Calif.: Stanford University Press, 2001.

Kim, Sue J. "Beyond Black and White: Race and Postmodernism in *The Lord of the Rings* Films." *MFS Modern Fiction Studies* 50, no. 4 (2004): 875–907.

Korematsu v. United States. 323 U.S. 214 (1944).

Kornbluth, Cyril. "Two Dooms." In *One Lamp*, edited by Gordon van Gelder, 1–58. New York: Four Walls Eight Windows, 2003.

Koselleck, Reinhardt. *The Practice of Conceptual History*. Stanford, Calif.: Stanford University Press, 2002.

Koshy, Susan. "Morphing Race into Ethnicity: Asian Americans and Critical Transformations of Whiteness." *Boundary 2* 28 (2001): 153–94

———. "Why the Humanities Matter for Race Studies Today." *PMLA* 123, no. 5 (2008): 1542–49.

Kray, Laura J., et al. "From What *Might* Have Been to What *Must* Have Been: Counterfactual Thinking Creates Meaning." *Journal of Personality and Social Psychology* 98, no. 1 (2010): 106–18.

Krishnan, Sanjay. "Reading Globalization from the Margin." *Representations* 99, no. 1 (Summer 2007): 40–73.

Lacan, Jacques. *The Seminar of Jacques Lacan, Book III: The Psychoses, 1955–56*. Translated by Russell Grigg. New York: W. W. Norton, 1993.

Lavender, Isiah. *Race in American Science Fiction*. Bloomington: Indiana University Press, 2011.

Lea, Homer. *The Valor of Ignorance*. New York: Harper and Brothers, 1942.

Lee, Chang-Rae. *Aloft*. New York: Riverhead Books, 2005.

Lee, Christopher. *The Semblance of Identity*. Stanford, Calif.: Stanford University Press, 2012.

Lee, James K. *Urban Triage*. Minneapolis: University of Minnesota Press, 2004.

Lieber, Fritz. "Howard's Style." In *The Spell of Conan*, edited by L. Sprague de Camp, 26–27. New York: Ace Books, 1980.

———. "Letter: On What We Should Call the Kind of Story This Magazine Is." *AMRA* 2, no. 16 (July 1961): 21. Transcribed from holdings of *AMRA* at Eaton Fanzine Collection, University of California, Riverside.

Locke, Alain. "Reason and Race: A Review of the Literature of the Negro for 1946." *Phylon* 8, no. 1 (1947): 17–27.

London, Jack. "Give Battle to Retard Enemy." In *Jack London Reports: War Correspondence, Sports Articles, and Miscellaneous Writings*, edited by King Hendricks and Irving Shepard, 99–107. New York: Doubleday, 1970.

———. "If Japan Wakens China." In *Jack London Reports: War Correspondence, Sports Articles, and Miscellaneous Writings*, edited by King Hendricks and Irving Shepard, 358–62. New York: Doubleday, 1970.

———. "The Yellow Peril." In *Jack London Reports: War Correspondence, Sports Articles, and Miscellaneous Writings*, edited by King Hendricks and Irving Shepard, 340–50. New York: Doubleday, 1970.

Loury, Glenn. *The Anatomy of Racial Inequality*. Cambridge, Mass.: Harvard University Press, 2002. Kindle edition.

———. "The Anatomy of Racial Inequality: A Clarification." In *Race, Liberalism, and Economics*, edited by David Colander, Robert E. Prasch, and Falguni A. Sheth, 238–59. Ann Arbor: University of Michigan Press, 2004.

———. "Relations before Transactions." *Georgia State University Law Review* 1, no. 3 (2006): 585–615.
Lovecraft, H. P. Letter to Donald Wollheim accompanying the manuscript pages of "The Hyborian Age." Transcribed from issue of *Hyborian Age* at Eaton Fanzine Collection, University of California, Riverside.
Lowe, Lisa. *The Intimacies of Four Continents.* Durham, N.C.: Duke University Press, 2015.
Luck, Chad. *The Body of Property.* New York: Fordham University Press, 2014.
Lukin, Josh. "The Wiggle Room of Theory: An Interview with Samuel R. Delany." In *Conversations with Samuel Delany*, edited by Carl Freedman, 166–86. Jackson: University of Mississippi Press, 2009.
Lye, Colleen. "The Afro-Asian Analogy." *PMLA* 123, no. 5 (2008): 1734–36.
———. *America's Asia: Racial Form and American Literature, 1893–1945.* Princeton, N.J.: Princeton University Press, 2005.
———. "Racial Form." *Representations* 104, no. 1 (2008): 92–101.
Lyman, Stanford. *Roads to Dystopia.* Fayetteville: University of Arkansas Press, 2001.
Manson, Marsden. *The Yellow Peril in Action: A Possible Chapter in History.* San Francisco: Britton and Rey, 1907.
Marvin, Taylor. "Game of Thrones, Racism, and White Saviors." *Smoke and Stir*, June 22, 2013. https://smokeandstir.org/2013/06/22/game-of-thrones-racism-and-white-saviors. Accessed June 11, 2014.
Marx, Karl. *Capital.* Vol. 1. Translated by Ben Fowkes. London: Penguin, 1990.
Massumi, Brian. *Parables for the Virtual.* Durham, N.C.: Duke University Press, 2002.
McCracken, Scott. *Pulp.* Manchester: Manchester University Press, 1998.
McKittrick, Katherine, ed. *Sylvia Wynter: On Being Human as Praxis.* Durham, N.C.: Duke University Press, 2015. Kindle edition.
McPherson, Tara. *Reconstructing Dixie: Race, Gender, and Nostalgia in the Imagined South.* Durham, N.C.: Duke University Press, 2003.
———. "Seeing in Black and White: Gender and Racial Visibility from *Gone with the Wind* to *Scarlett*." In *Hop on Pop: The Politics and Pleasures of Popular Culture*, edited by Henry Jenkins et al., 517–35. Durham, N.C.: Duke University Press, 2002.
Melamed, Jodi. *Represent and Destroy: Rationalizing Violence in the New Racial Capitalism.* Minneapolis: University of Minnesota Press, 2011.
Mendlesohn, Farah. *Rhetorics of Fantasy.* Middletown, Conn.: Wesleyan University Press, 2013.
Metro Broadcasting, Inc. v. FCC. 497 U.S. 547 (1990).
Mieville, China. "Marxism and Fantasy." *Historical Materialism* 10, no. 4 (2002): 39–49.

Miller, P. Schuyler. "Lord of the Black Throne." In *The Blade of Conan*, edited by L. Sprague de Camp, 78. New York: Ace Books, 1979.

Miner, Earl. "Hearn and Japan: An Attempt at Interpretation." In *Rediscovering Lafcadio Hearn*, edited by Sukehiro Hirakawa, 58–72. Kent, U.K.: Global Oriental, 1997.

Mitchell, Margaret. *Gone with the Wind.* New York: Scribner, 1964.

Mollmann, Steven. "Air-Ships and the Technological Revolution: Detached Violence in George Griffith and H. G. Wells." *Science Fiction Studies* 42, no. 1 (2015): 20–41.

Moore, Jack B. "The Guilt of the Victim: Racial Themes in Some Frank Yerby Novels." *Journal of Popular Culture* 8, no. 4 (1975): 745–56.

Moore, Ward. *Bring the Jubilee.* New York: Ballantine Books, 1953.

Morse, A. Reynolds, ed. *Shiel in Diverse Hands: A Collection of Essays on M. P. Shiel.* Cleveland: Reynolds Morse Foundation, 1983.

Mulhall, Stephen. *On Being in the World: Wittgenstein and Heidegger on Seeing Aspects.* London: Routledge, 1990.

Mullen, Bill. *Afro-Orientalism.* Minneapolis: University of Minnesota Press, 2004.

Obasogie, Osagie. *Blinded by Sight: Seeing Race through the Eyes of the Blind.* Stanford, Calif.: Stanford University Press, 2014. Kindle edition.

O'Brien, Kenneth. "Race, Romance, and the Southern Literary Tradition." In *Recasting: "Gone with the Wind" in American Culture*, edited by Darden Asbury Pyron, 153–66. Gainesville: University Presses of Florida, 1983.

Okihiro, Gary. *Margins and Mainstreams.* Seattle: University of Washington Press, 1994.

Omi, Michael, and Howard Winant. *Racial Formation in the United States: From the 1960s to the 1990s.* New York: Routledge, 1994.

———. *Racial Formation in the United States.* 3rd ed. Routledge: London, 2015.

Pak, Susie J., and Elda Tsou. "Introduction." *Journal of Asian American Studies* 14, no. 2 (2011): 172–73.

Parrinder, Patrick. *Shadows of the Future.* Liverpool: Liverpool University Press, 1995.

Pavel, Thomas. *Fictional Worlds.* Cambridge, Mass.: Harvard University Press, 1989.

Pearce, Lynn. *Romance Writing.* Oxford: Polity, 2006.

Pearson, Charles. *National Life and Character: A Forecast.* London: Macmillan, 1893.

Peirce, Charles. *Philosophical Writings of Peirce.* Edited by Justus Buchler. New York: Dover, 1955. Kindle edition.

———. "What Is a Sign." In *The Essential Peirce: Selected Philosophical Writings*, vol. 2, *1893–1913*, edited by Nathan Houser, 4–11. Bloomington: Indiana University Press, 1998.

Perry, Imani. *More Beautiful and More Terrible: The Embrace and Transcendence of Racial Inequality in the United States.* New York: New York University Press, 2011. Kindle edition.

Piper, Adrian. "Impartiality, Compassion, and Modal Imagination." *Ethics* 101, no. 4 (1991): 726–57.

———. *Out of Order, Out of Sight.* Vol. 1, *Selected Writings in Meta-Art, 1968–1992.* Cambridge, Mass.: MIT Press, 1996.

———. *Out of Order, Out of Sight.* Vol. 2, *Selected Writings in Art Criticism, 1967–1992.* Cambridge, Mass.: MIT Press, 1996.

Pitt, James. "The White World." *Sunday Magazine* 6 (1877): 128.

Porter, Eric. *The Problem of the Future World: W. E. B. DuBois and the Race Concept at Midcentury.* Durham, N.C.: Duke University Press, 2010.

Prashad, Vijay. *Everybody Was Kung Fu Fighting: Afro-Asian Connections and the Myth of Cultural Purity.* Boston: Beacon Press, 2001.

Prince, Gerald. *Narrative as Theme.* Lincoln: University of Nebraska Press, 1992.

"Proposals on the Biological Aspects of Race." In *Four Statements on the Race Question.* France: UNESCO, 1969.

Radway, Janice. *Reading the Romance.* Chapel Hill: University of North Carolina Press, 1984.

Ramirez, Catherine S. "Afrofuturism/Chicanafuturism: Fictive Kin." *Aztlán: A Journal of Chicano Studies* 33, no. 1 (2008): 185–94

———. "El fantasma en la máquina: El arte chicanafuturista de Marion C. Martínez y la descolonización del futuro." In *Suturas y fragmentos: cuerpos y territorias en la ciencia-ficción*, edited by Fundació Antoni Tàpies and Universidad Internacional de Andalucía, Sevilla, translated by Isaïes Fanlo, 54–65. Barcelona: Fundació Antoni Tàpies, 2006.

Rastogi, Nina. "Is 'Game of Thrones' Racist?" *Slate*, April 20, 2011. http://www.slate.com/blogs/browbeat/2011/04/20/is_game_of_thrones_racist.html. Accessed June 11, 2014.

Reardon, Jenny. *Race to the Finish: Identity and Governance in an Age of Genomics.* Princeton, N.J.: Princeton University Press, 2005.

Rearick, Anderson, III. "Why Is the Only Good Orc a Dead Orc?: The Dark Face of Racism Examined in Tolkien's World." *MFS Modern Fiction Studies* 50, no. 4 (Winter 2004): 861–74.

Reed, Christopher Robert. *"All the World Is Here!": The Black Presence at White City.* Bloomington: Indiana University Press, 2000.

Regents of the University of California v. Bakke. 438 U.S. 265 (1978).

Reynolds, David S. *John Brown, Abolitionist: The Man Who Killed Slavery, Sparked the Civil War, and Seeded Civil Rights.* New York: Alfred A. Knopf, 2005.

Ricci v. Destefano. 557 U.S. 557 (2009). Trans. Lexis 34 (oral argumentation).

Richardson, Riché. "Mammy's 'Mules' and the Rules of Marriage in *Gone with the Wind*." In *American Cinema and the Southern Imaginary*, edited by Deborah Barker and Kathryn McKee, 52–78. Athens: University of Georgia Press, 2011.

Rieder, John. *Colonialism and the Emergence of Science Fiction*. Middletown, Conn.: Wesleyan University Press, 2008.

———. "John Henry Palmer's *The Invasion of New York; or, How Hawaii Was Annexed:* Political Discourse and Emergent Mass Culture in 1897." In *Future Wars*, edited by David Seed, 85–103. Liverpool: Liverpool University Press, 2012.

———. "The Metafictive World of *The Man in the High Castle*: Hermeneutics, Ethics, and Political Ideology." *Science Fiction Studies* 15, no. 2 (1988): 214–25.

Roberts, Diane. *The Myth of Aunt Jemima: Representations of Race and Region*. London: Routledge, 1994.

Roberts, Thomas. *An Aesthetics of Junk Fiction*. Athens: University of Georgia Press, 1990.

Robinson, Cedric. *Black Marxism: The Making of the Black Radical Tradition*. Chapel Hill: University of North Carolina Press, 1983.

Robinson, Kim Stanley. "The Novels of Philip K. Dick." Ph.D. diss., University of California, San Diego, 1982.

Roediger, David R. *Wages of Whiteness: Race and the Makings of the American Working Class*. London: Verso, 1991.

Roh, David S., Betsy Huang, and Greta A. Niu, eds. *Techno-Orientalism: Imagining Asia in Speculative Fiction, History and Media*. New Brunswick, N.J.: Rutgers University Press, 2015.

Rose, Mark. *Alien Encounters: Anatomy of Science Fiction*. Cambridge, Mass.: Harvard University Press, 1981.

Rosenberg, Jordana, and Brit Rusert. "Framing Finance: Rebellion, Dispossession, and the Geopolitics of Enclosure in Samuel Delany's *Nevèrÿon Series*." *Radical History Review* 2014, no. 118 (2014): 64–91.

Rosenfeld, Gavriel D. "Why Do We Ask 'What If?': Reflections on the Function of Alternate History." *History and Theory* 41 (2002): 90–103.

———. *The World Hitler Never Made: Alternate History and the Memory of Nazism*. Cambridge: Cambridge University Press, 2011.

Rowden, Terry, ed. "Special Issue: Delany Lately." *African American Review* 48, no. 3 (Fall 2015): 225–377.

Rugh, Jacob S. and Douglas S. Massey. "Racial Segregation and the American Foreclosure Crisis." *American Sociological Review* 75, no. 5 (2010): 629–51.

Rusert, Brit, and Adrienne Brown. "The Princess Steel: Introduction." *PMLA* 130, no. 3 (2015): 819–21.

Ryan, Marie-Laure. *Possible Worlds, Artificial Intelligence, and Narrative Theory*. Bloomington: Indiana University Press, 1992.

Ryan, Tim. *Calls and Responses: The American Novel of Slavery Since "Gone with the Wind."* Baton Rouge: Louisiana State University Press, 2008.

Saldívar, Ramón. "Historical Fantasy, Speculative Realism, and Postrace Aesthetics in Contemporary American Fiction." *American Literary History* 23, no. 3 (2011): 574–99.

———. "The Second Elevation of the Novel: Race, Form and the Postrace Aesthetic in Contemporary Narrative." *Narrative* 21, no. 1 (January 2013): 1–18.

Saler, Michael. *As If: Modern Enchantment and the Literary Prehistory of Virtual Reality*. Oxford: Oxford University Press, 2012.

Saunders, Charles R. "Die Black Dog!" February 12, 2011. http://reindeermotel.com/CHARLES/charles_blog42_dieblackdog.html. Accessed May 15, 2014.

Saxton, Alexander. *The Indispensable Enemy: Labor and the Anti-Chinese Movement in California*. Berkeley: University of California Press, 1995.

Scarry, Elaine. *Dreaming by the Book*. New York: Farrar, Straus and Giroux, 1999. E-book edition.

Schuyler, George S. "The Negro-Art Hokum." In *African American Literary Theory*, edited by Winston Napier, 24–26. New York: New York University Press, 2000.

Scithers, G. H. "Balthus of the Tauran and Robert of Cross Plains." *AMRA* 3 (1959): 20. Transcribed from holdings of *AMRA* at Eaton Fanzine Collection, University of California, Riverside.

Scott, Darieck. *Extravagant Abjection*. New York: New York University Press, 2010.

———. "The Not-Yet Justice League: Fantasy, Redress and Transatlantic Black History on the Comic Book Page." Paper presented at the annual meeting of the American Studies Association, Los Angeles, November 7, 2014.

Shanks, Jeffrey. "Hyborian Age Archaeology: Unearthing Historical and Anthropological Foundations." In *Conan Meets the Academy*, edited by Jonas Prida, 13–34. Jefferson, N.C.: McFarland, 2013.

Shelley v. Kraemer. 334 U.S. 1 (1948).

Shiel, M. P. *The Yellow Danger*. Charleston, S.C: Nabu Press, 2010. Kindle edition. Originally published in 1898.

———. *The Yellow Wave*. London: Ward, Lock, 1905.

Shippey, Tom. *The Road to Middle-Earth*. London: Allen and Unwin, 1982.

Shirer, William. "If Hitler Had Won World War II." *Look Magazine*, December 19, 1961, 28–36, 41–43.

Shockley, Evie. *Renegade Poetics: Black Aesthetics and Formal Innovation in African American Poetry.* Iowa City: University of Iowa Press, 2011.

Silber, Nina. *The Romance of Reunion: Northerners and the South, 1865–1900.* Chapel Hill: University of North Carolina Press, 1993.

Simmel, Georg. *The Philosophy of Money.* London: Routledge, 1978.

Singh, Anita. "Avatar Hit by Accusations of Racism." *Telegraph*, January 11, 2010. http://www.telegraph.co.uk/culture/film/film-news/6968020/Avatar-hit-by-claims-of-racism.html. Accessed December 10, 2016.

Smedley, Audrey. *Race in North America: Origin and Evolution of a World View.* Boulder: Westview Press, 1993.

Sohn, Stephen. "Alien/Asian: Imagining the Racialized Future." *MELUS* 33, no. 4 (2008): 5–23.

———. *Racial Asymmetries: Asian American Fictional Worlds.* New York: New York University Press, 2014.

Spencer, Kathleen. "Deconstructing Tales of Nevèrÿon: Delany, Derrida, and the 'Modular Calculus,' Parts I–IV." *Essays in Arts and Sciences* 14 (1985): 59–89.

Spillers, Hortense, Saidiya Hartman, Farah Jasmine Griffin, Shelly Eversley, and Jennifer L. Morgan. "'Whatcha Gonna Do?': Revisiting 'Mama's Baby, Papa's Maybe': An American Grammar Book." *Women's Studies Quarterly* 35, no. 1/2 (2007): 299–309.

Squires, John D. Afterword to *China in Arms: The Final Revision of Yellow Danger*, by M. P. Shiel, edited by John Squires. Kettering, Ohio: The Vainglory Press, 1998. Reproduced at http://www.alangullette.com/lit/shiel/essays/YellowDangerRevisited.htm. Accessed September 12, 2014.

———. "Some Contemporary Themes in Shiel's Early Novels" and "The Dragon's Tale: M.P. Shiel on the Emergence of Modern China." In *Shiel in Diverse Hands: A Collection of Essays on M. P. Shiel*, edited by A. Reynolds Morse, 249–326. Cleveland: Reynolds Morse Foundation, 1983.

Stableford, Brian. "The Politics of Evolution: Philosophical Themes in the Speculative Fiction of M. P. Shiel." In *Shiel in Diverse Hands: A Collection of Essays on M. P. Shiel*, edited by A. Reynolds Morse, 360–92. Cleveland: Reynolds Morse Foundation, 1983.

Stanley, Amy Dru. *From Bondage to Contract: Wage Labor, Marriage and the Market in the Age of Slave Emancipation.* Cambridge: Cambridge University Press, 1998.

Stanton, William. *The Leopard's Spots: Scientific Attitudes toward Race in America, 1815–1859.* Chicago: University of Chicago Press, 1960.

"Statement on the Nature of Race and Race Differences, Paris, June 1951." In *Four Statements on the Race Question.* France: UNESCO, 1969.

"Statement on Race, Paris, July 1950." In *Four Statements on the Race Question.* France: UNESCO, 1969.

Stead, W. T., ed. *Review of Reviews* 29 (January–June 1904).

Stecopoulos, Harilaos. *Reconstructing the World: Southern Fictions and U.S. Imperialisms, 1898–1976.* Ithaca, N.Y.: Cornell University Press, 2008.

Stepan, Nancy. *The Idea of Race in Science.* New York: Macmillan Press, 1982.

Stocking, George. *Race, Culture, and Evolution.* Chicago: University of Chicago Press, 1982.

Stoddard, Lothrop. *The Rising Tide of Color against White World Supremacy.* New York: Charles Scribner's Sons, 1920.

Stoler, Ann Laura. "Racial Histories and Their Regimes of Truth." *Political Power and Social Theory* 11 (1997): 183–206.

Strassfeld, Robert N. "If . . . : Counterfactuals in the Law." In *George Washington Law Review* 60, no. 339 (1992): 340–416.

Suvin, Darko. *Metamorphoses of Science Fiction: On the Poetics and History of a Literary Genre.* Edited by Gerry Canavan. Switzerland: Peter Lang, 2016.

Swaine, Jon, Paul Lewis, and Dan Roberts. "Grand Jury Decline to Charge Darren Wilson for Killing Michael Brown." *Guardian*, November 25, 2014, www.theguardian.com /us-news/2014/nov/24/ferguson-police-darren-wilson-michael-brown-no-charges. Accessed December 10, 2016.

Takaki, Ronald. *Strangers from a Different Shore.* Boston: Little, Brown, 1989.

Teskey, Gordon. *Allegory and Violence.* Ithaca, N.Y.: Cornell University Press, 1996.

Thoma, Pamela. *Asian American Women's Popular Literature: Feminizing Genres and National Belonging.* Philadelphia: Temple University Press, 2014.

Thompson, Richard Austin. *The Yellow Peril, 1890–1924.* Ann Arbor: University Microfilms, 1970.

A Time to Kill. Directed by Joel Schumacher. Burbank, CA: Warner Brothers, 1996.

Todorov, Tzvetan. *The Fantastic: A Structural Approach to a Literary Genre.* Ithaca, N.Y.: Cornell University Press, 1975.

Trodd, Zoe, and John Stauffer, eds. *Meteor of War: The John Brown Story.* Maplecrest, N.Y.: Brandywine Press, 2004.

Tsou, Elda. *Unquiet Tropes: Form, Race, and Asian American Literature.* Philadelphia: Temple University Press, 2015.

Tsouras, Peter. "Confederate Black and Grey." In *Dixie Victorious: An Alternate History of the Civil War*, edited by Peter Tsouras. New York: Skyhorse, 2004.

Tsouras, Peter, ed. *Rising Sun Victorious: An Alternate History of the Pacific War.* Novato, Calif.: Presidio Press, 2007. Kindle edition.

Tucker, Irene. *The Moment of Racial Sight.* Chicago: University of Chicago Press, 2012.

Tucker, Jeffrey. *A Sense of Wonder*. Middletown, Conn.: Wesleyan University Press, 2004.

Turner, Darwin T. "Frank Yerby as Debunker." *Massachusetts Review* 9, no. 3 (1968): 569–77.

Turner, Jack. *Awakening to Race*. Ithaca, N.Y.: Cornell University Press, 2012.

Turtledove, Harry. *Days of Infamy*. New York: Berkley Publishing Group, 2004. Kindle edition.

———. *Guns of the South*. New York: Del Rey, 1992.

Ular, Alexander. "Europe's Failure, Japan's Opportunity." *Review of Reviews* 29 (1904).

Uncertain Commons. *Speculate This!* Durham, N.C.: Duke University Press, 2013.

Vint, Sherryl. "Only by Experience: Embodiment and the Limitations of Realism in Neo-Slave Narratives." *Science Fiction Studies* 34, no. 2 (2007): 241–61.

Visweswaran, Kamala. "Race and the Culture of Anthropology." *American Anthropologist* 100, no. 1 (1998): 70–83.

Wainwright, F. T., ed. *The Problem of the Picts*. New York: Philosophical Library, 1956.

Wang, Dorothy. *Thinking Its Presence*. Stanford, Calif.: Stanford University Press, 2013.

Weale, B. L. Putnam. *The Coming Struggle in Eastern Asia*. New York: Macmillan, 1908.

———. "The Conflict of Color: The World Today and How Color Divides It." *World's Work* 18, no. 5 (1909): 12023–29, 12111–25.

———. *The Conflict of Colour*. New York: Macmillan, 1910.

Weheliye, Alexander. *Habeas Victus*. Durham, N.C.: Duke University Press, 2014.

Wells, H. G. Preface to *The Sleeper Awakes*. In *H. G. Wells's Literary Criticism*, edited by Patrick Parrinder and Robert Philmus, 238. Sussex: Harvester Press, 1980.

———. *The War in the Air*. London: George Bell and Sons, 1908.

———. *The War in the Air*. London: Penguin, 2005.

Wells, Jeremy. *Romances of the White Man's Burden: Race, Empire, and the Plantation in American Literature, 1880–1936*. Nashville: Vanderbilt University Press, 2011.

Wendt, Lloyd. "Amber Hued Romances in Delta County." *Chicago Tribune*, February 10, 1946, G3.

Wiegman, Robyn. *American Anatomies: Theorizing Race and Gender*. Durham, N.C.: Duke University Press, 1995.

Williams, Eric. *Slavery and Capitalism*. Chapel Hill: University of North Carolina Press, 1994.

Williams, F. P. *Hallie Marshall: A True Daughter of the South*. New York: Abbey Press, 1900.

Williams, Patricia. *The Alchemy of Race and Rights*. Cambridge, Mass.: Harvard University Press, 1991.

———. *Open House: Of Family, Friends, Food, Piano Lessons, and the Search for a Room of My Own*. New York: Picador, 2004.

———. *The Rooster's Egg*. Cambridge, Mass.: Harvard University Press, 1997.

———. *Seeing a Color-Blind Future: The Paradox of Race*. New York: Noonday Press, 1997.

Williams, Raymond. *Marxism and Literature*. Oxford: Oxford University Press, 1977.

Williamson, Joel. "How Black Was Rhett Butler?" In *The Evolution of Southern Culture*, edited by Numan V. Bartley, 187–207. Athens: University of Georgia Press, 1988.

Winant, Howard. "Race and Racism: Towards a Global Future." *Ethnic and Racial Studies* 29, no. 5 (2006): 986–1003.

Wittgenstein, Ludwig. *Philosophical Investigations*. Translated by G. E. M. Anscombe. Oxford: Blackwell, 1953.

Wolf, Mark J. P. *Building Imaginary Worlds: The Theory and History of Subcreation*. New York: Routledge, 2012.

Woloch, Alex. "Partial Representation." In *The Work of Genre*, edited by Robyn Warhol, 227–57. Cambridge: English Institute in collaboration with the American Council of Learned Societies, 2011. http://quod.lib.umich.edu/cgi/t/text/text-idx?c=acls;idno=heb90055.0001.001. Accessed September 26, 2013.

Wong, Edlie. "In a Future Tense: Immigration Law, Counterfactual Histories, and Chinese Invasion Fiction." *American Literary History* 26, no. 3 (2014): 511–35.

———. *Racial Reconstruction: Black Inclusion, Chinese Exclusion, and the Fictions of Citizenship*. Baltimore: Johns Hopkins University Press, 2009.

Woodward, C. Vann. *Origins of the New South, 1877–1913*. Baton Rouge: Louisiana State University Press, 1951.

Woolf, Virginia. "How Should One Read a Book." In *The Second Common Reader*, vol. 2. New York: Harcourt Brace, 1932.

Worth, Aaron. "The Reversible Empire: Race, Technology, and Irreversible Time in the Future-War Novel." In *Studies in Irreversibility: Texts and Contexts*, edited by Benjamin Schreier, 99–118. Newcastle upon Tyne, U.K.: Cambridge Scholars, 2007.

Wu, Willliam F. *The Yellow Peril: Chinese-Americans in American Fiction, 1850–1940*. Hamden, Conn.: Archon Books, 1982.

Wyly, Elvin K., Mona Atia, Elizabeth Lee, and Pablo Mendez. "Race, Gender and Statistical Representation: Predatory Mortgage Lending and the US Community Reinvestment Movement." *Environment and Planning* A 39 (2007): 2139–66.

Wynter, Jay. Introduction to *The War in the Air*, by H. G. Wells, xxiii–xxv. London: Penguin, 2005.

Wynter, Sylvia. "Unsettling the Coloniality of Being/Power/Truth/ Freedom." *CR: The New Centennial Review* 3, no. 3 (2003): 257–337.

Yamamura, Tim. "Science Fiction Futures and the Ocean as History: Literature, Diaspora, and the Pacific War." Ph.D. diss., University of California, Santa Cruz, 2014.

Yaszek, Lisa. "An Afrofuturist Reading of Ralph Ellison's *Invisible Man*." *Rethinking History* 9, nos. 2/3 (2005): 297–313.

Yerby, Frank. *Foxes of Harrow*. New York: Dell, 1946.

———. "Notes of Background Material from Historical Works." Frank Yerby Collection, Howard Gottlieb Archival Research Center, Boston University.

Young, Elizabeth. *Disarming the Nation: Women's Writing and the American Civil War*. Chicago: University of Chicago Press, 1999.

Young, Geoffrey Winthrop. "The Third Reich in Alternate History." *Journal of Popular Culture* 39, no. 5 (2006): 878–96.

Young, Helen. "Diversity and Difference: Cosmopolitanism and *The Lord of the Rings*." *Journal of the Fantastic in the Arts* 21, no. 3 (2010): 351–65.

INDEX